# NEW GAME! volume 7

Shotaro Tokuno

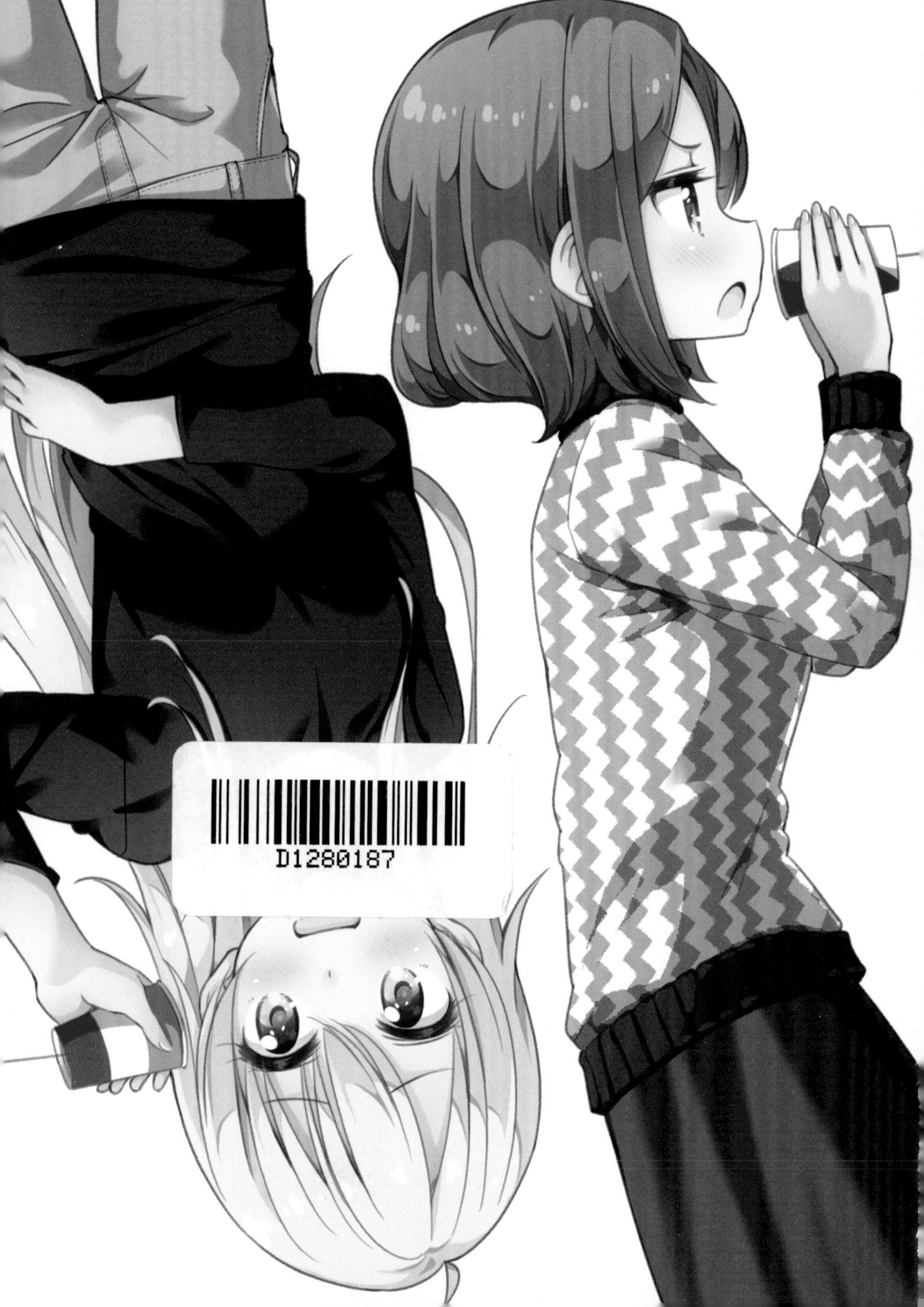

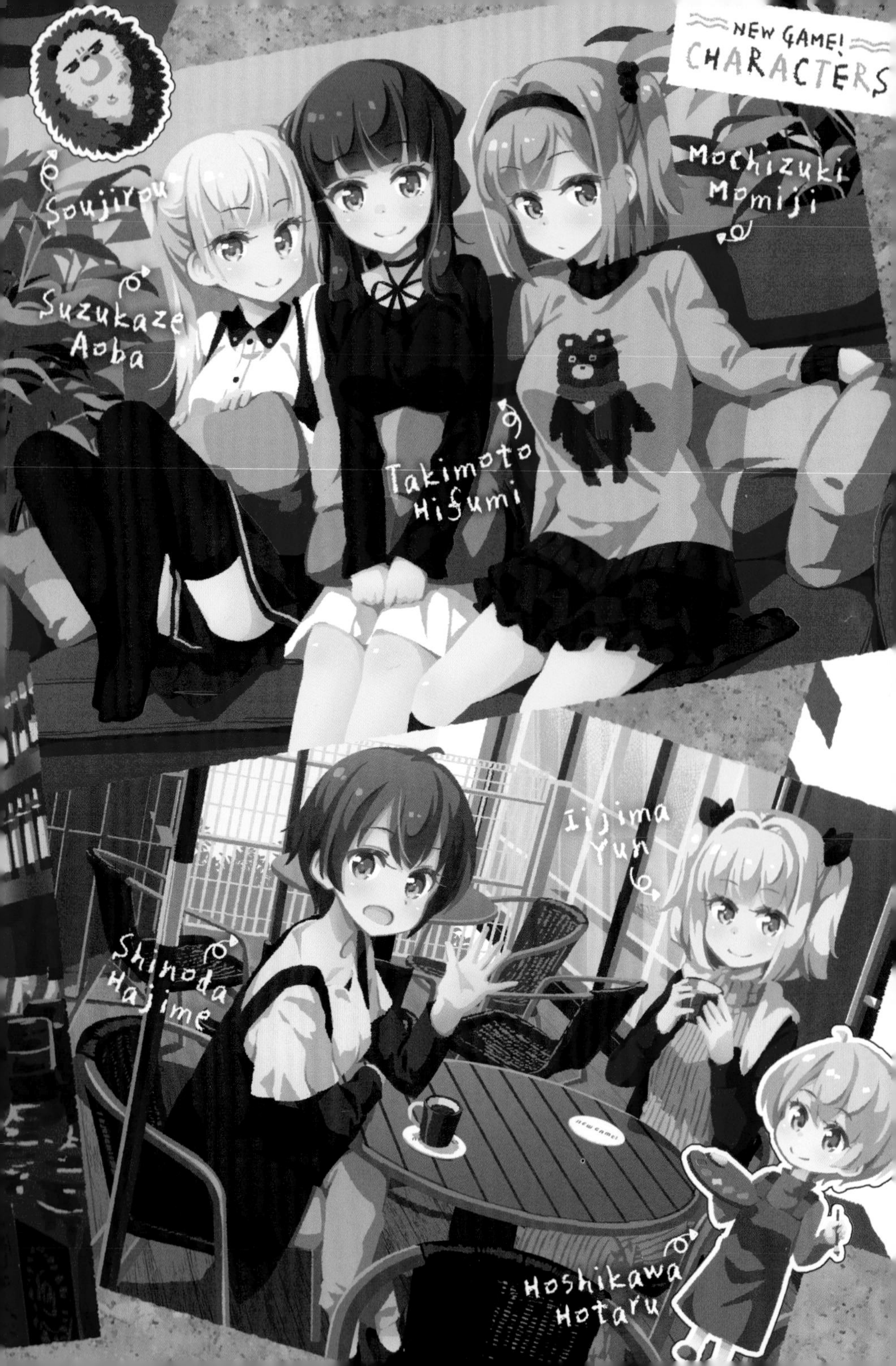
NEW GAME!
CHARACTERS
Soujirou
Suzukaze Aoba
Takimoto Hifumi
Mochizuki Momiji
Iijima Yun
Shinoda Hajime
Hoshikawa Hotaru
new game!

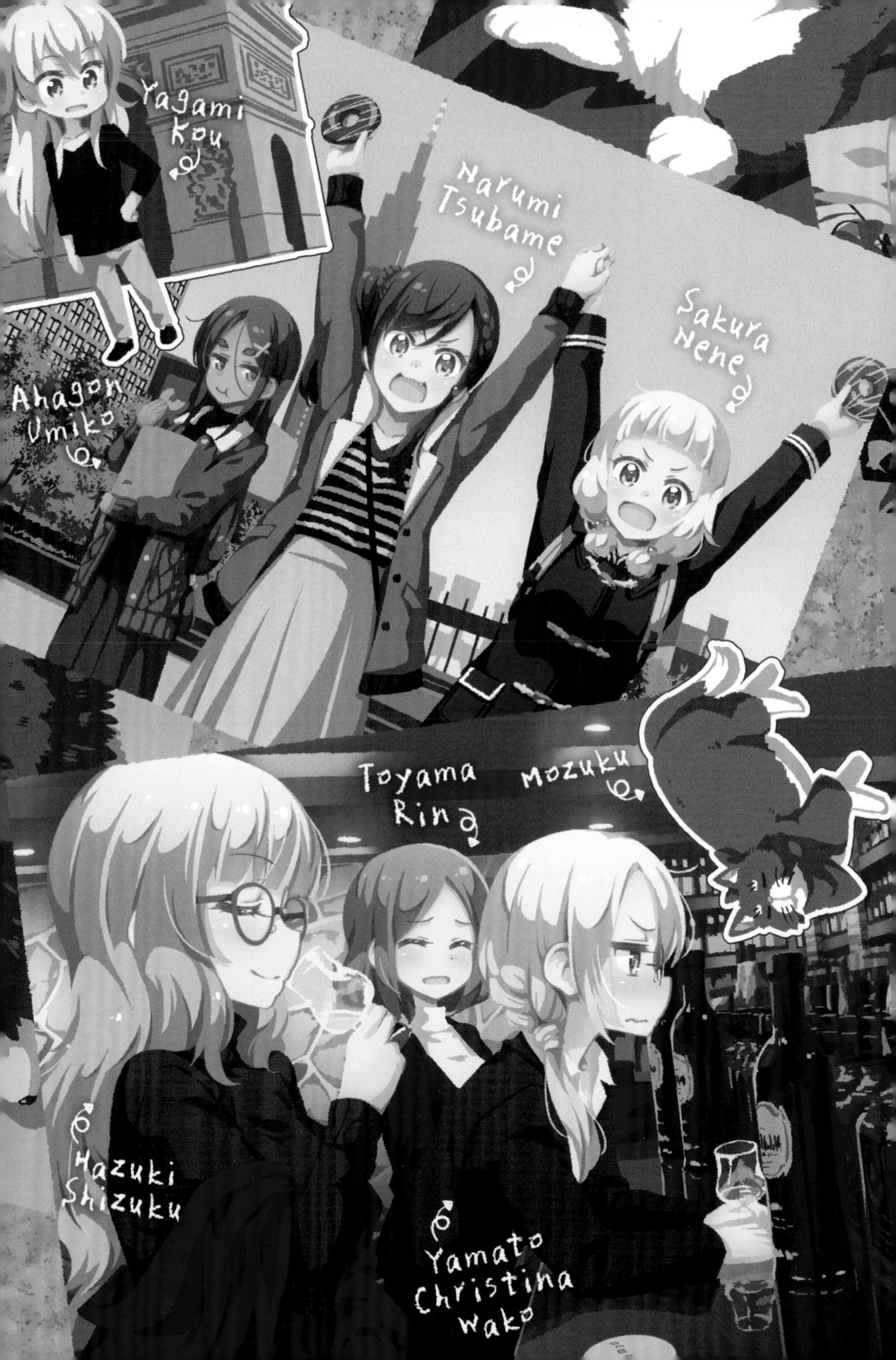
Yagami Kou
Narumi Tsubame
Sakura Nene
Ahagon Umiko
Toyama Rin
Mozuku
Hazuki Shizuku
Yamato Christina Wako

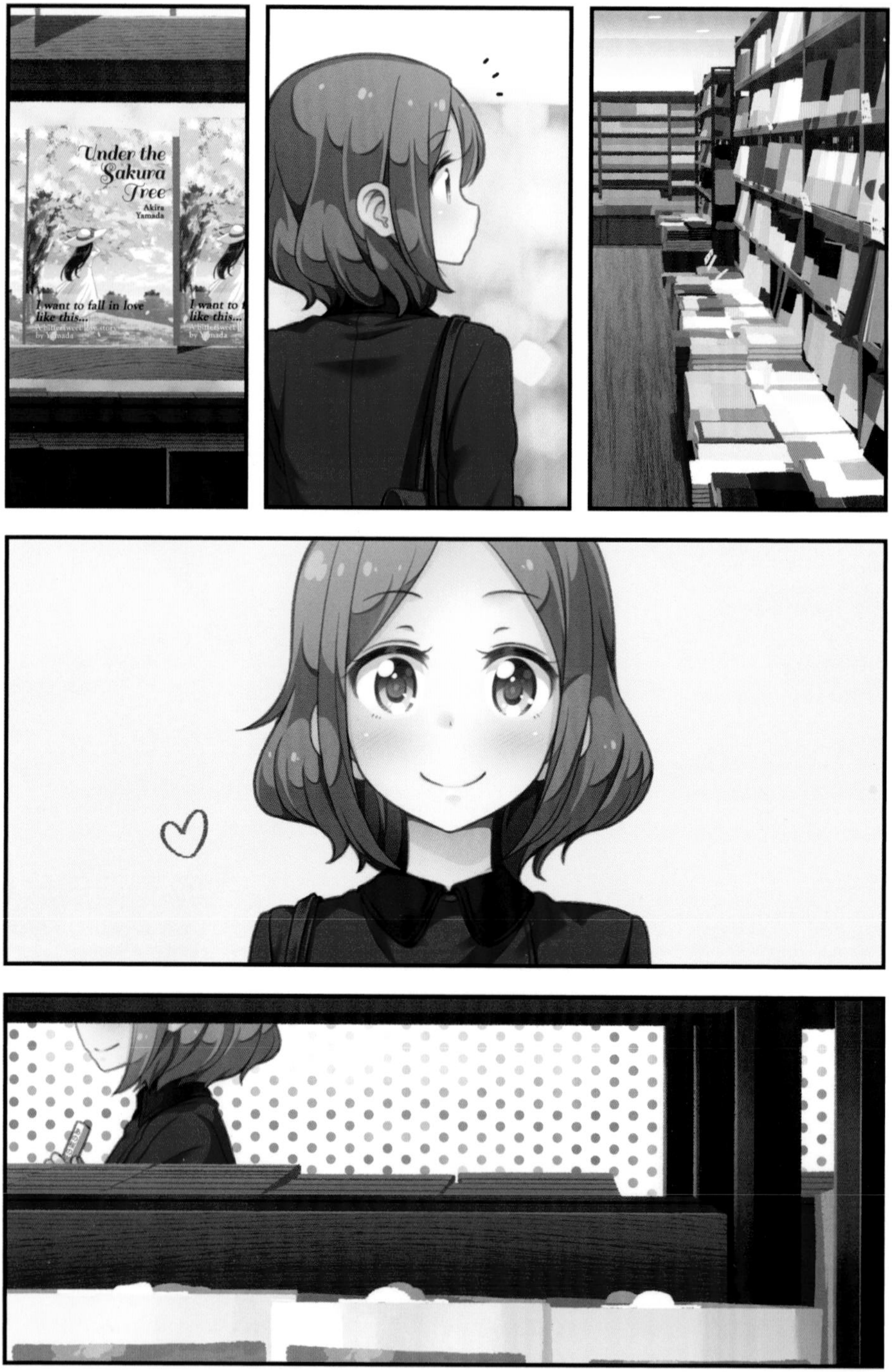
Under the Sakura Tree
Akira Yamada
I want to fall in love like this...

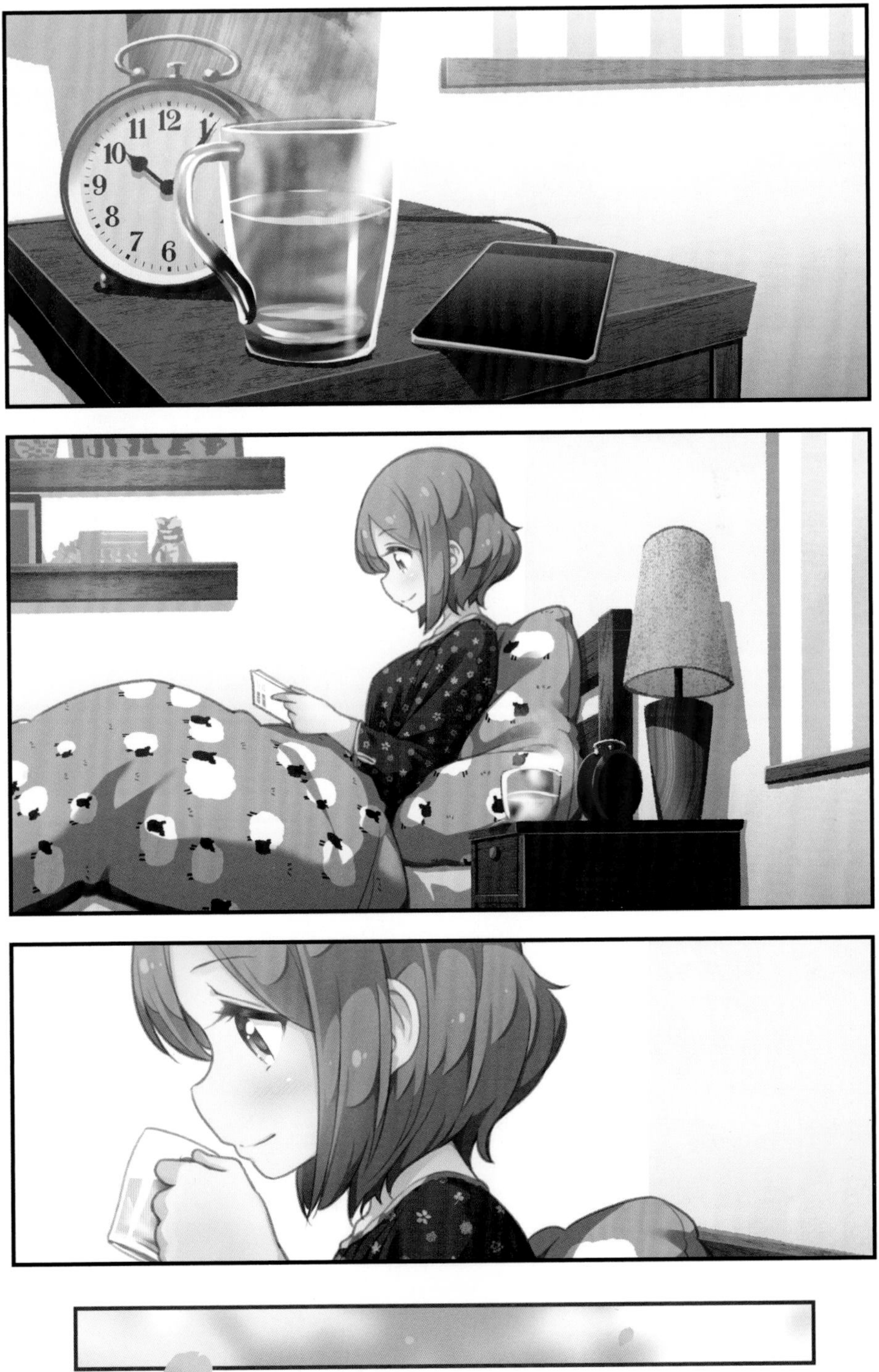

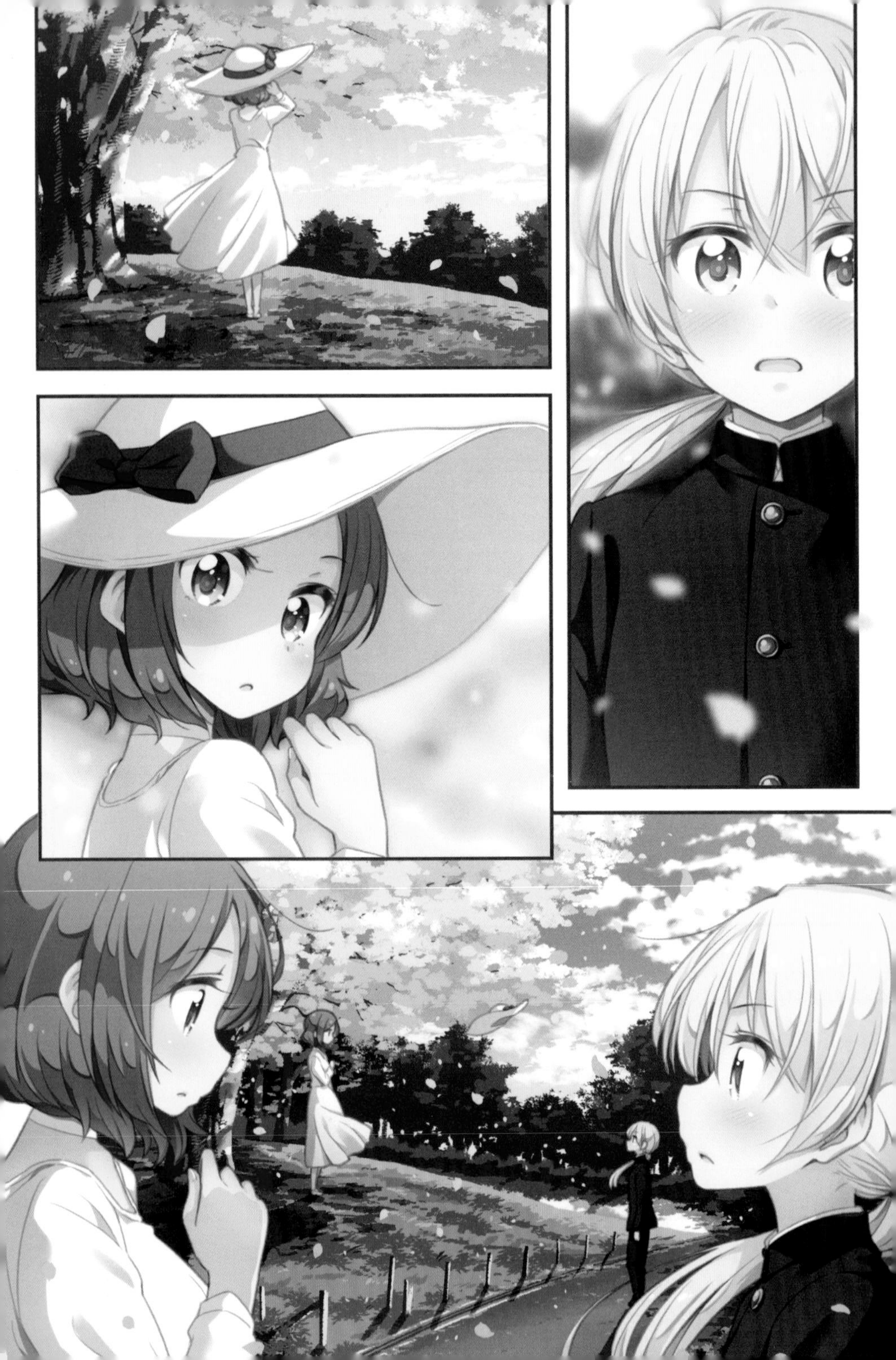

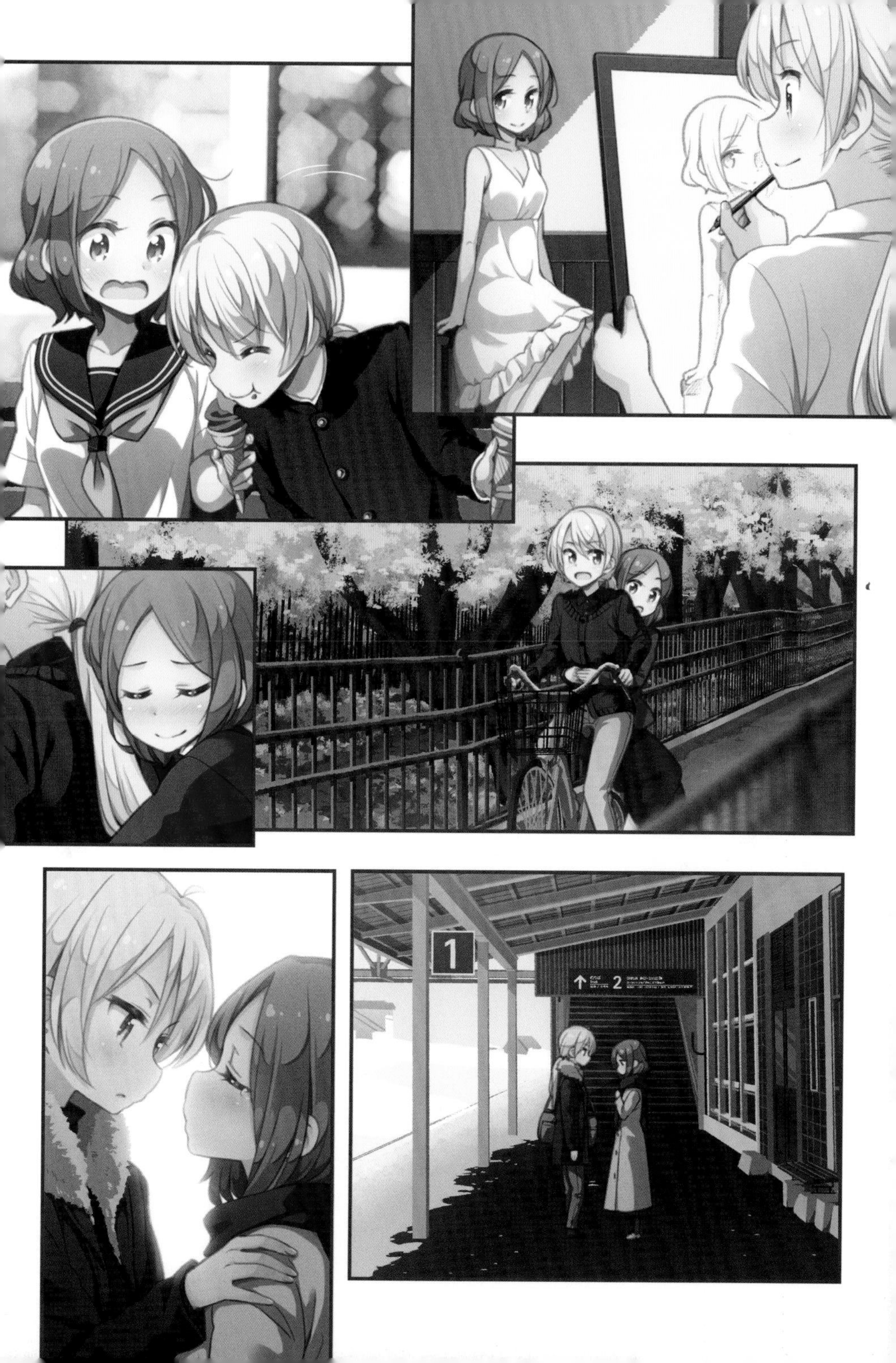
1
2

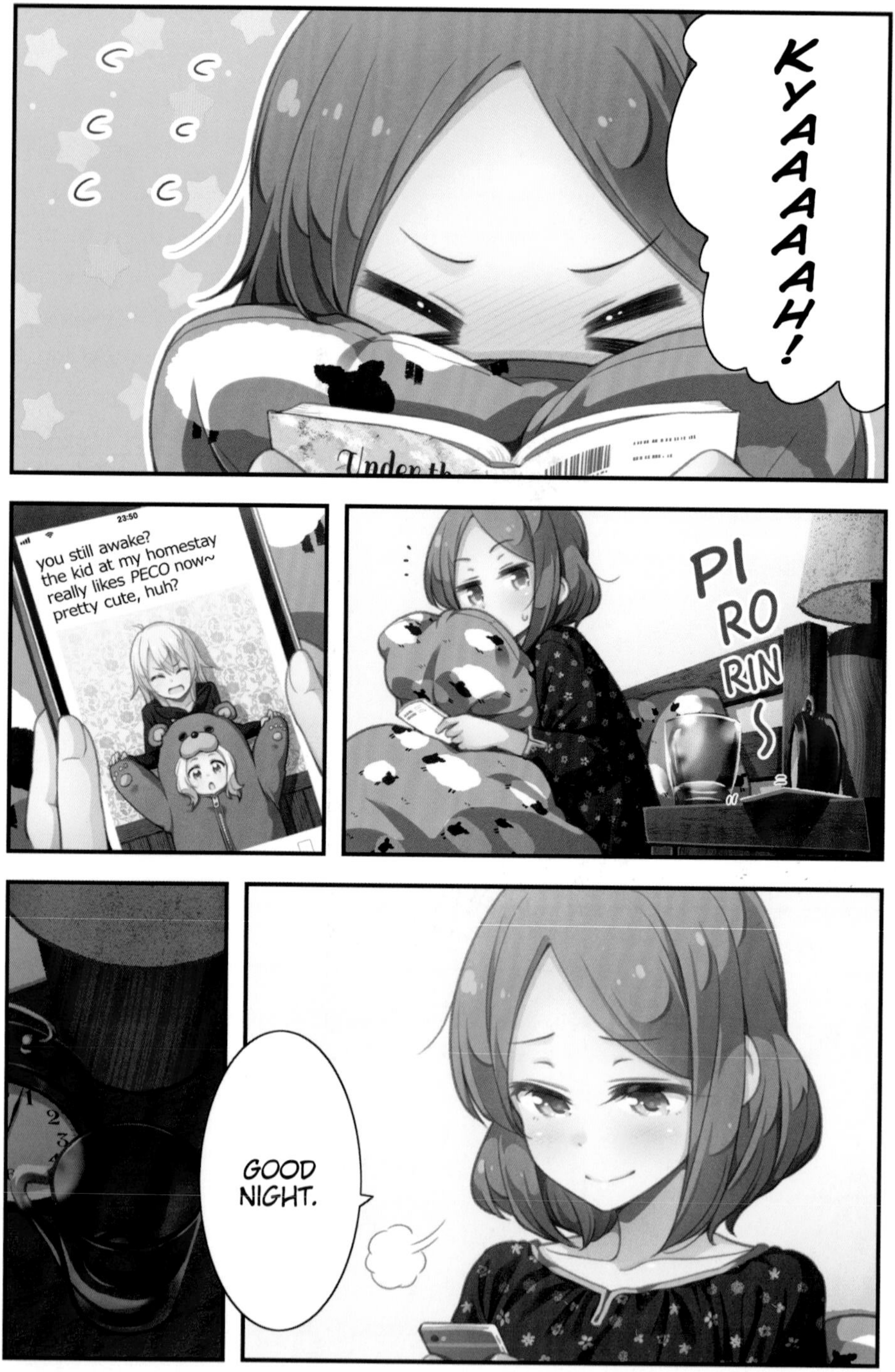
KYAAAAAAH!
PI RO RIN ~
23:50
you still awake?
the kid at my homestay really likes PECO now~
pretty cute, huh?
GOOD NIGHT.

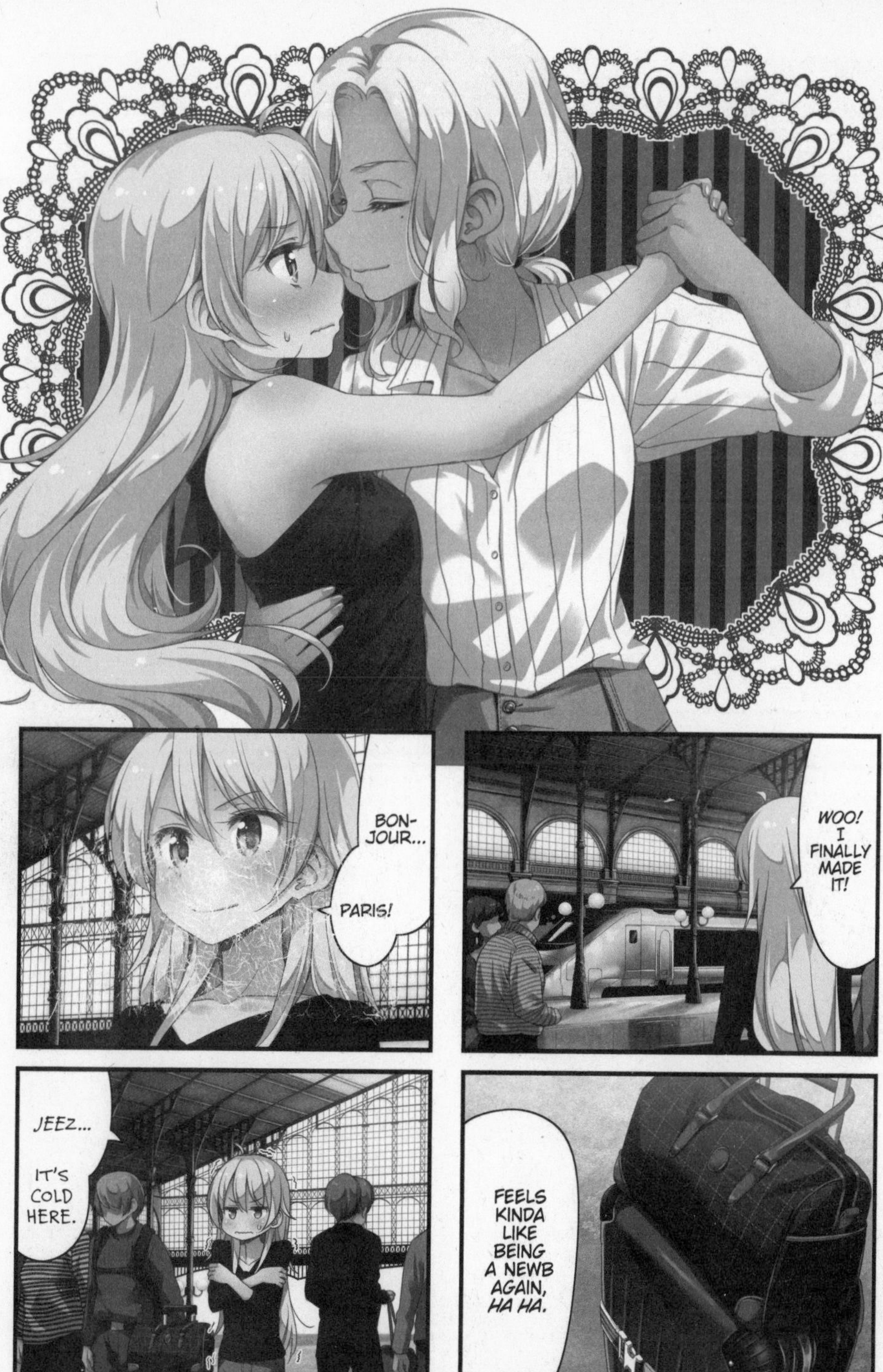
WOO! I FINALLY MADE IT!
BON-JOUR...
PARIS!
FEELS KINDA LIKE BEING A NEWB AGAIN, HA HA.
JEEZ...
IT'S COLD HERE.

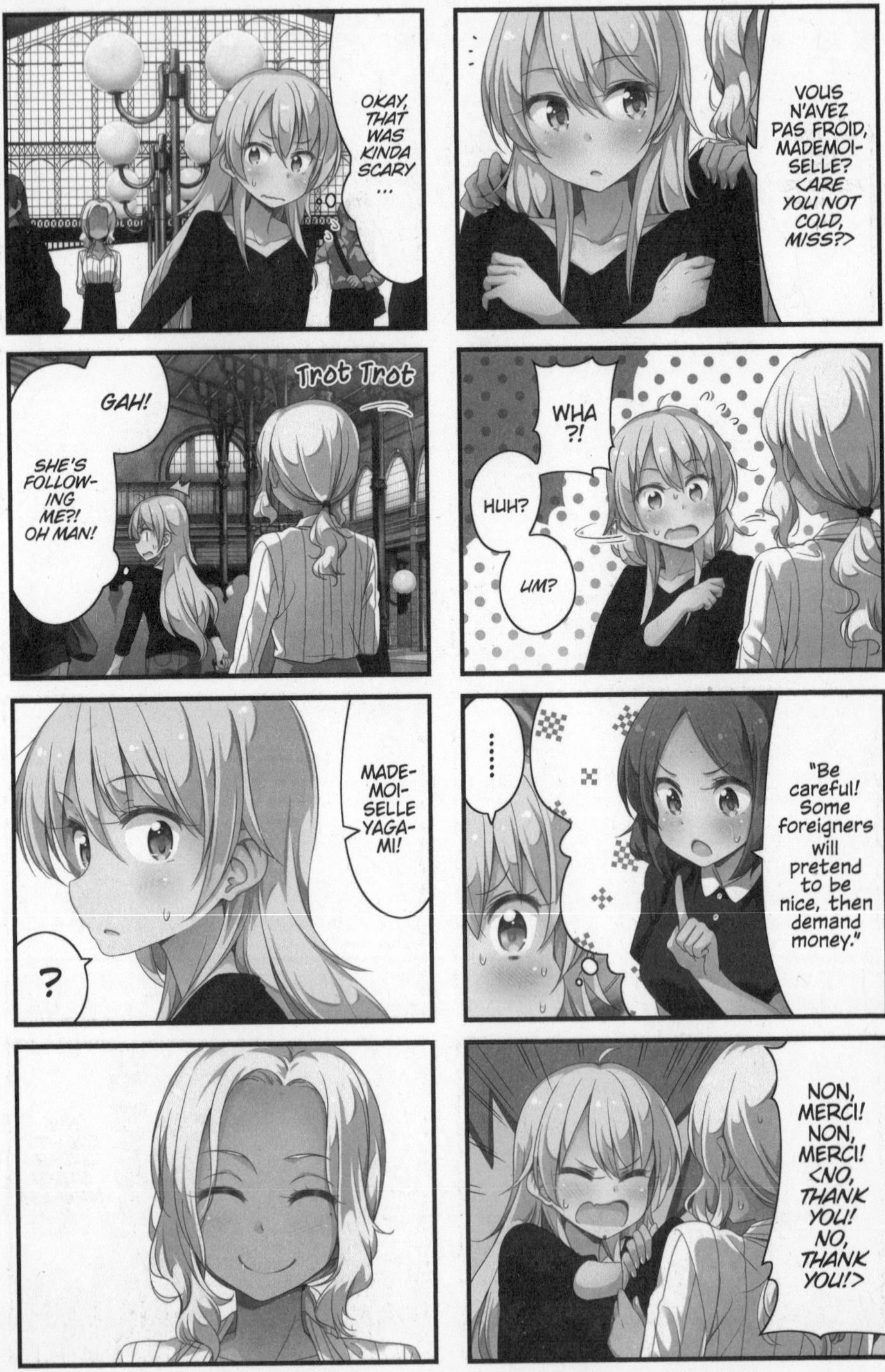
VOUS N'AVEZ PAS FROID, MADEMOISELLE? <ARE YOU NOT COLD, MISS?>
OKAY, THAT WAS KINDA SCARY...
WHA?!
HUH?
UM?
Trot Trot
GAH!
SHE'S FOLLOWING ME?! OH MAN!
"Be careful! Some foreigners will pretend to be nice, then demand money."
......
MADEMOISELLE YAGAMI!
?
NON, MERCI! NON, MERCI! <NO, THANK YOU! NO, THANK YOU!>

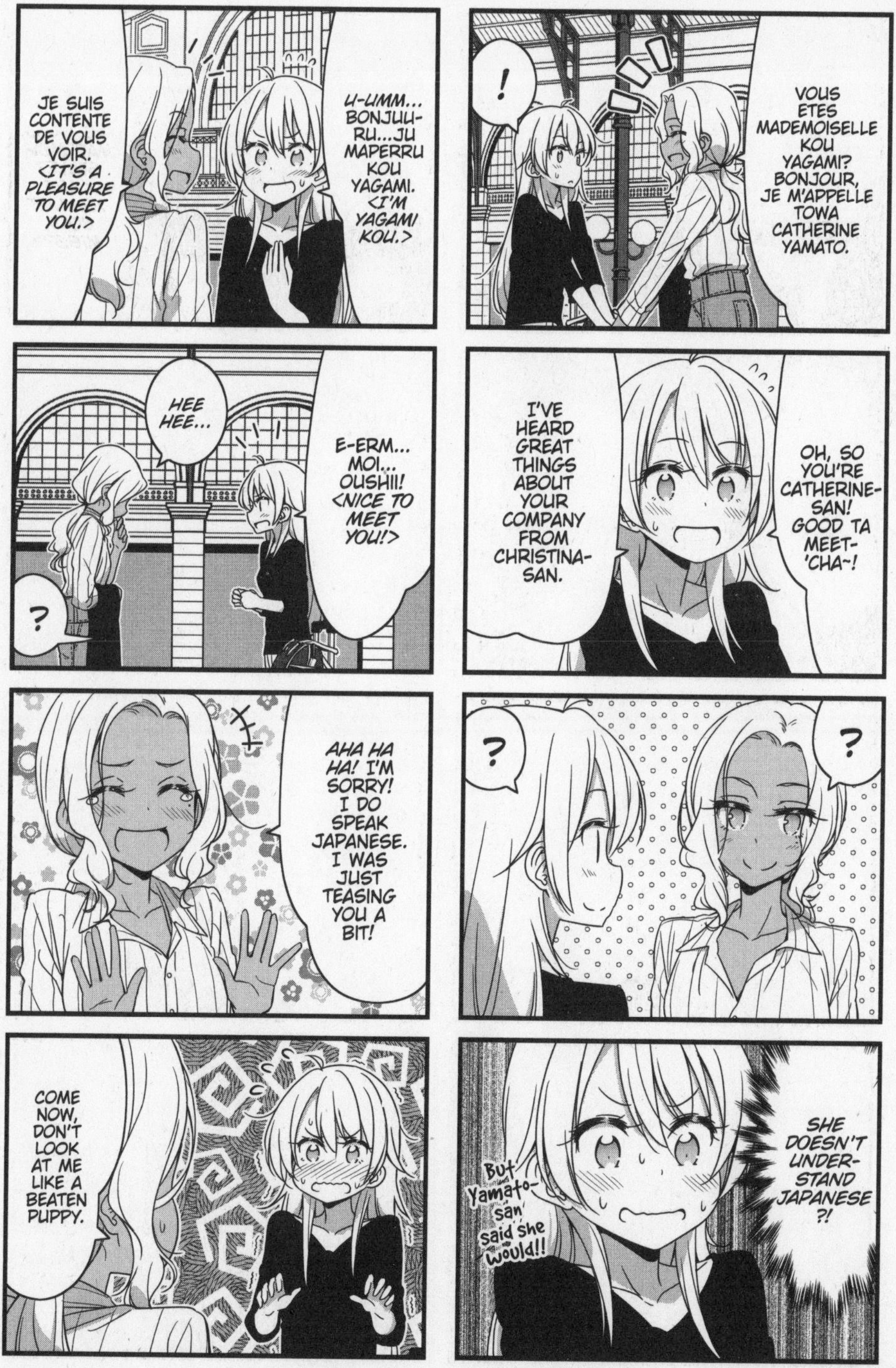
!
VOUS ETES MADEMOISELLE KOU YAGAMI? BONJOUR, JE M'APPELLE TOWA CATHERINE YAMATO.
U-UMM... BONJUURU...JU MAPERRU KOU YAGAMI. <I'M YAGAMI KOU.>
JE SUIS CONTENTE DE VOUS VOIR. <IT'S A PLEASURE TO MEET YOU.>
OH, SO YOU'RE CATHERINE-SAN! GOOD TA MEET-'CHA~!
I'VE HEARD GREAT THINGS ABOUT YOUR COMPANY FROM CHRISTINA-SAN.
E-ERM... MOI... OUSHII! <NICE TO MEET YOU!>
HEE HEE...
?
?
?
AHA HA HA! I'M SORRY! I DO SPEAK JAPANESE. I WAS JUST TEASING YOU A BIT!
SHE DOESN'T UNDER-STAND JAPANESE?!
But Yamato-san said she would!!
COME NOW, DON'T LOOK AT ME LIKE A BEATEN PUPPY.

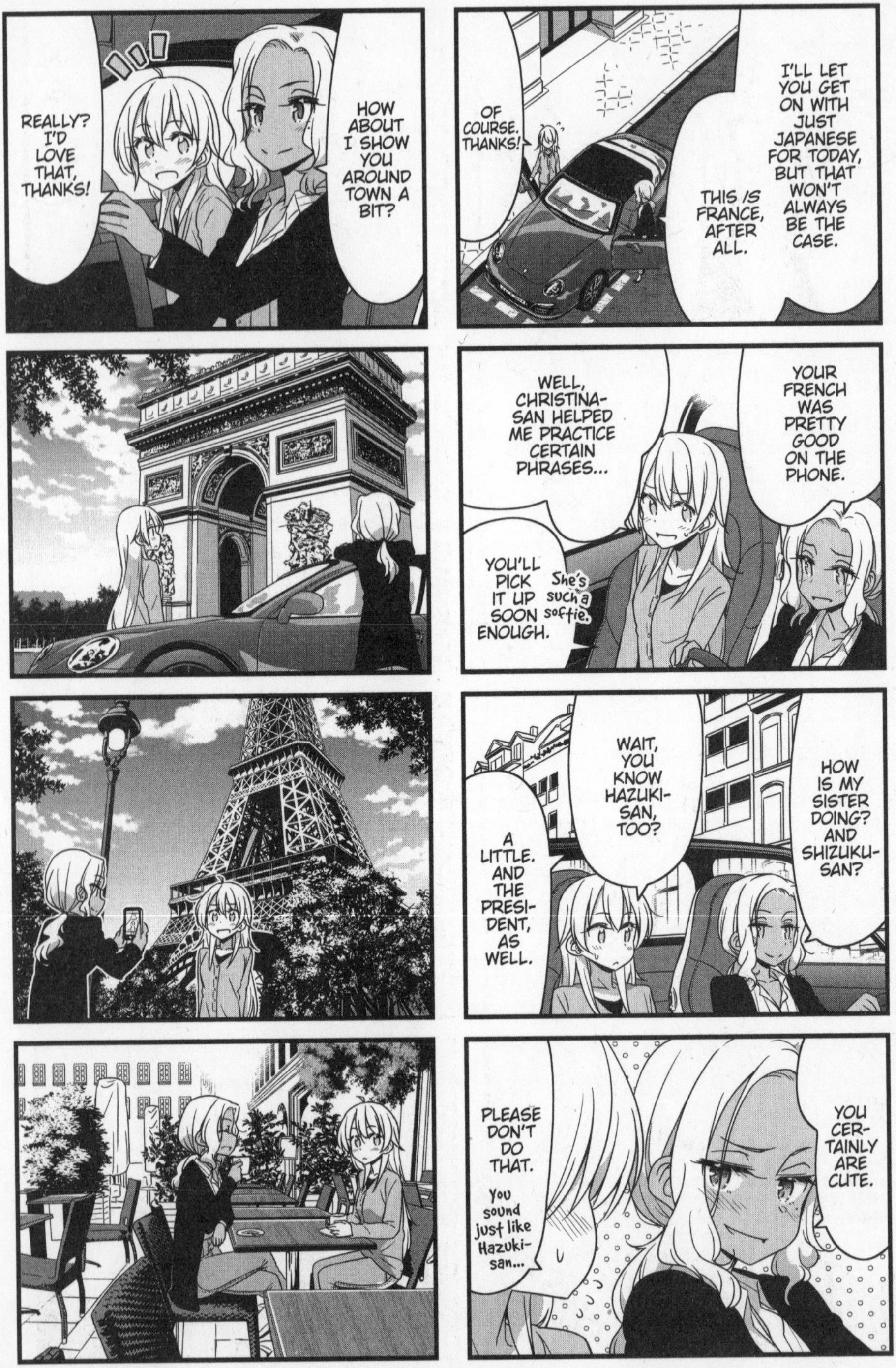
I'LL LET YOU GET ON WITH JUST JAPANESE FOR TODAY, BUT THAT WON'T ALWAYS BE THE CASE.
THIS IS FRANCE, AFTER ALL.
OF COURSE. THANKS!
HOW ABOUT I SHOW YOU AROUND TOWN A BIT?
REALLY? I'D LOVE THAT, THANKS!
YOUR FRENCH WAS PRETTY GOOD ON THE PHONE.
WELL, CHRISTINA-SAN HELPED ME PRACTICE CERTAIN PHRASES...
YOU'LL PICK IT UP SOON ENOUGH.
She's such a softie.
HOW IS MY SISTER DOING? AND SHIZUKU-SAN?
WAIT, YOU KNOW HAZUKI-SAN, TOO?
A LITTLE. AND THE PRESI-DENT, AS WELL.
YOU CER-TAINLY ARE CUTE.
PLEASE DON'T DO THAT.
You sound just like Hazuki-san...

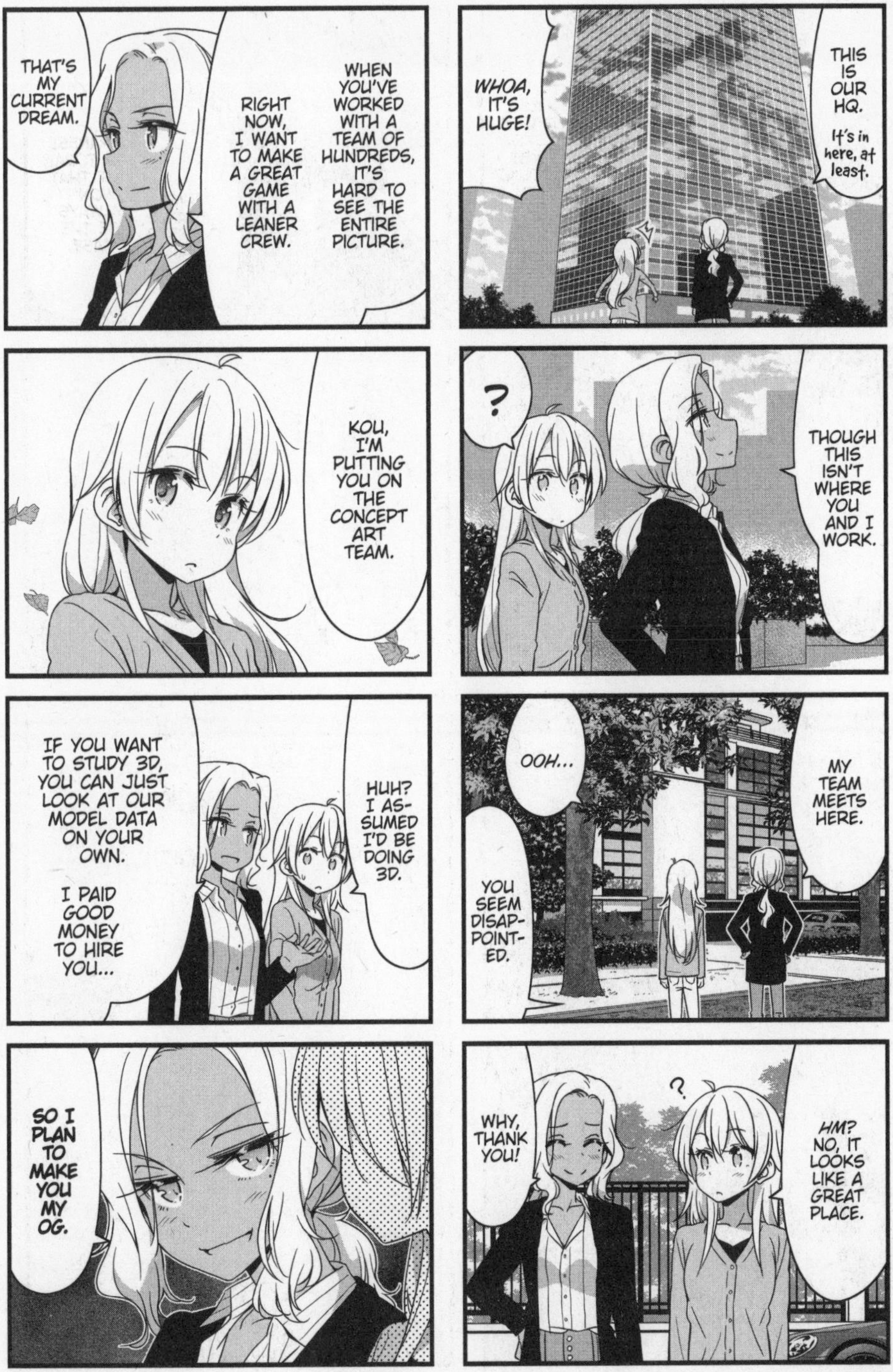
THIS IS OUR HQ.
It's in here, at least.
*WHOA*, IT'S HUGE!
THOUGH THIS ISN'T WHERE YOU AND I WORK.
?
MY TEAM MEETS HERE.
*OOH...*
YOU SEEM DISAPPOINTED.
*HM?* NO, IT LOOKS LIKE A GREAT PLACE.
WHY, THANK YOU!
WHEN YOU'VE WORKED WITH A TEAM OF HUNDREDS, IT'S HARD TO SEE THE ENTIRE PICTURE.
RIGHT NOW, I WANT TO MAKE A GREAT GAME WITH A LEANER CREW.
THAT'S MY CURRENT DREAM.
KOU, I'M PUTTING YOU ON THE CONCEPT ART TEAM.
HUH? I ASSUMED I'D BE DOING 3D.
IF YOU WANT TO STUDY 3D, YOU CAN JUST LOOK AT OUR MODEL DATA ON YOUR OWN.
I PAID GOOD MONEY TO HIRE YOU...
SO I PLAN TO MAKE YOU MY OG.

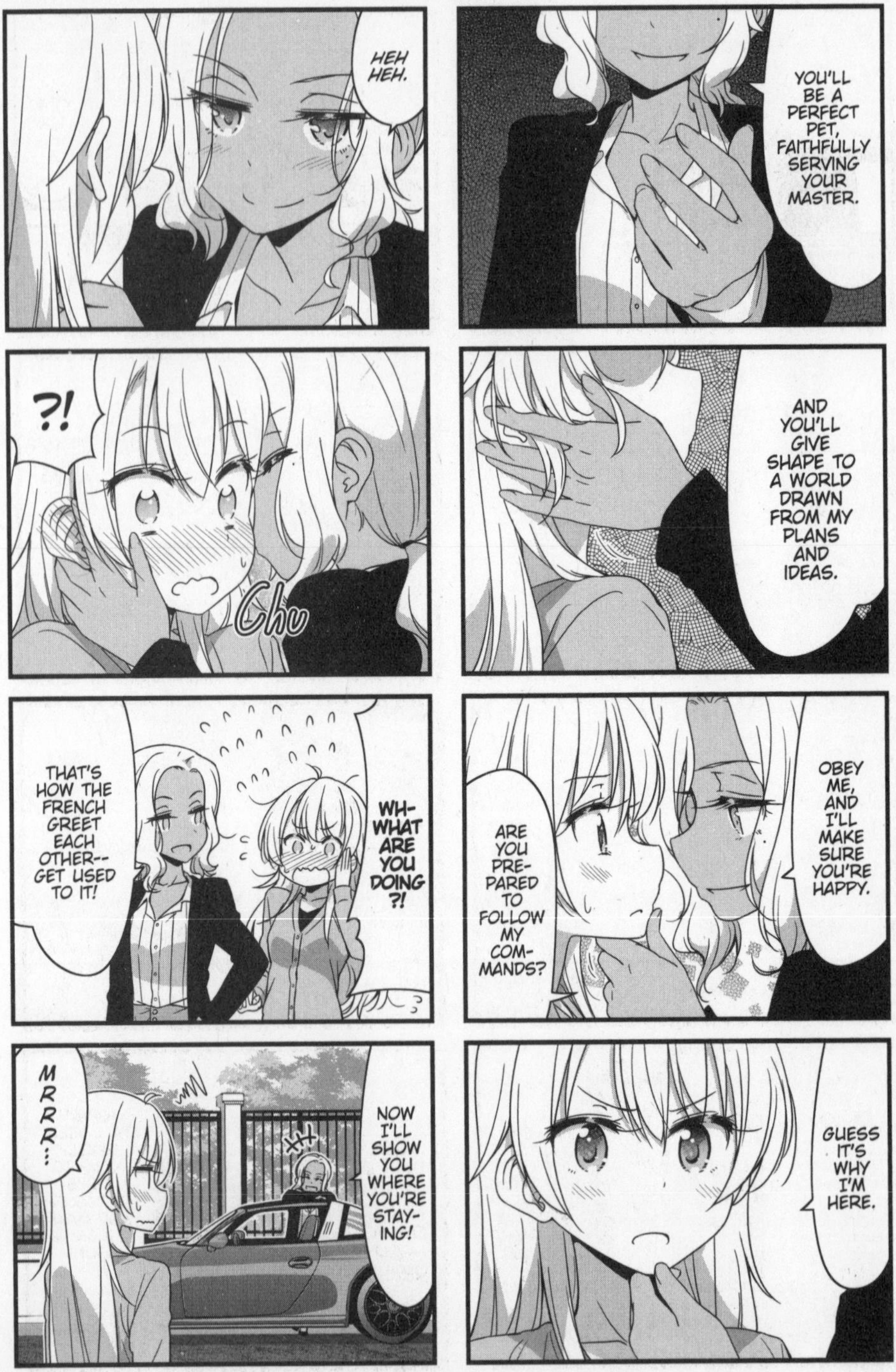
YOU'LL BE A PERFECT PET, FAITHFULLY SERVING YOUR MASTER.
HEH HEH.
AND YOU'LL GIVE SHAPE TO A WORLD DRAWN FROM MY PLANS AND IDEAS.
?!
Chu
OBEY ME, AND I'LL MAKE SURE YOU'RE HAPPY.
ARE YOU PREPARED TO FOLLOW MY COMMANDS?
WH- WHAT ARE YOU DOING?!
THAT'S HOW THE FRENCH GREET EACH OTHER-- GET USED TO IT!
GUESS IT'S WHY I'M HERE.
NOW I'LL SHOW YOU WHERE YOU'RE STAYING!
MRRR...

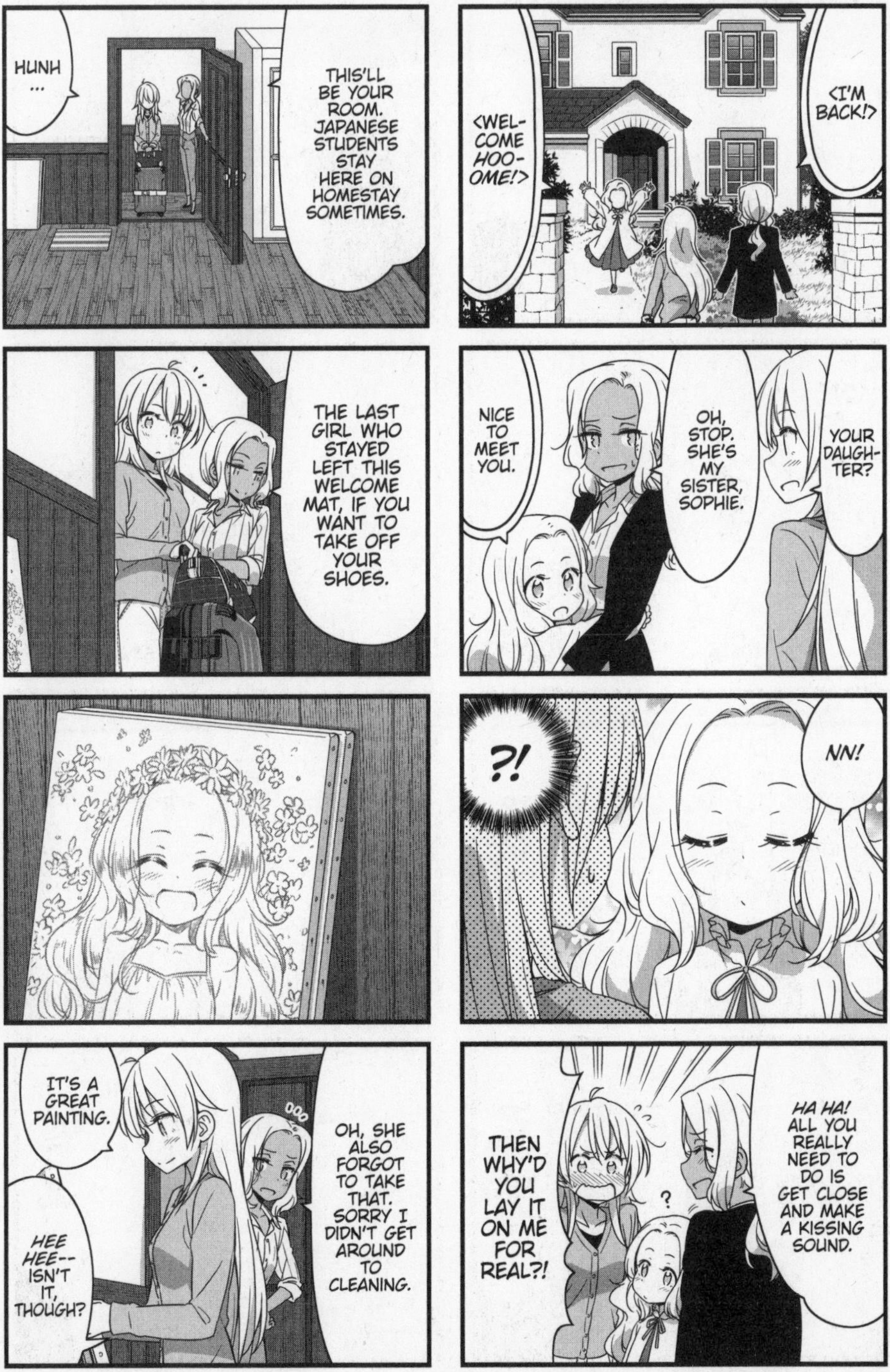
<I'M BACK!>
<WEL-COME HOO-OME!>
THIS'LL BE YOUR ROOM. JAPANESE STUDENTS STAY HERE ON HOMESTAY SOMETIMES.
HUNH ...
YOUR DAUGHTER?
OH, STOP. SHE'S MY SISTER, SOPHIE.
NICE TO MEET YOU.
THE LAST GIRL WHO STAYED LEFT THIS WELCOME MAT, IF YOU WANT TO TAKE OFF YOUR SHOES.
NN!
?!
HA HA! ALL YOU REALLY NEED TO DO IS GET CLOSE AND MAKE A KISSING SOUND.
?
THEN WHY'D YOU LAY IT ON ME FOR REAL?!
OH, SHE ALSO FORGOT TO TAKE THAT. SORRY I DIDN'T GET AROUND TO CLEANING.
IT'S A GREAT PAINTING.
HEE HEE-- ISN'T IT, THOUGH?

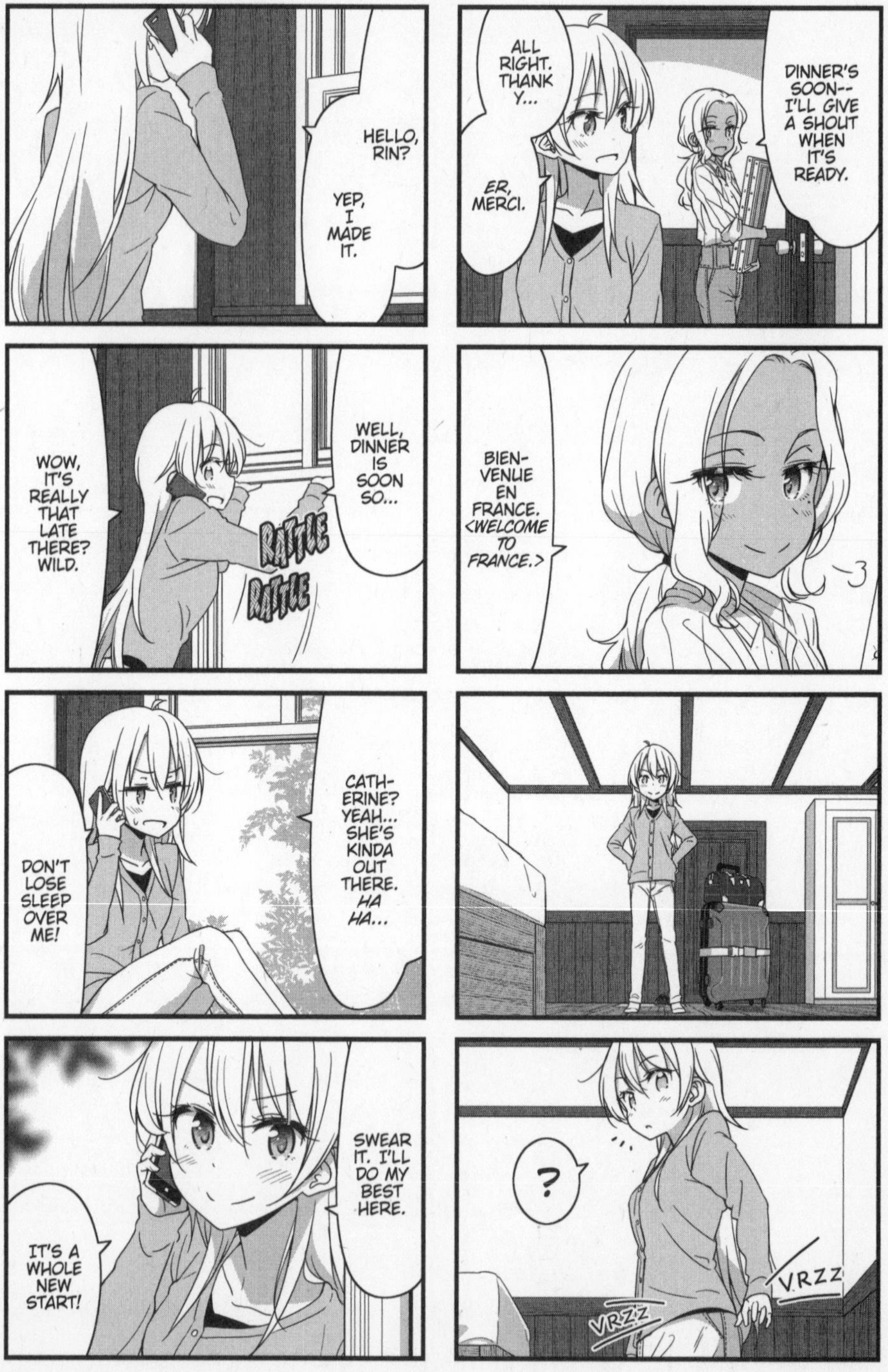
DINNER'S SOON-- I'LL GIVE A SHOUT WHEN IT'S READY.
ALL RIGHT. THANK Y...
ER, MERCI.
HELLO, RIN?
YEP, I MADE IT.
BIEN-VENUE EN FRANCE. <WELCOME TO FRANCE.>
WELL, DINNER IS SOON SO...
RATTLE
RATTLE
WOW, IT'S REALLY THAT LATE THERE? WILD.
CATH-ERINE? YEAH... SHE'S KINDA OUT THERE. HA HA...
DON'T LOSE SLEEP OVER ME!
?
VRZZ
VRZZ
SWEAR IT. I'LL DO MY BEST HERE.
IT'S A WHOLE NEW START!

# NEW GAME!

NEW GAME!

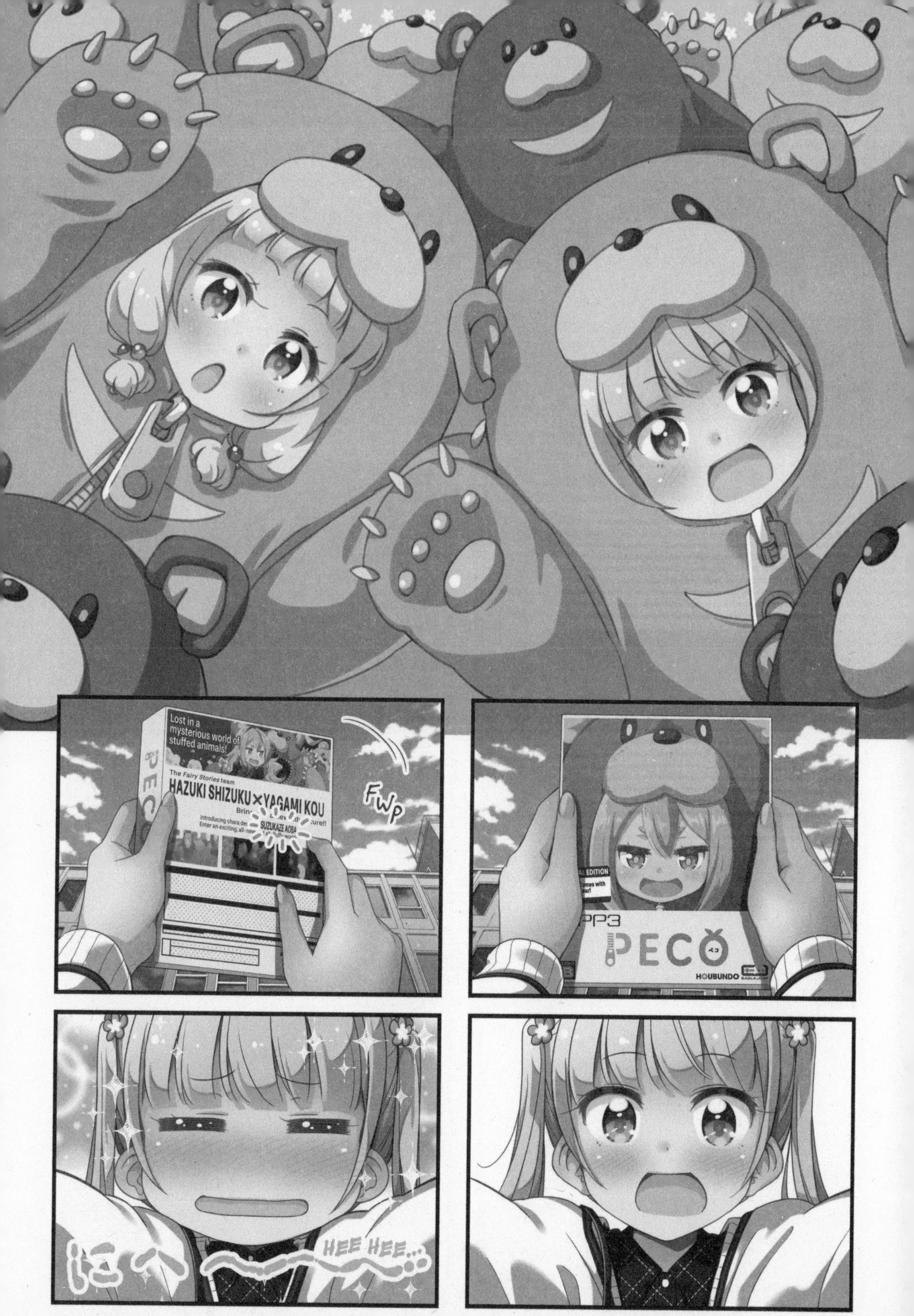
PP3
PECO
HOUBUNDO
Lost in a mysterious world of stuffed animals!
The Fairy Stories team
HAZUKI SHIZUKU × YAGAMI KOU
SUZUKAZE AOBA
FWP
にへ〜〜〜
HEE HEE...

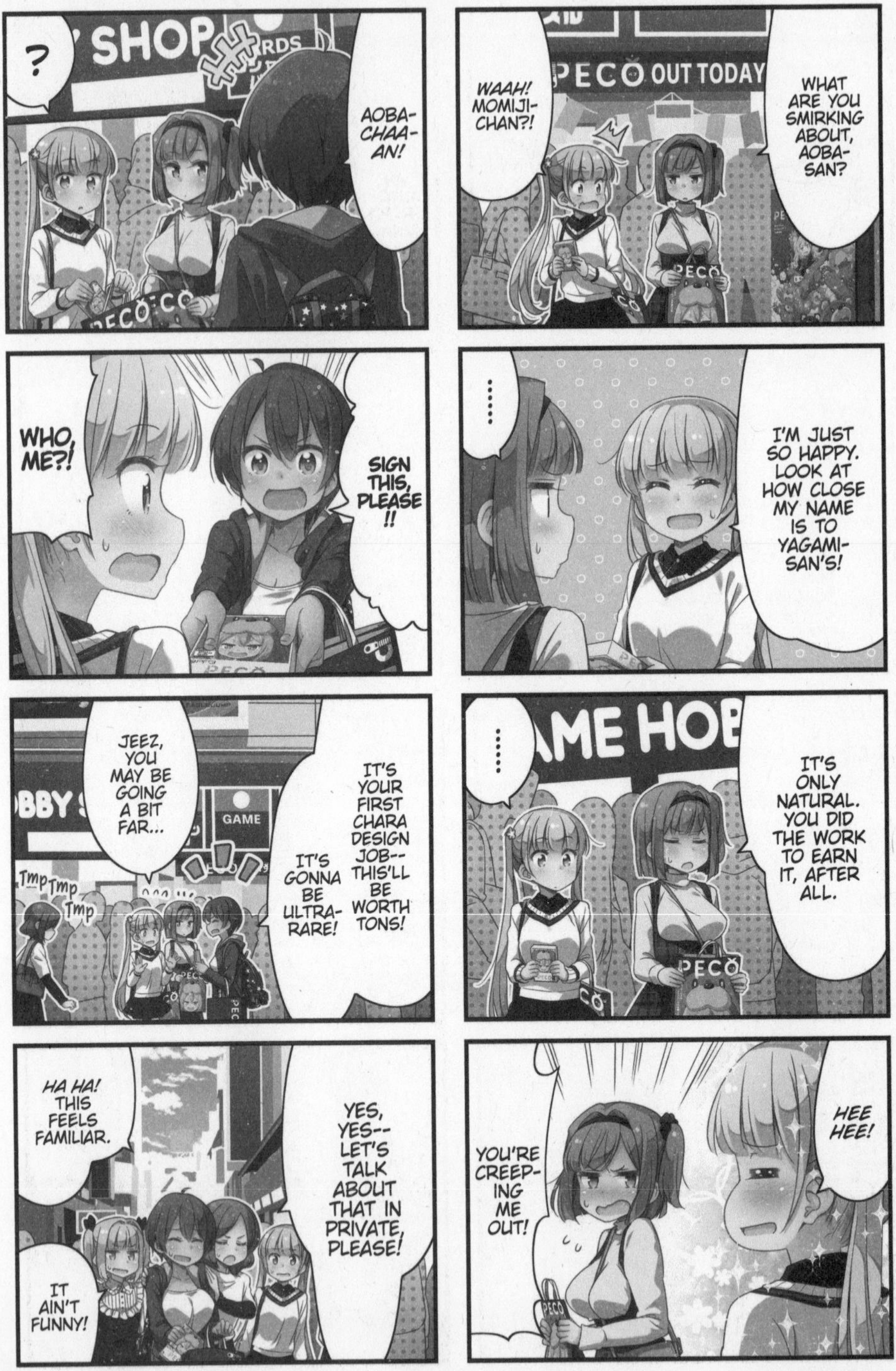
PECO OUT TODAY
WHAT ARE YOU SMIRKING ABOUT, AOBA-SAN?
WAAH! MOMIJI-CHAN?!
SHOP
AOBA-CHAA-AN!
?
I'M JUST SO HAPPY. LOOK AT HOW CLOSE MY NAME IS TO YAGAMI-SAN'S!
......
SIGN THIS, PLEASE!!
WHO, ME?!
AME HOB
IT'S ONLY NATURAL. YOU DID THE WORK TO EARN IT, AFTER ALL.
......
IT'S YOUR FIRST CHARA DESIGN JOB-- THIS'LL BE WORTH TONS!
IT'S GONNA BE ULTRA-RARE!
JEEZ, YOU MAY BE GOING A BIT FAR...
Tmp Tmp Tmp
HEE HEE!
YOU'RE CREEPING ME OUT!
YES, YES-- LET'S TALK ABOUT THAT IN PRIVATE, PLEASE!
HA HA! THIS FEELS FAMILIAR.
IT AIN'T FUNNY!

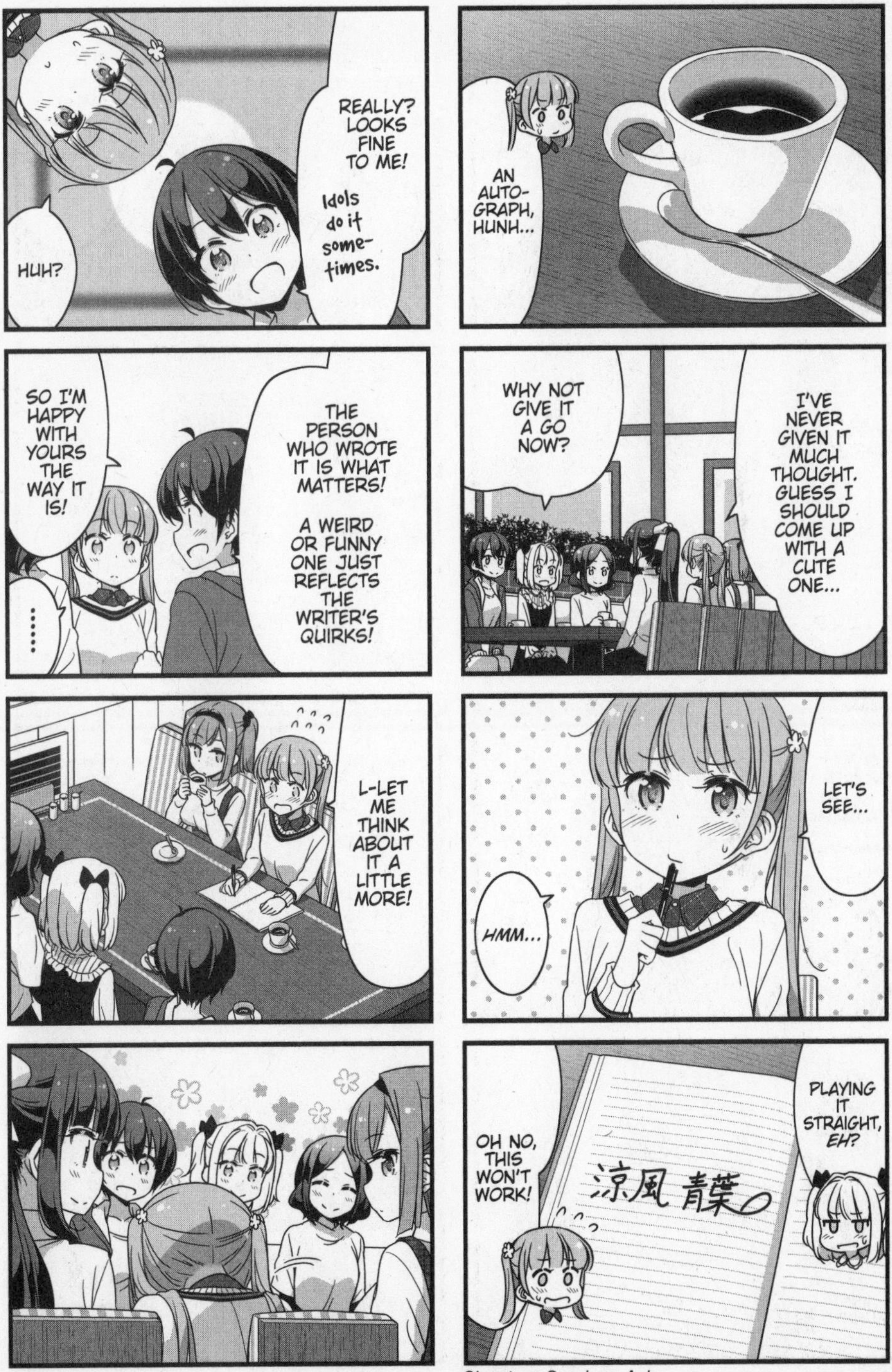
AN AUTOGRAPH, HUNH...
REALLY? LOOKS FINE TO ME!
Idols do it sometimes.
HUH?
I'VE NEVER GIVEN IT MUCH THOUGHT. GUESS I SHOULD COME UP WITH A CUTE ONE...
WHY NOT GIVE IT A GO NOW?
THE PERSON WHO WROTE IT IS WHAT MATTERS!
A WEIRD OR FUNNY ONE JUST REFLECTS THE WRITER'S QUIRKS!
SO I'M HAPPY WITH YOURS THE WAY IT IS!
......
LET'S SEE...
HMM...
L-LET ME THINK ABOUT IT A LITTLE MORE!
PLAYING IT STRAIGHT, EH?
OH NO, THIS WON'T WORK!
涼風 青葉

*Signature: Suzukaze Aoba.*

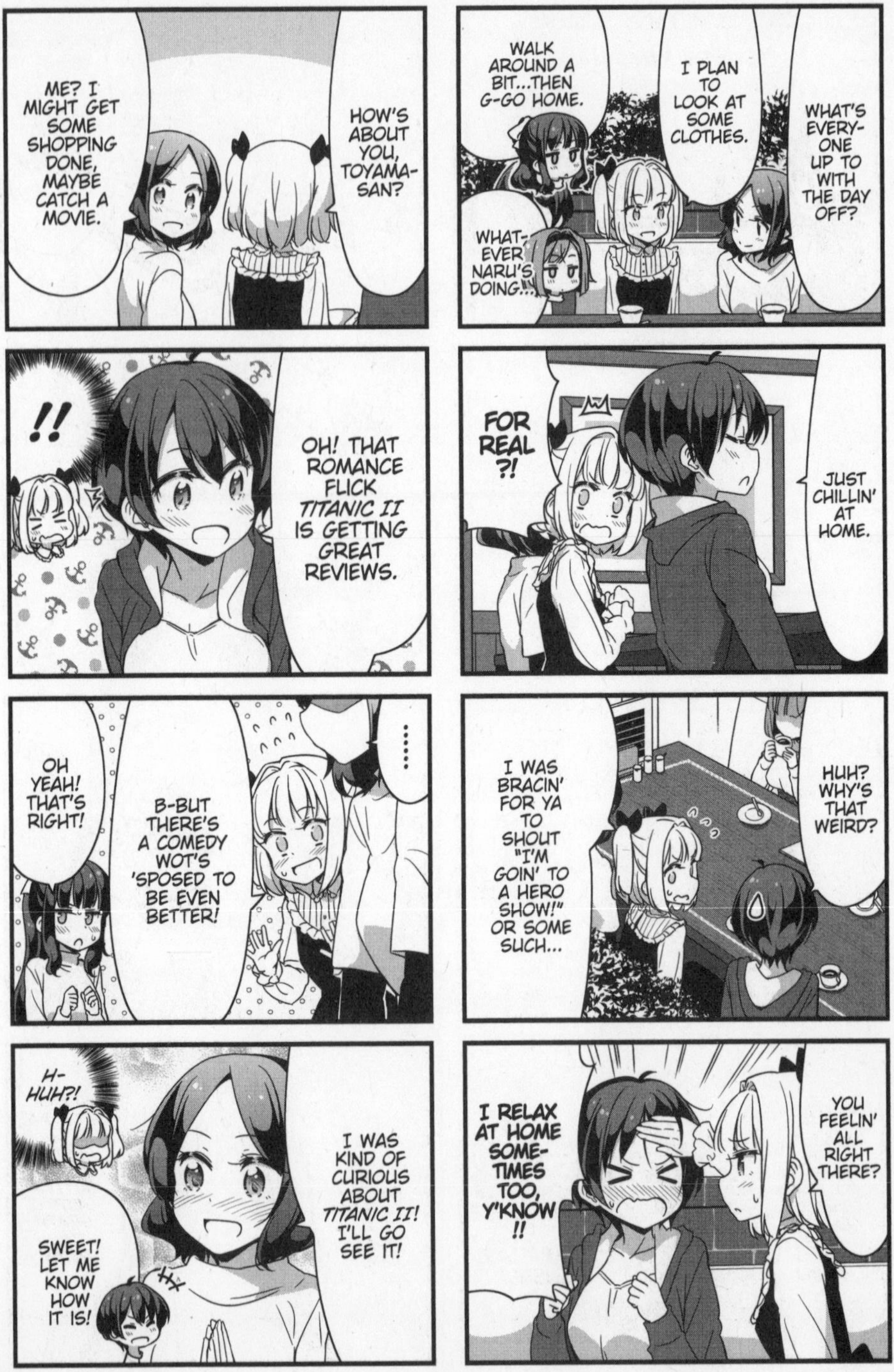
WHAT'S EVERYONE UP TO WITH THE DAY OFF?
I PLAN TO LOOK AT SOME CLOTHES.
WALK AROUND A BIT...THEN G-GO HOME.
WHATEVER NARU'S DOING...
JUST CHILLIN' AT HOME.
FOR REAL ?!
HUH? WHY'S THAT WEIRD?
I WAS BRACIN' FOR YA TO SHOUT "I'M GOIN' TO A HERO SHOW!" OR SOME SUCH...
YOU FEELIN' ALL RIGHT THERE?
I RELAX AT HOME SOMETIMES TOO, Y'KNOW!!
HOW'S ABOUT YOU, TOYAMA-SAN?
ME? I MIGHT GET SOME SHOPPING DONE, MAYBE CATCH A MOVIE.
OH! THAT ROMANCE FLICK *TITANIC II* IS GETTING GREAT REVIEWS.
!!
......
B-BUT THERE'S A COMEDY WOT'S 'SPOSED TO BE EVEN BETTER!
OH YEAH! THAT'S RIGHT!
I WAS KIND OF CURIOUS ABOUT *TITANIC II*! I'LL GO SEE IT!
H-HUH?!
SWEET! LET ME KNOW HOW IT IS!

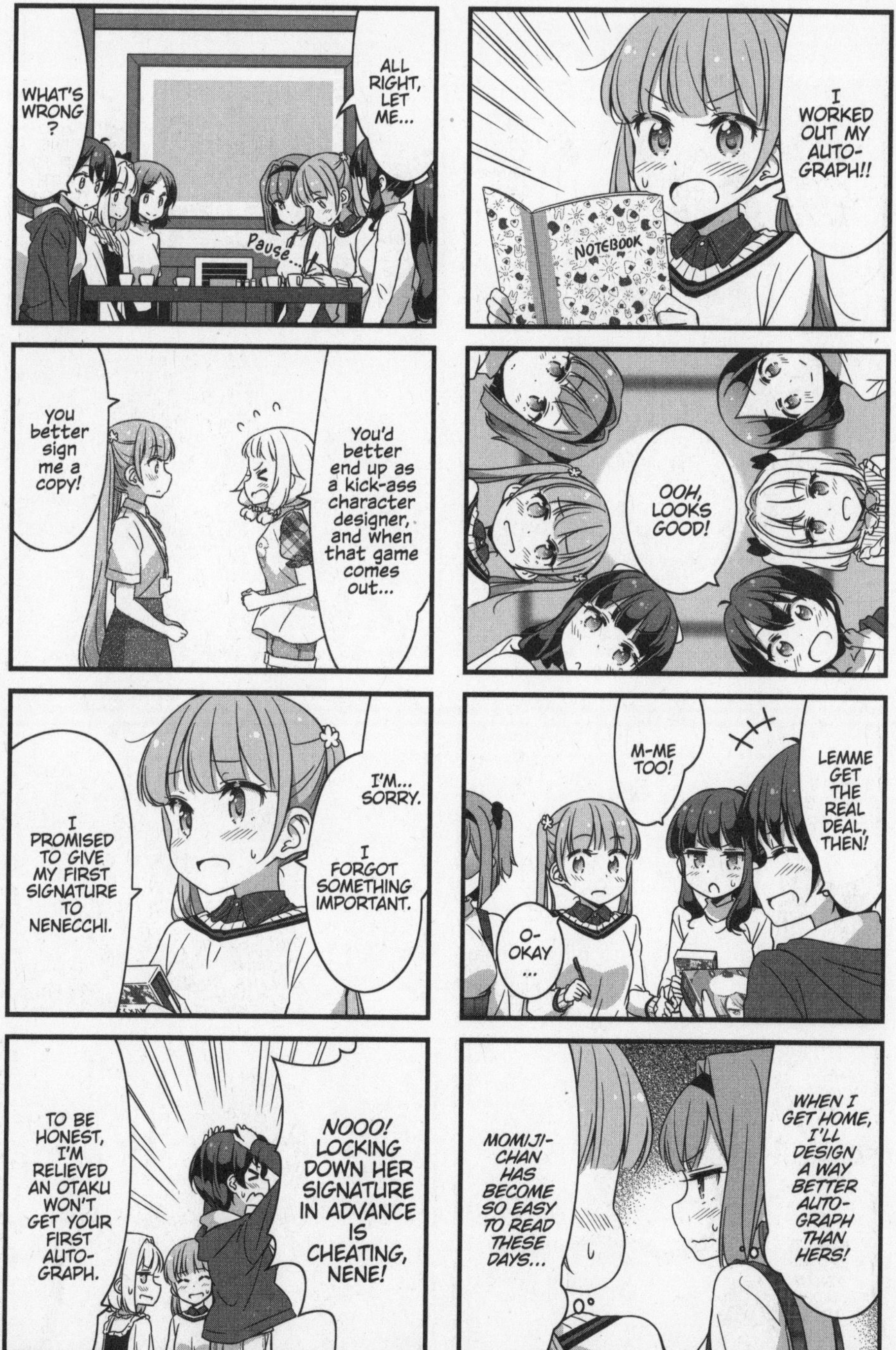
I WORKED OUT MY AUTO-GRAPH!!
NOTEBOOK
ALL RIGHT, LET ME...
Pause...
WHAT'S WRONG?
OOH, LOOKS GOOD!
You'd better end up as a kick-ass character designer, and when that game comes out...
You better sign me a copy!
LEMME GET THE REAL DEAL, THEN!
M-ME TOO!
O-OKAY...
I'M... SORRY.
I FORGOT SOMETHING IMPORTANT.
I PROMISED TO GIVE MY FIRST SIGNATURE TO NENECCHI.
WHEN I GET HOME, I'LL DESIGN A WAY BETTER AUTO-GRAPH THAN HERS!
MOMIJI-CHAN HAS BECOME SO EASY TO READ THESE DAYS...
NOOO! LOCKING DOWN HER SIGNATURE IN ADVANCE IS CHEATING, NENE!
TO BE HONEST, I'M RELIEVED AN OTAKU WON'T GET YOUR FIRST AUTO-GRAPH.

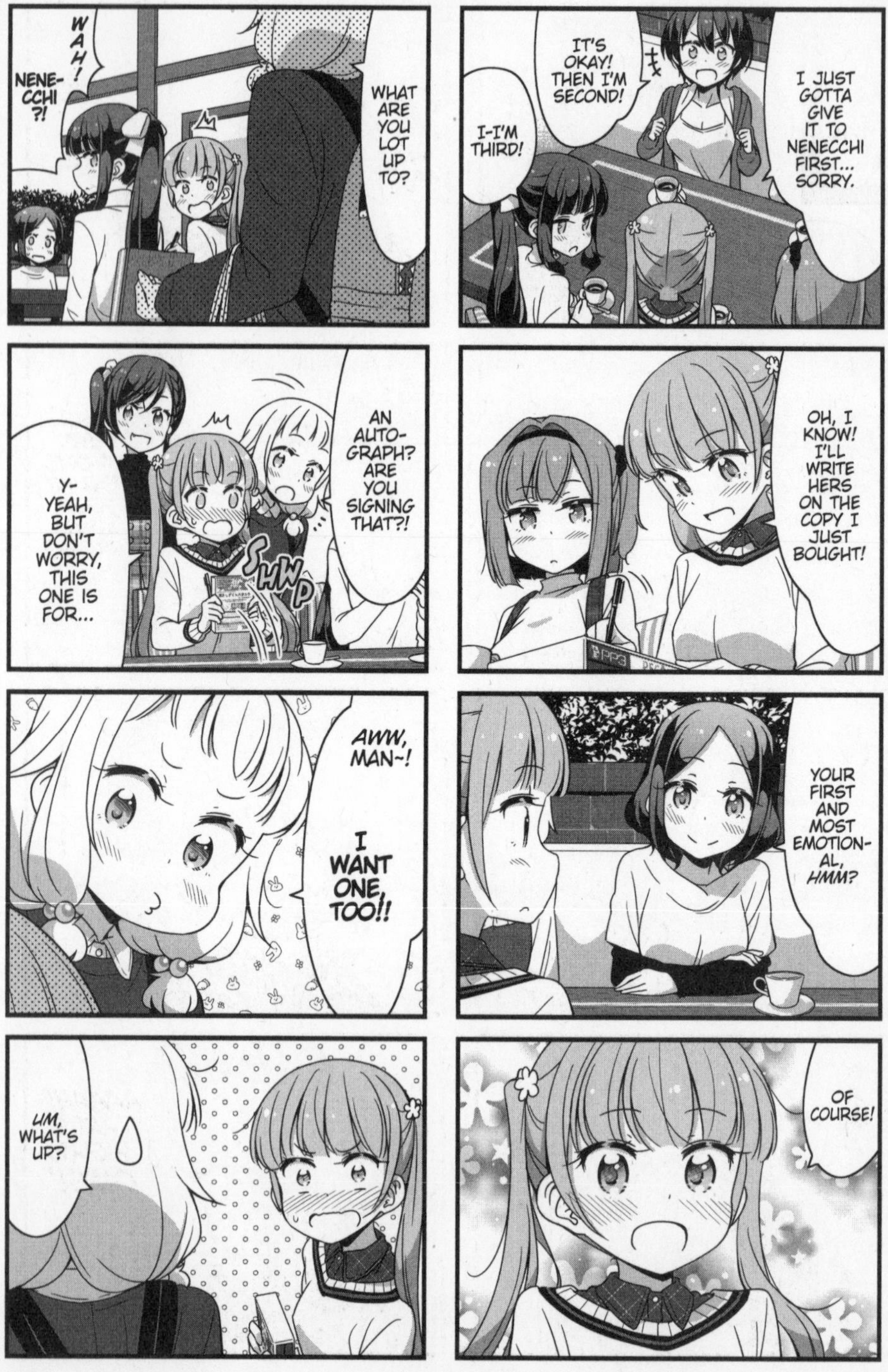
I JUST GOTTA GIVE IT TO NENECCHI FIRST... SORRY.
IT'S OKAY! THEN I'M SECOND!
I-I'M THIRD!
WHAT ARE YOU LOT UP TO?
WAH!
NENECCHI?!
OH, I KNOW! I'LL WRITE HERS ON THE COPY I JUST BOUGHT!
AN AUTOGRAPH? ARE YOU SIGNING THAT?!
SHWP
Y-YEAH, BUT DON'T WORRY, THIS ONE IS FOR...
YOUR FIRST AND MOST EMOTIONAL, HMM?
AWW, MAN~!
I WANT ONE TOO!!
OF COURSE!
UM, WHAT'S UP?

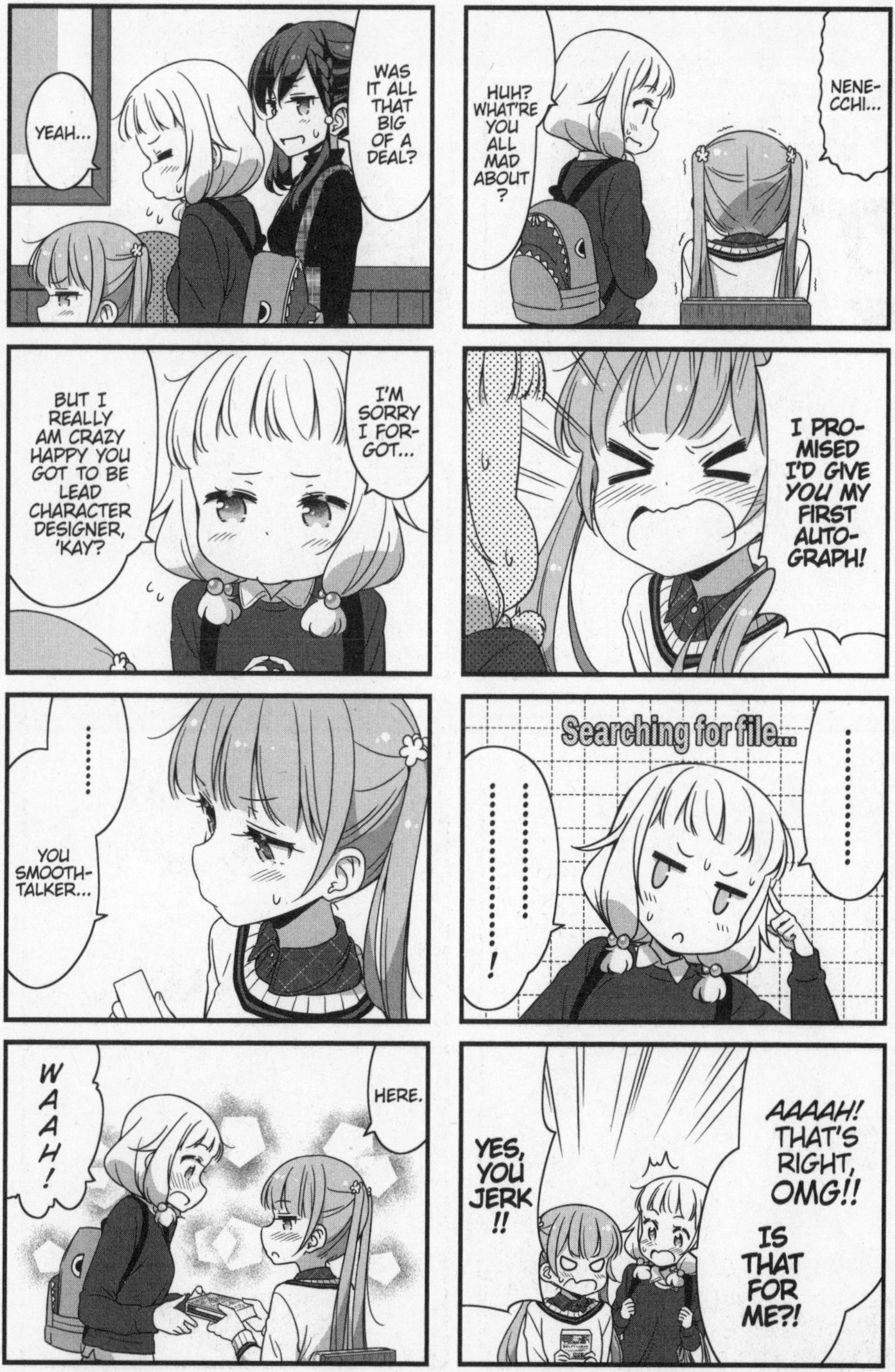
NENE-CCHI...
HUH? WHAT'RE YOU ALL MAD ABOUT?
WAS IT ALL THAT BIG OF A DEAL?
YEAH...
I PRO-MISED I'D GIVE *YOU* MY FIRST AUTO-GRAPH!
I'M SORRY I FOR-GOT...
BUT I REALLY AM CRAZY HAPPY YOU GOT TO BE LEAD CHARACTER DESIGNER, 'KAY?
Searching for file...
..........
..........!
......
YOU SMOOTH-TALKER...
AAAAH! THAT'S RIGHT, OMG!!
IS THAT FOR ME?!
YES, YOU JERK!!
HERE.
WAAH!

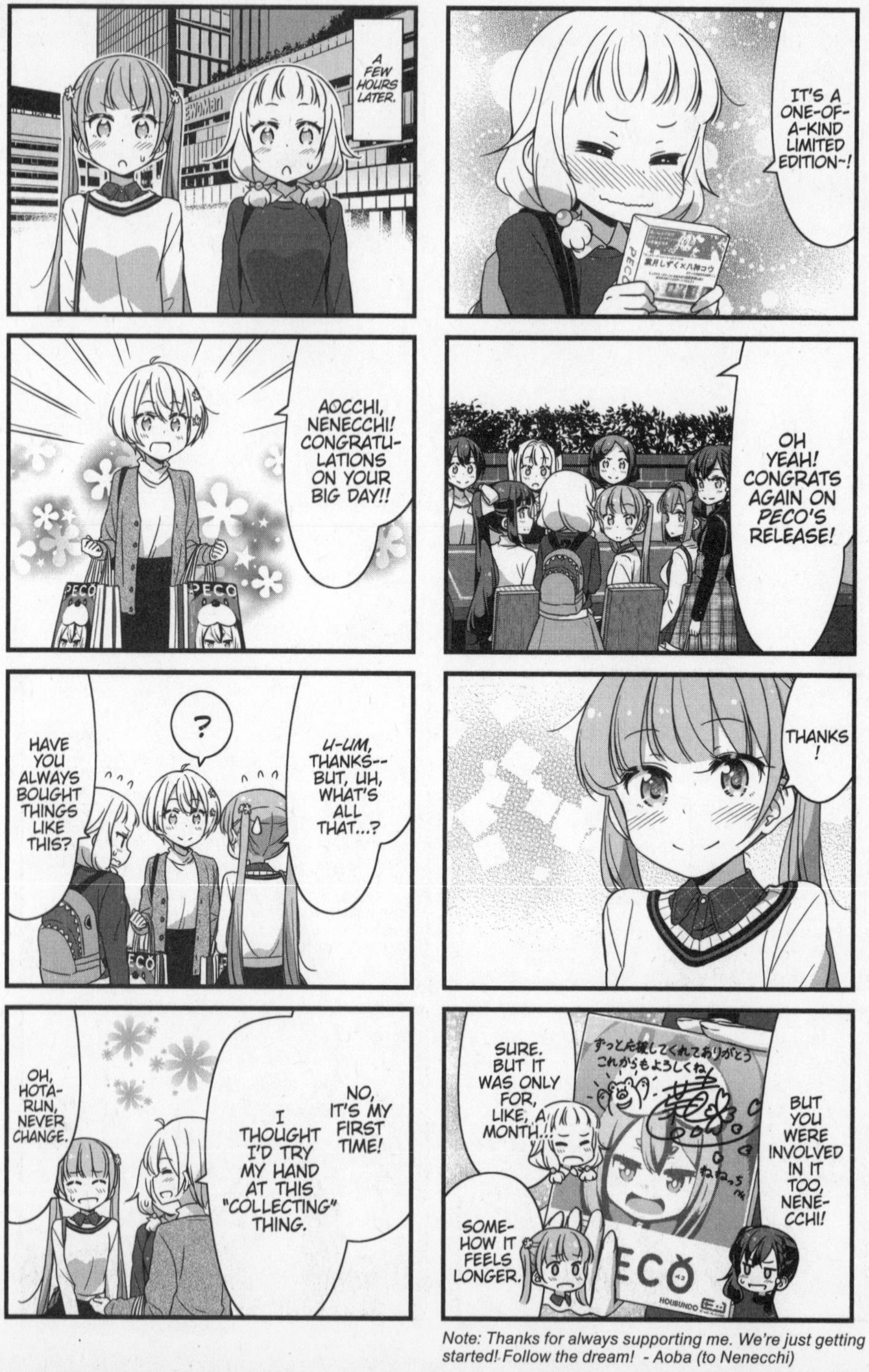
IT'S A ONE-OF-A-KIND LIMITED EDITION~!
OH YEAH! CONGRATS AGAIN ON PECO'S RELEASE!
THANKS!
BUT YOU WERE INVOLVED IN IT TOO, NENECCHI!
SURE. BUT IT WAS ONLY FOR, LIKE, A MONTH...!
SOMEHOW IT FEELS LONGER.
ずっと応援してくれてありがとう
これからもよろしくね。
ECO
HOUBUNDO
A FEW HOURS LATER.
AOCCHI, NENECCHI! CONGRATULATIONS ON YOUR BIG DAY!!
PECO
U-UM, THANKS-- BUT, UH, WHAT'S ALL THAT...?
?
HAVE YOU ALWAYS BOUGHT THINGS LIKE THIS?
NO, IT'S MY FIRST TIME!
I THOUGHT I'D TRY MY HAND AT THIS "COLLECTING" THING.
OH, HOTA-RUN, NEVER CHANGE.

Note: Thanks for always supporting me. We're just getting started! Follow the dream! - Aoba (to Nenecchi)

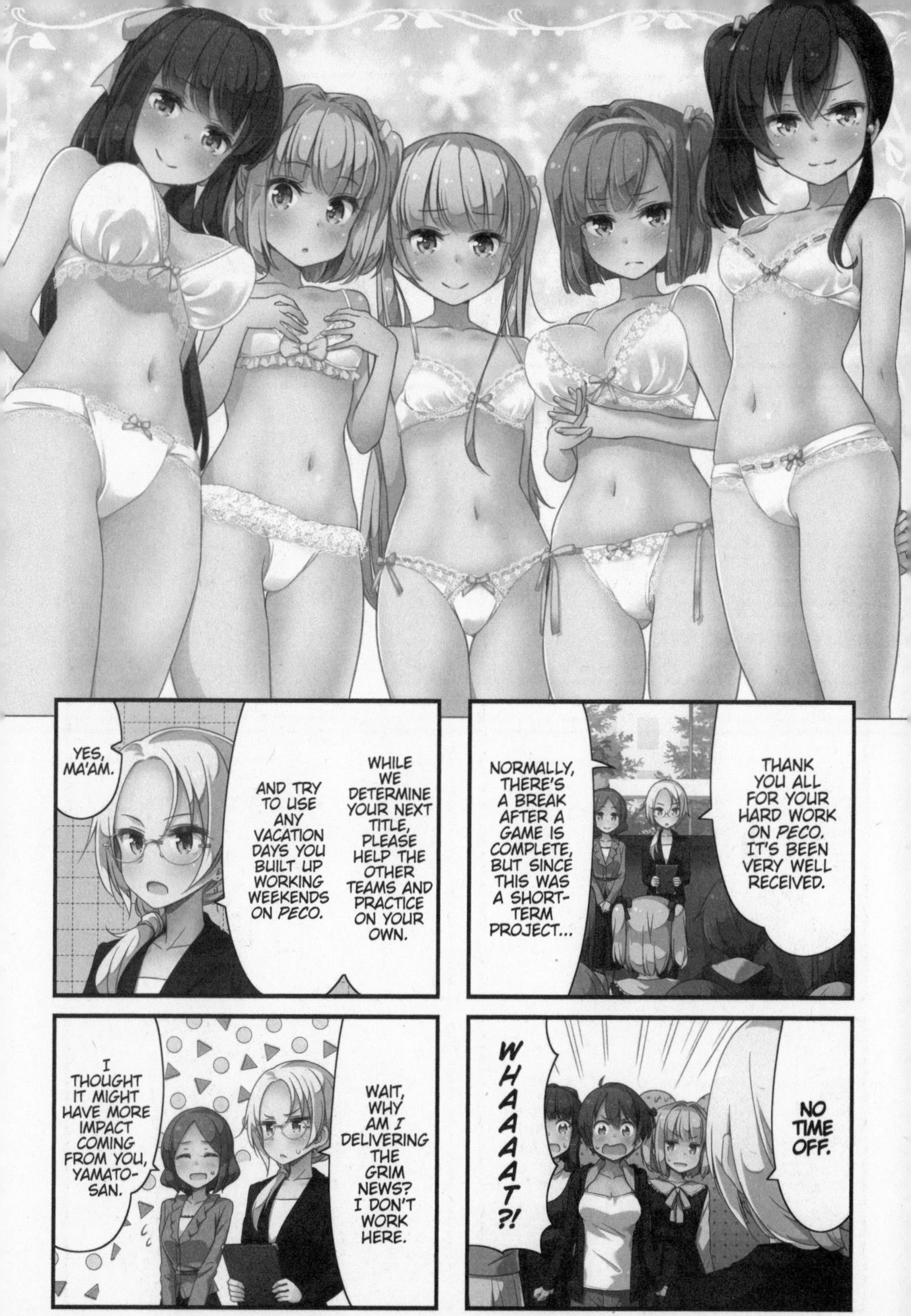

THANK YOU ALL FOR YOUR HARD WORK ON *PECO*. IT'S BEEN VERY WELL RECEIVED.
NORMALLY, THERE'S A BREAK AFTER A GAME IS COMPLETE, BUT SINCE THIS WAS A SHORT-TERM PROJECT...
WHILE WE DETERMINE YOUR NEXT TITLE, PLEASE HELP THE OTHER TEAMS AND PRACTICE ON YOUR OWN.
AND TRY TO USE ANY VACATION DAYS YOU BUILT UP WORKING WEEKENDS ON *PECO*.
YES, MA'AM.
NO TIME OFF.
WHAAAAAT?!
WAIT, WHY AM *I* DELIVERING THE GRIM NEWS? I DON'T WORK HERE.
I THOUGHT IT MIGHT HAVE MORE IMPACT COMING FROM YOU, YAMATO-SAN.

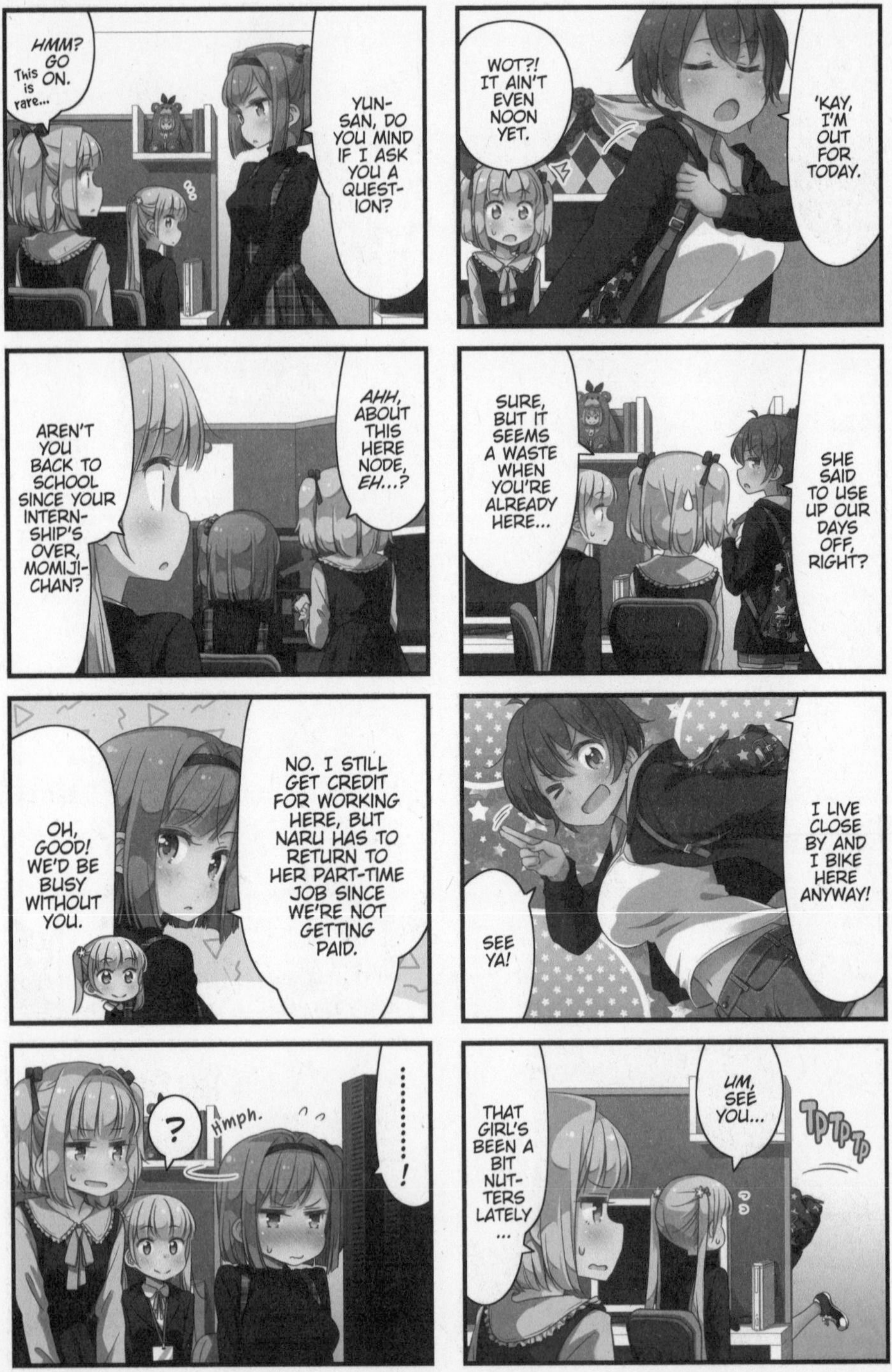
'KAY, I'M OUT FOR TODAY.
WOT?! IT AIN'T EVEN NOON YET.
YUN-SAN, DO YOU MIND IF I ASK YOU A QUEST-ION?
HMM? GO ON.
This is rare...
SHE SAID TO USE UP OUR DAYS OFF, RIGHT?
SURE, BUT IT SEEMS A WASTE WHEN YOU'RE ALREADY HERE...
AHH, ABOUT THIS HERE NODE, EH...?
AREN'T YOU BACK TO SCHOOL SINCE YOUR INTERN-SHIP'S OVER, MOMIJI-CHAN?
I LIVE CLOSE BY AND I BIKE HERE ANYWAY!
SEE YA!
NO. I STILL GET CREDIT FOR WORKING HERE, BUT NARU HAS TO RETURN TO HER PART-TIME JOB SINCE WE'RE NOT GETTING PAID.
OH, GOOD! WE'D BE BUSY WITHOUT YOU.
UM, SEE YOU...
TPTPTP
THAT GIRL'S BEEN A BIT NUTTERS LATELY...
.........!
Hmph.
?

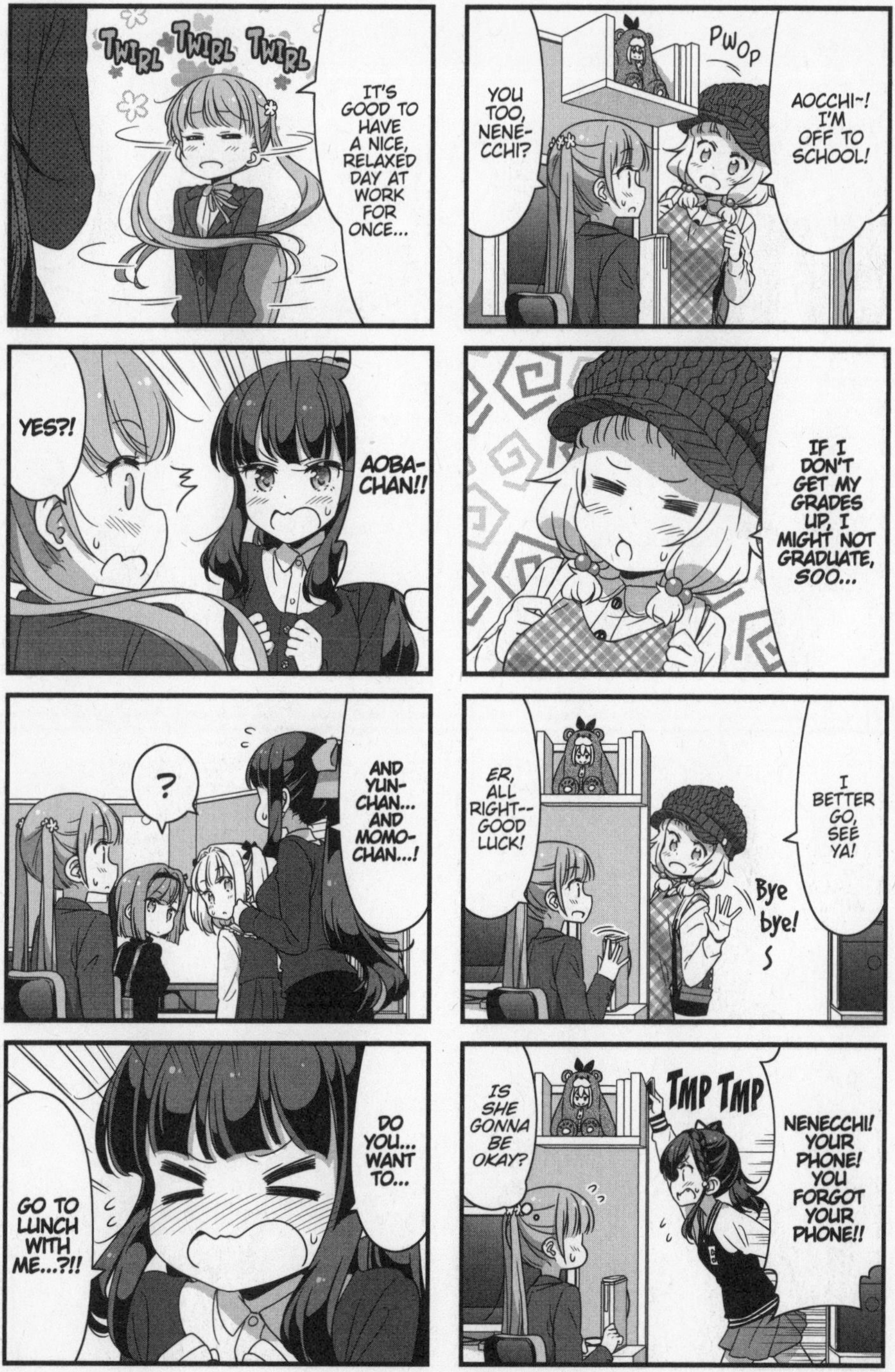
PWOP
AOCCHI~! I'M OFF TO SCHOOL!
YOU TOO, NENE-CCHI?
IF I DON'T GET MY GRADES UP, I MIGHT NOT GRADUATE, SOO...
I BETTER GO, SEE YA!
Bye bye!
ER, ALL RIGHT-- GOOD LUCK!
NENECCHI! YOUR PHONE! YOU FORGOT YOUR PHONE!!
TMP TMP
IS SHE GONNA BE OKAY?
TWIRL TWIRL TWIRL
IT'S GOOD TO HAVE A NICE, RELAXED DAY AT WORK FOR ONCE...
AOBA-CHAN!!
YES?!
AND YUN-CHAN... AND MOMO-CHAN...!
?
DO YOU... WANT TO...
GO TO LUNCH WITH ME...?!!

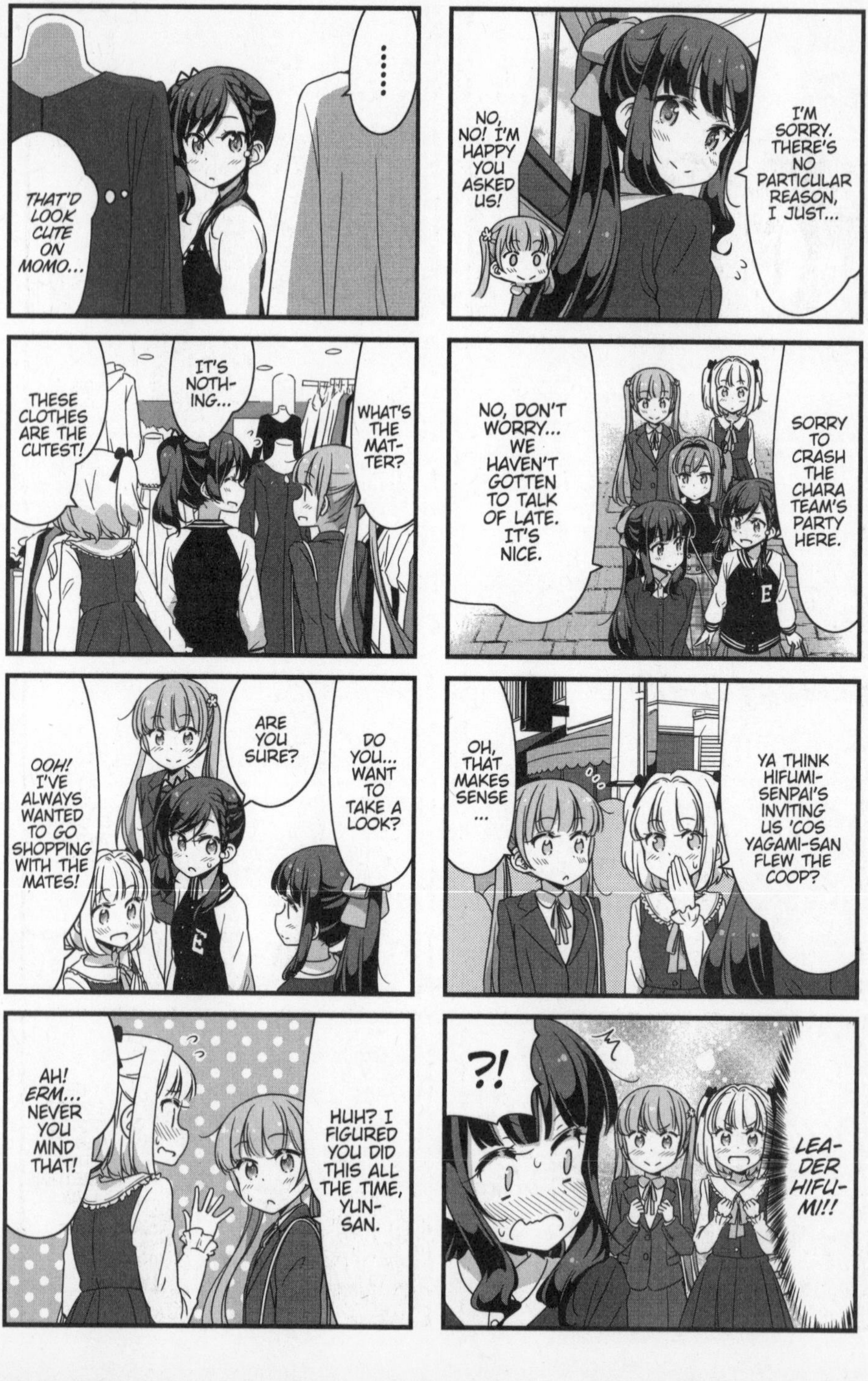
I'M SORRY. THERE'S NO PARTICULAR REASON, I JUST...
NO, NO! I'M HAPPY YOU ASKED US!
......
THAT'D LOOK CUTE ON MOMO...
SORRY TO CRASH THE CHARA TEAM'S PARTY HERE.
NO, DON'T WORRY... WE HAVEN'T GOTTEN TO TALK OF LATE. IT'S NICE.
WHAT'S THE MATTER?
IT'S NOTHING...
THESE CLOTHES ARE THE CUTEST!
YA THINK HIFUMI-SENPAI'S INVITING US 'COS YAGAMI-SAN FLEW THE COOP?
OH, THAT MAKES SENSE...
DO YOU... WANT TO TAKE A LOOK?
ARE YOU SURE?
OOH! I'VE ALWAYS WANTED TO GO SHOPPING WITH THE MATES!
LEADER HIFUMI!!
?!
HUH? I FIGURED YOU DID THIS ALL THE TIME, YUN-SAN.
AH! ERM... NEVER YOU MIND THAT!

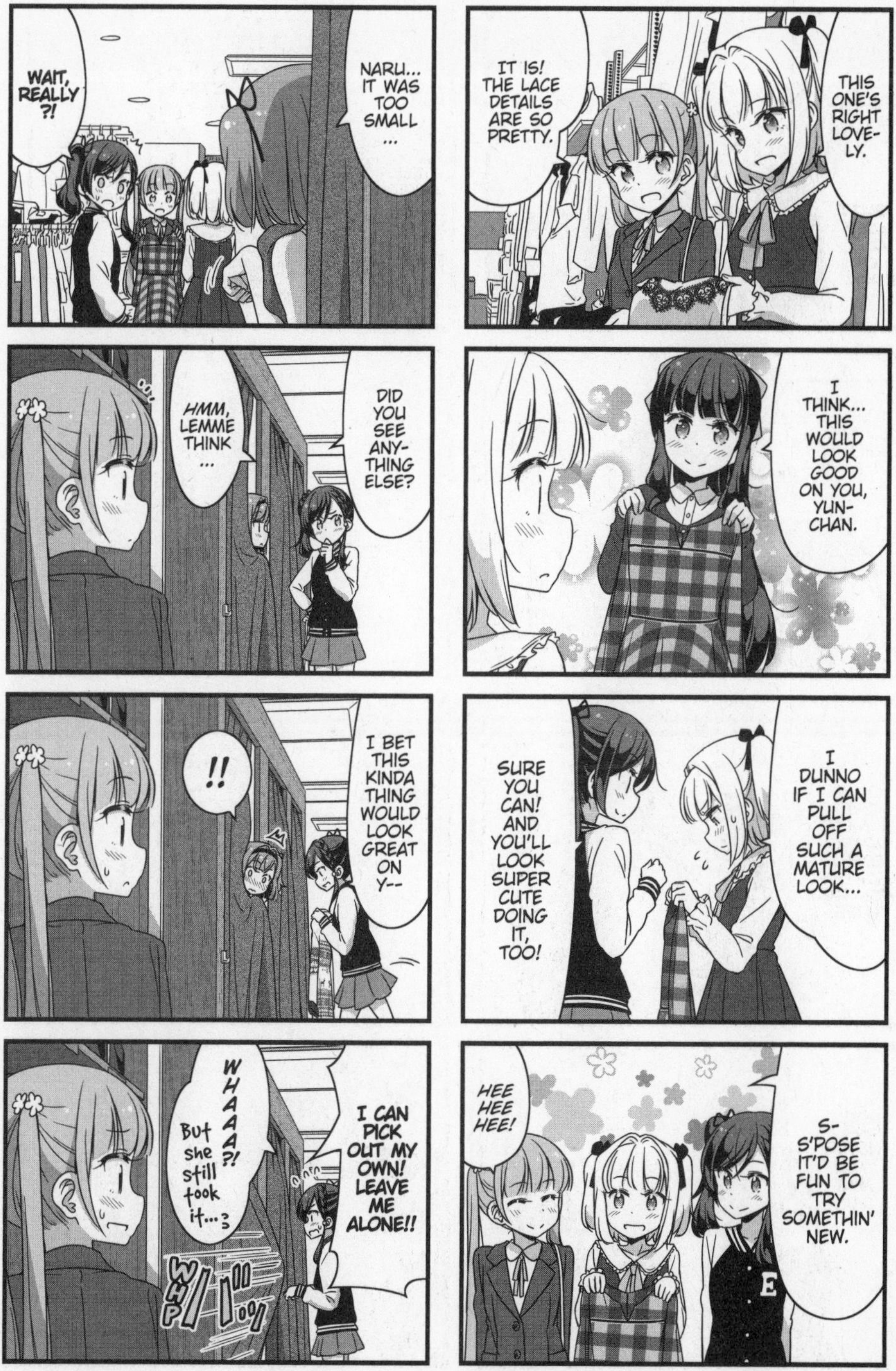
THIS ONE'S RIGHT LOVELY.
IT IS! THE LACE DETAILS ARE SO PRETTY.
I THINK... THIS WOULD LOOK GOOD ON YOU, YUN-CHAN.
I DUNNO IF I CAN PULL OFF SUCH A MATURE LOOK...
SURE YOU CAN! AND YOU'LL LOOK SUPER CUTE DOING IT, TOO!
S-S'POSE IT'D BE FUN TO TRY SOMETHIN' NEW.
HEE HEE HEE!
NARU... IT WAS TOO SMALL...
WAIT, REALLY?!
DID YOU SEE ANYTHING ELSE?
HMM, LEMME THINK...
I BET THIS KINDA THING WOULD LOOK GREAT ON Y--
!!
I CAN PICK OUT MY OWN! LEAVE ME ALONE!!
WHAAAA?!
But she still took it...?
WHIP

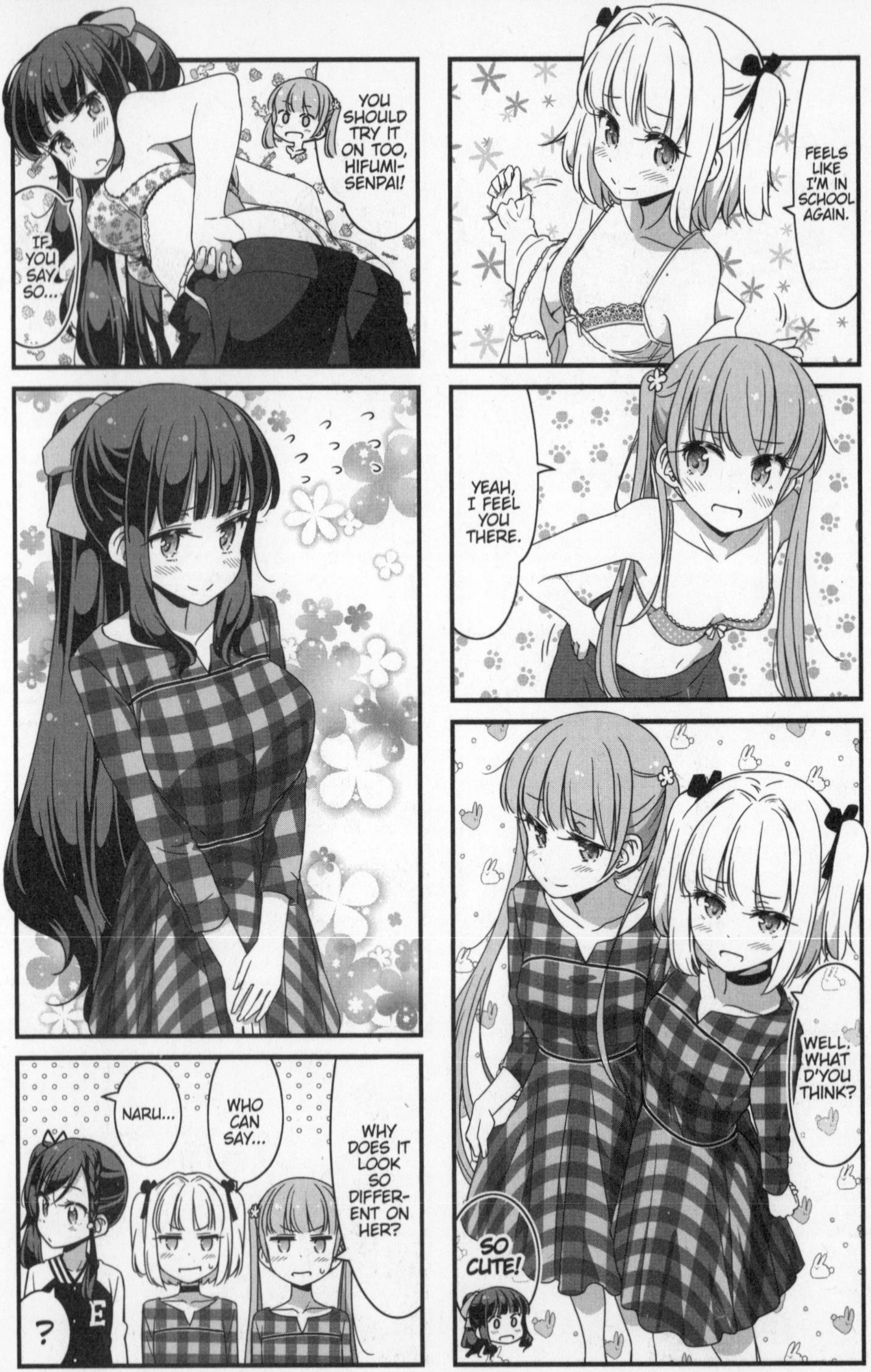
FEELS LIKE I'M IN SCHOOL AGAIN.
YOU SHOULD TRY IT ON TOO, HIFUMI-SENPAI!
IF YOU SAY SO...
YEAH, I FEEL YOU THERE.
WELL, WHAT D'YOU THINK?
SO CUTE!
WHY DOES IT LOOK SO DIFFERENT ON HER?
WHO CAN SAY...
NARU...
?

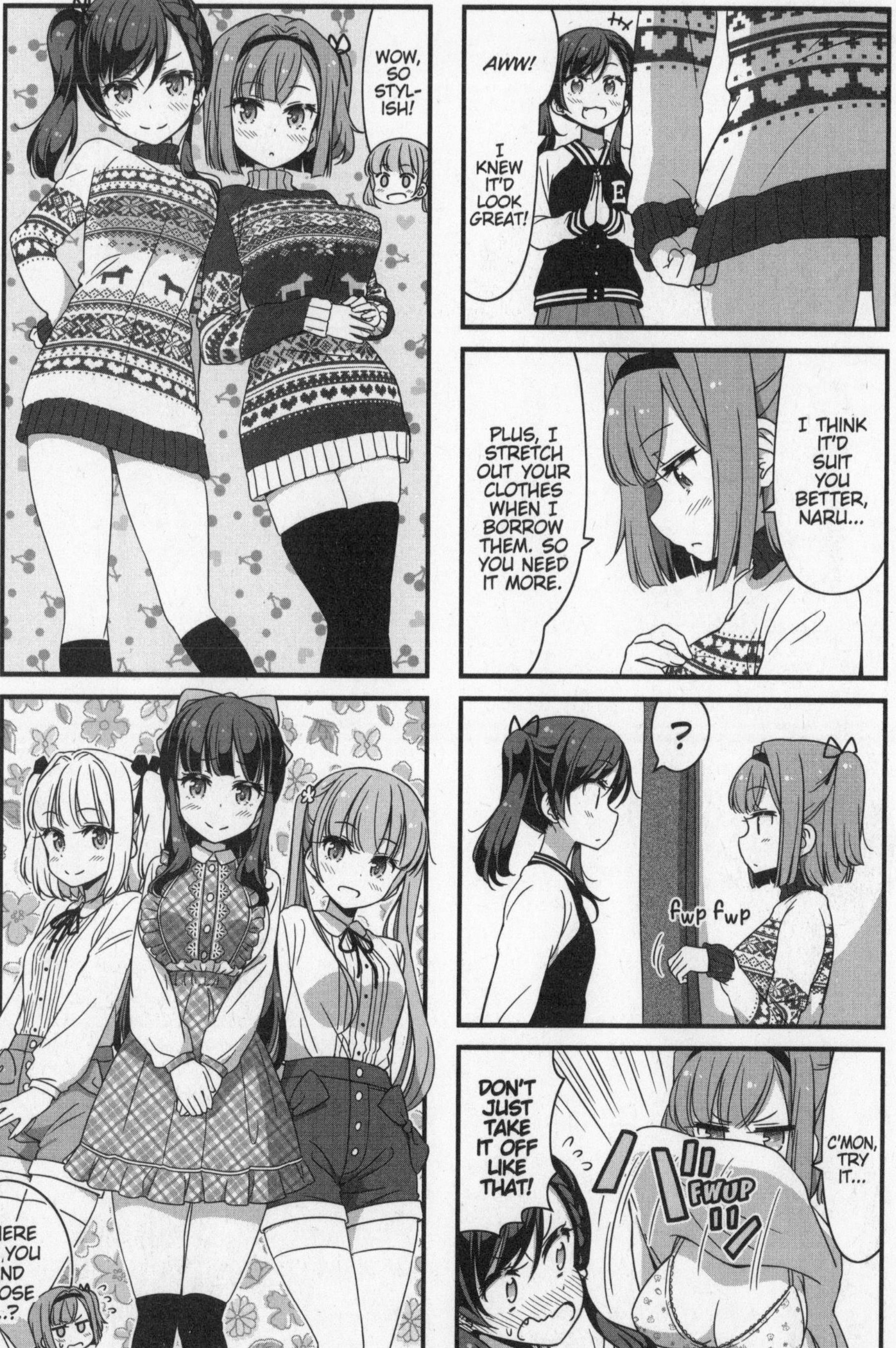
AWW!
I KNEW IT'D LOOK GREAT!
I THINK IT'D SUIT YOU BETTER, NARU...
PLUS, I STRETCH OUT YOUR CLOTHES WHEN I BORROW THEM. SO YOU NEED IT MORE.
WOW, SO STYLISH!
?
fwp fwp
C'MON, TRY IT...
FWUP
DON'T JUST TAKE IT OFF LIKE THAT!
WHERE DID YOU FIND THOSE ...?

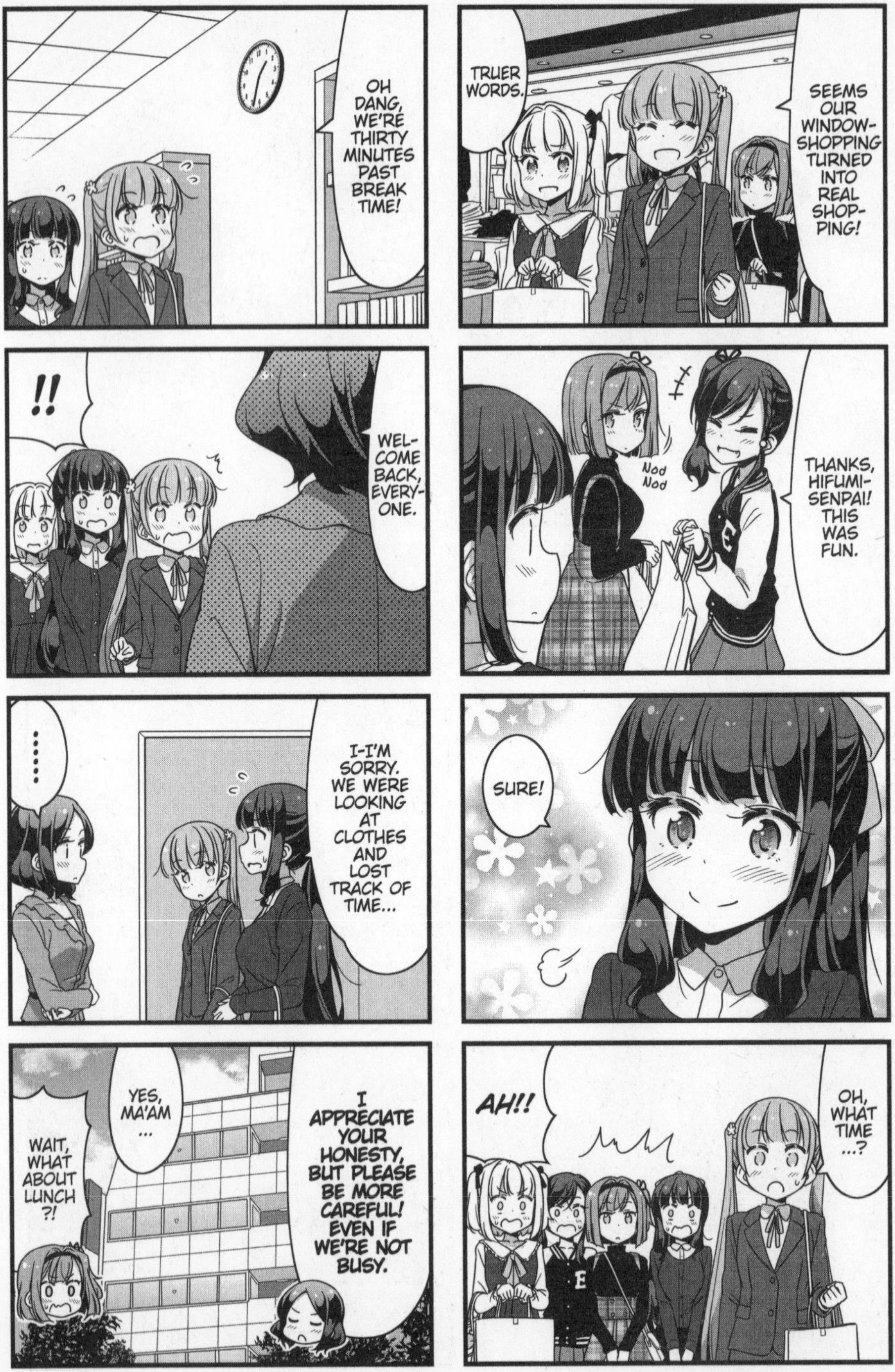
SEEMS OUR WINDOW-SHOPPING TURNED INTO REAL SHOPPING!
TRUER WORDS.
OH DANG, WE'RE THIRTY MINUTES PAST BREAK TIME!
THANKS, HIFUMI-SENPAI! THIS WAS FUN.
Nod Nod
WELCOME BACK, EVERYONE.
!!
SURE!
I-I'M SORRY. WE WERE LOOKING AT CLOTHES AND LOST TRACK OF TIME...
......
OH, WHAT TIME ...?
AH!!
I APPRECIATE YOUR HONESTY, BUT PLEASE BE MORE CAREFUL! EVEN IF WE'RE NOT BUSY.
YES, MA'AM ...
WAIT, WHAT ABOUT LUNCH ?!

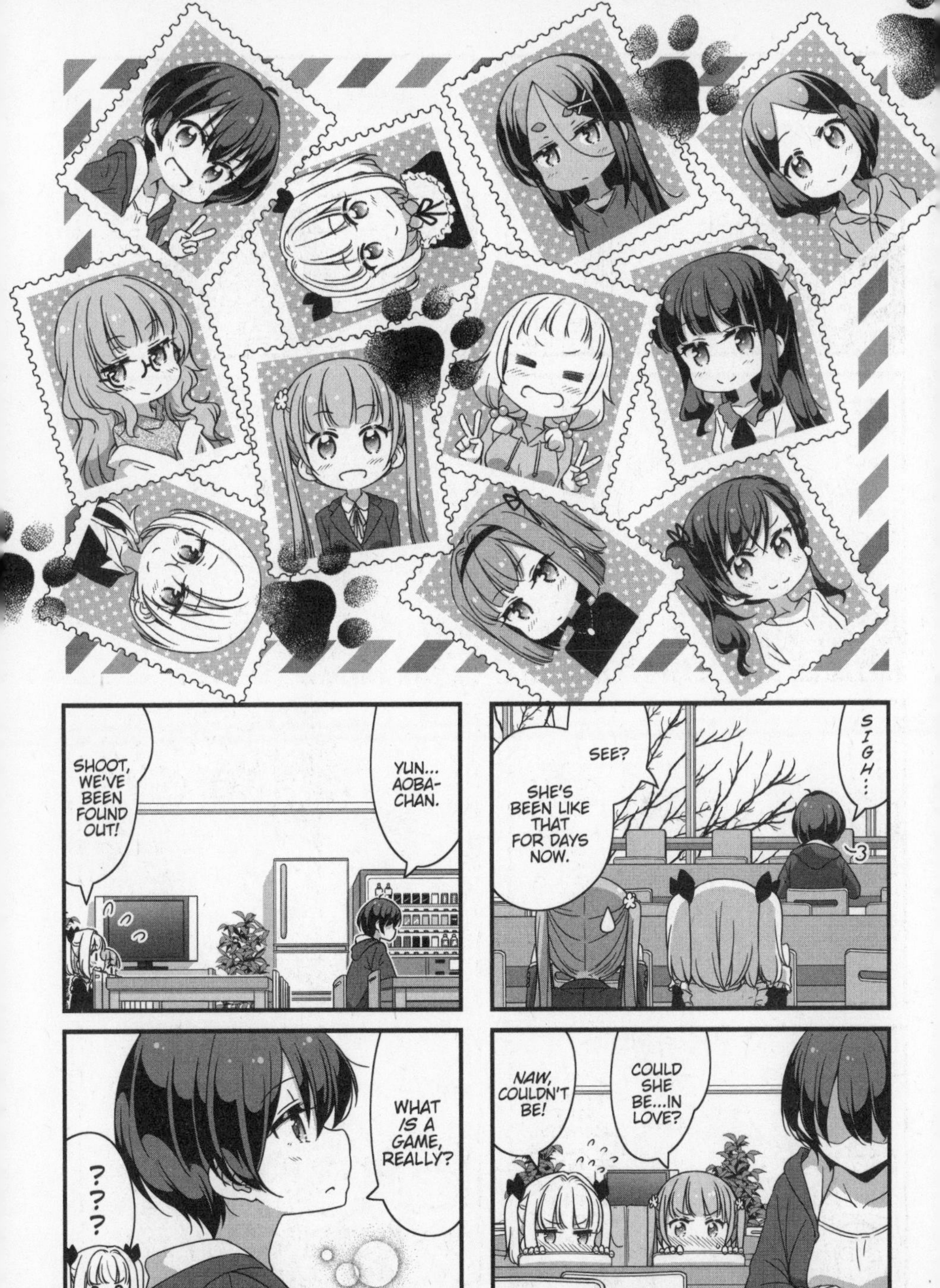
SIGH...
SEE?
SHE'S BEEN LIKE THAT FOR DAYS NOW.
YUN... AOBA-CHAN.
SHOOT, WE'VE BEEN FOUND OUT!
COULD SHE BE...IN LOVE?
*NAW*, COULDN'T BE!
WHAT *IS* A GAME, REALLY?
?.?.?

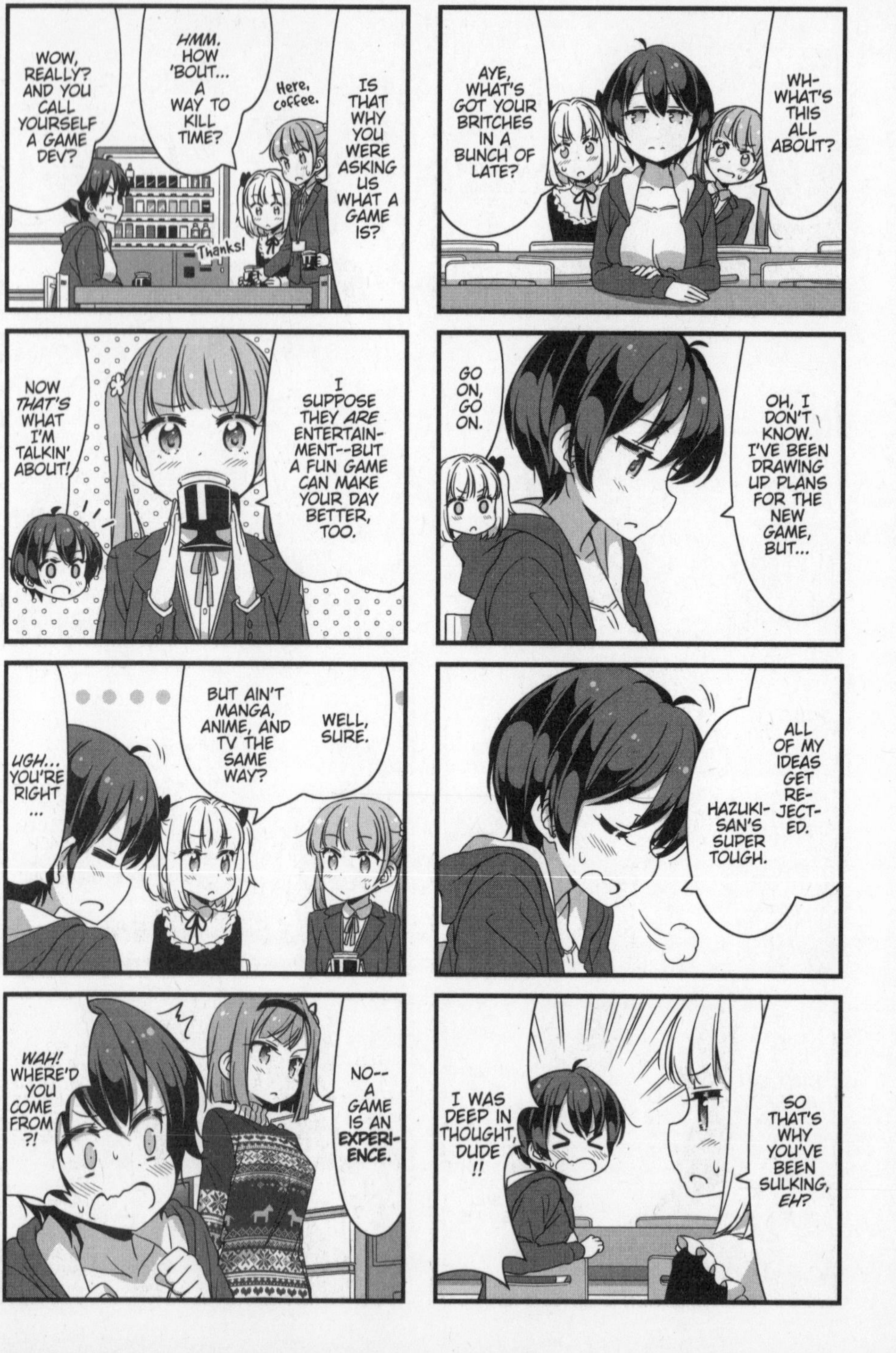
WH-WHAT'S THIS ALL ABOUT?
AYE, WHAT'S GOT YOUR BRITCHES IN A BUNCH OF LATE?
IS THAT WHY YOU WERE ASKING US WHAT A GAME IS?
Here, coffee.
HMM. HOW 'BOUT... A WAY TO KILL TIME?
Thanks!
WOW, REALLY? AND YOU CALL YOURSELF A GAME DEV?
OH, I DON'T KNOW. I'VE BEEN DRAWING UP PLANS FOR THE NEW GAME, BUT...
GO ON, GO ON.
I SUPPOSE THEY *ARE* ENTERTAINMENT--BUT A FUN GAME CAN MAKE YOUR DAY BETTER, TOO.
NOW *THAT'S* WHAT I'M TALKIN' ABOUT!
ALL OF MY IDEAS GET RE-JECT-ED.
HAZUKI-SAN'S SUPER TOUGH.
WELL, SURE.
BUT AIN'T MANGA, ANIME, AND TV THE SAME WAY?
*UGH*... YOU'RE RIGHT...
SO THAT'S WHY YOU'VE BEEN SULKING, *EH*?
I WAS DEEP IN THOUGHT, DUDE!!
NO--A GAME IS AN **EXPERIENCE**.
*WAH!* WHERE'D YOU COME FROM?!

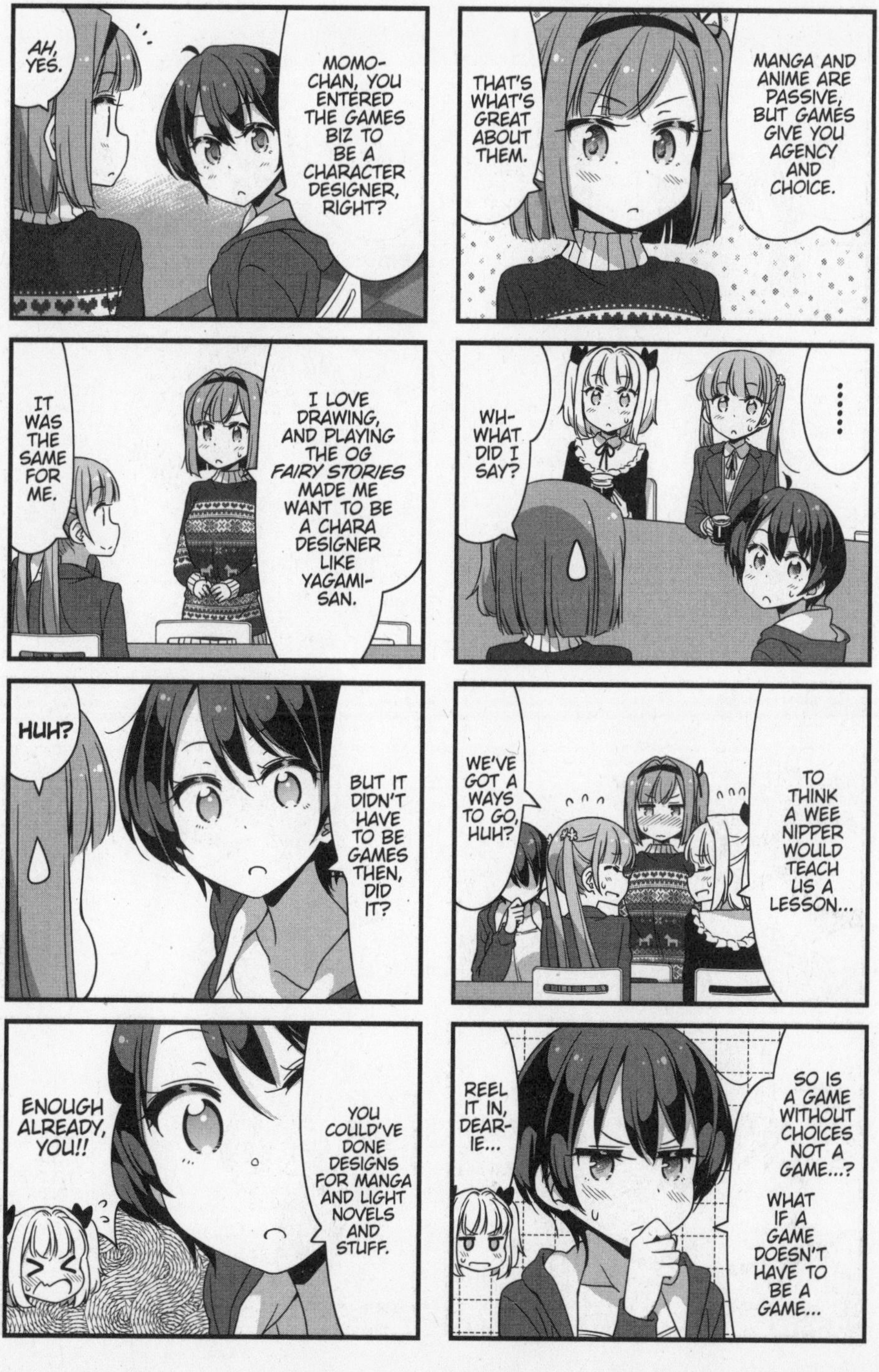
MANGA AND ANIME ARE PASSIVE, BUT GAMES GIVE YOU AGENCY AND CHOICE.
THAT'S WHAT'S GREAT ABOUT THEM.
......
WH-WHAT DID I SAY?
TO THINK A WEE NIPPER WOULD TEACH US A LESSON...
WE'VE GOT A WAYS TO GO, HUH?
SO IS A GAME WITHOUT CHOICES NOT A GAME...?
WHAT IF A GAME DOESN'T HAVE TO BE A GAME...
REEL IT IN, DEAR-IE...
MOMO-CHAN, YOU ENTERED THE GAMES BIZ TO BE A CHARACTER DESIGNER, RIGHT?
AH, YES.
I LOVE DRAWING, AND PLAYING THE OG *FAIRY STORIES* MADE ME WANT TO BE A CHARA DESIGNER LIKE YAGAMI-SAN.
IT WAS THE SAME FOR ME.
BUT IT DIDN'T HAVE TO BE GAMES THEN, DID IT?
HUH?
YOU COULD'VE DONE DESIGNS FOR MANGA AND LIGHT NOVELS AND STUFF.
ENOUGH ALREADY, YOU!!

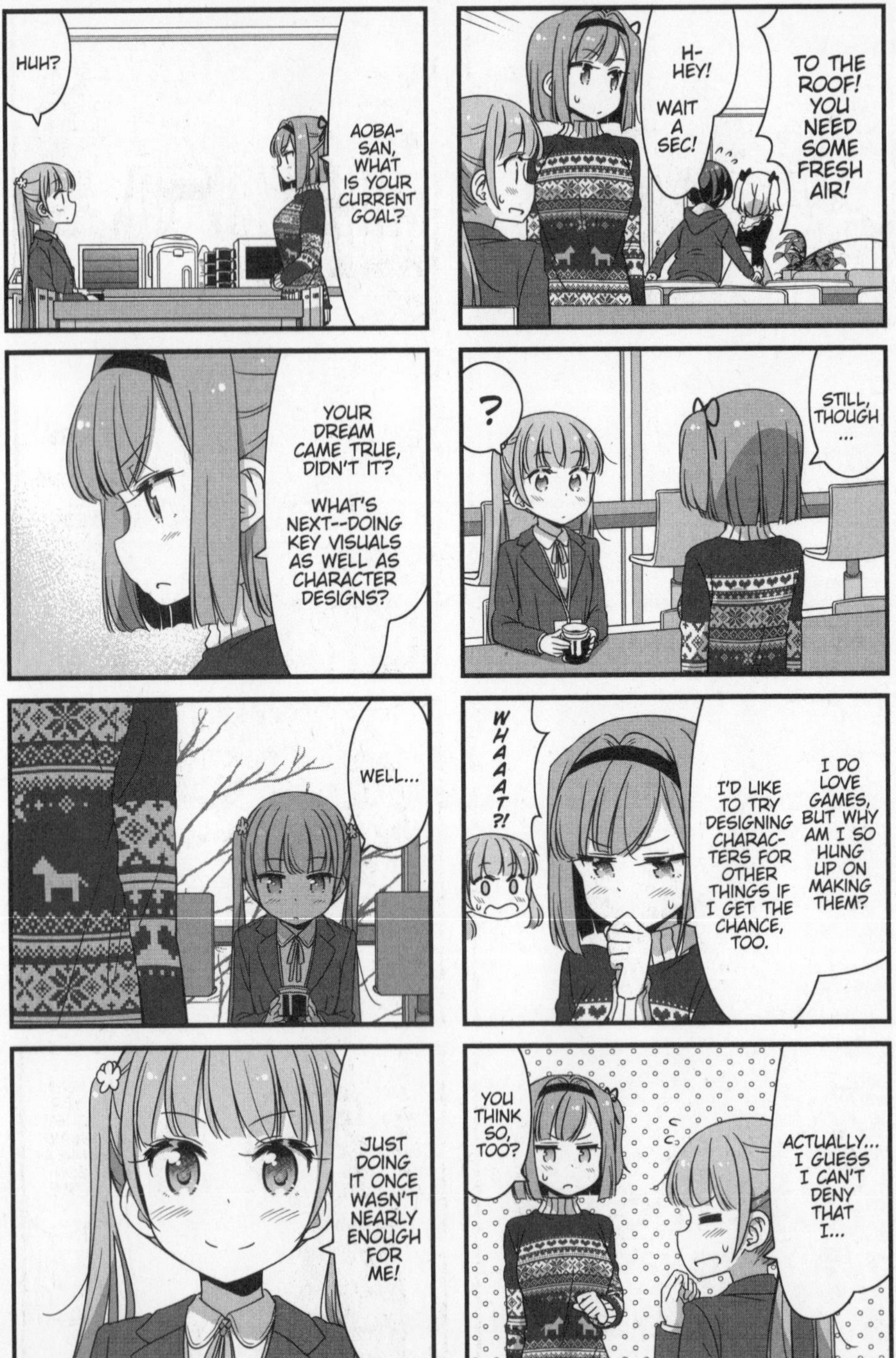
TO THE ROOF! YOU NEED SOME FRESH AIR!
H-HEY! WAIT A SEC!
STILL, THOUGH...
?
I DO LOVE GAMES, BUT WHY AM I SO HUNG UP ON MAKING THEM?
I'D LIKE TO TRY DESIGNING CHARACTERS FOR OTHER THINGS IF I GET THE CHANCE, TOO.
WHAAAAT?!
ACTUALLY... I GUESS I CAN'T DENY THAT I...
YOU THINK SO, TOO?
AOBA-SAN, WHAT IS YOUR CURRENT GOAL?
HUH?
YOUR DREAM CAME TRUE, DIDN'T IT?
WHAT'S NEXT--DOING KEY VISUALS AS WELL AS CHARACTER DESIGNS?
WELL...
JUST DOING IT ONCE WASN'T NEARLY ENOUGH FOR ME!

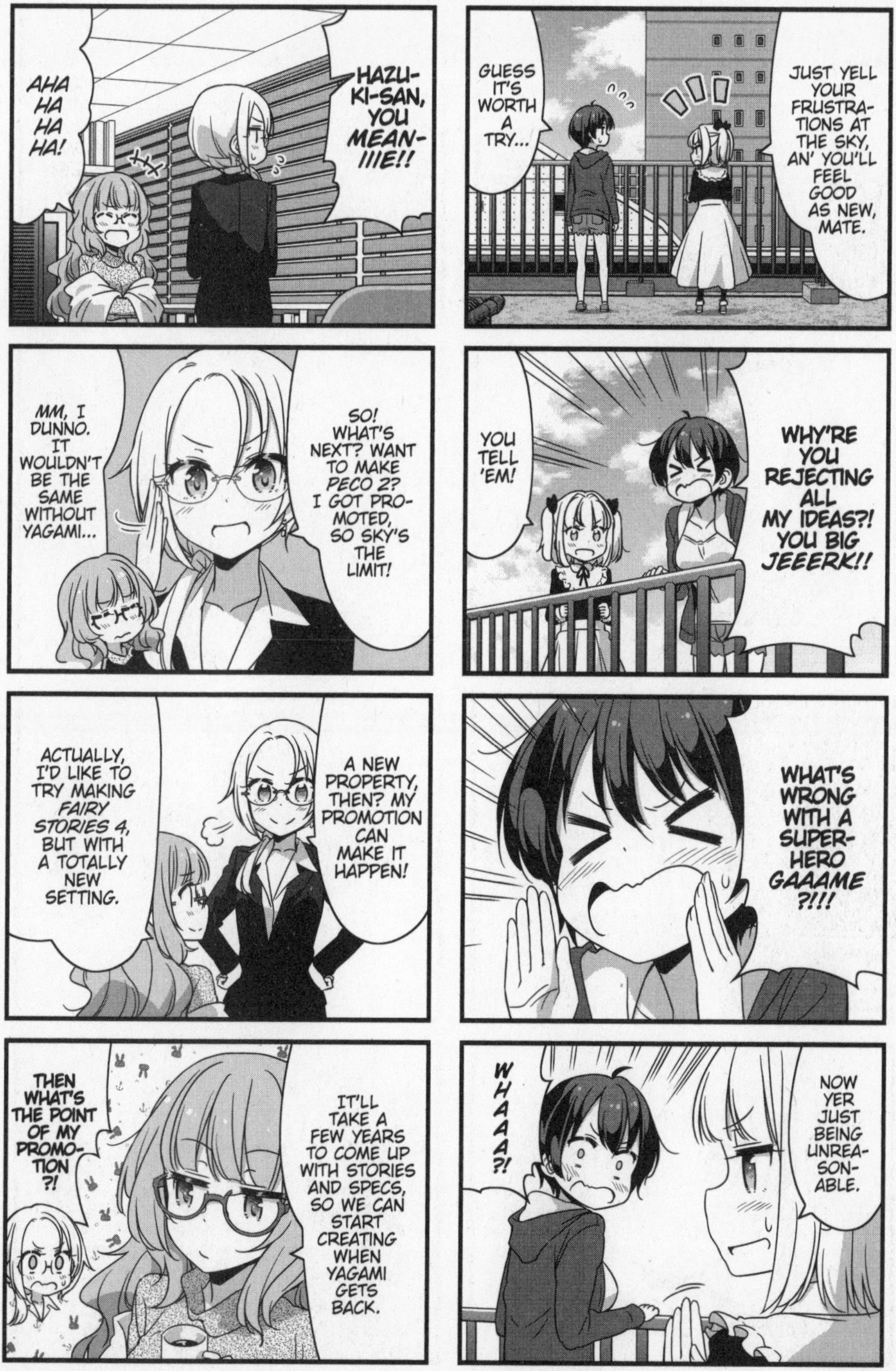
JUST YELL YOUR FRUSTRATIONS AT THE SKY, AN' YOU'LL FEEL GOOD AS NEW, MATE.
GUESS IT'S WORTH A TRY...
WHY'RE YOU REJECTING ALL MY IDEAS?! YOU BIG JEEERK!!
YOU TELL 'EM!
WHAT'S WRONG WITH A SUPERHERO GAAAME?!!!
NOW YER JUST BEING UNREASONABLE.
WHAAAA?!
HAZUKI-SAN, YOU MEANIIIE!!
AHA HA HA HA!
SO! WHAT'S NEXT? WANT TO MAKE PECO 2? I GOT PROMOTED, SO SKY'S THE LIMIT!
MM, I DUNNO. IT WOULDN'T BE THE SAME WITHOUT YAGAMI...
A NEW PROPERTY, THEN? MY PROMOTION CAN MAKE IT HAPPEN!
ACTUALLY, I'D LIKE TO TRY MAKING FAIRY STORIES 4, BUT WITH A TOTALLY NEW SETTING.
IT'LL TAKE A FEW YEARS TO COME UP WITH STORIES AND SPECS, SO WE CAN START CREATING WHEN YAGAMI GETS BACK.
THEN WHAT'S THE POINT OF MY PROMOTION?!

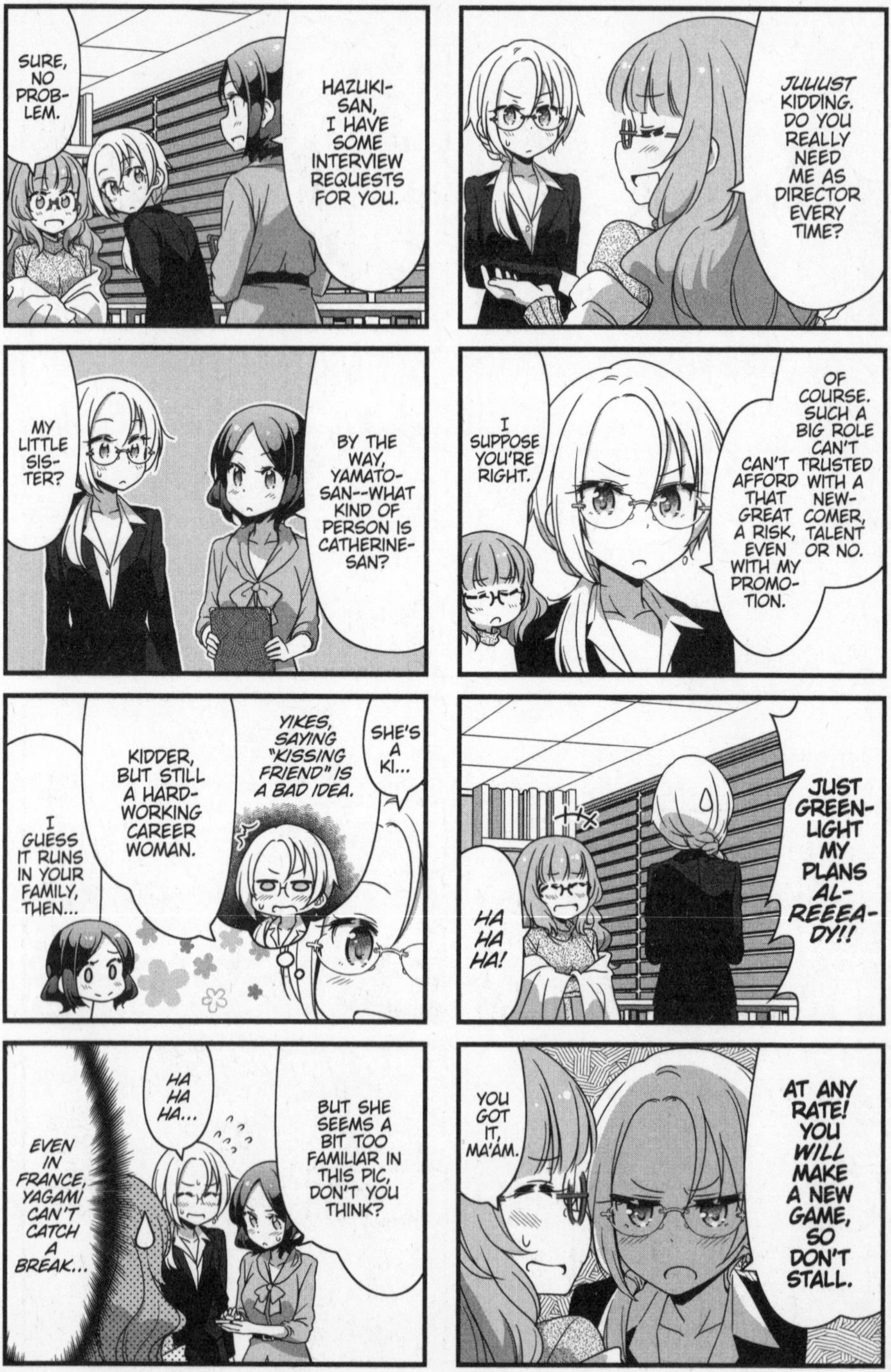
JUUUST KIDDING. DO YOU REALLY NEED ME AS DIRECTOR EVERY TIME?
OF COURSE. SUCH A BIG ROLE CAN'T TRUSTED WITH A NEWCOMER, TALENT OR NO.
CAN'T AFFORD THAT GREAT A RISK, EVEN WITH MY PROMOTION.
I SUPPOSE YOU'RE RIGHT.
JUST GREENLIGHT MY PLANS ALREEEADY!!
HA HA HA!
AT ANY RATE! YOU WILL MAKE A NEW GAME, SO DON'T STALL.
YOU GOT IT, MA'AM.
HAZUKI-SAN, I HAVE SOME INTERVIEW REQUESTS FOR YOU.
SURE, NO PROBLEM.
BY THE WAY, YAMATO-SAN--WHAT KIND OF PERSON IS CATHERINE-SAN?
MY LITTLE SISTER?
SHE'S A KI...
YIKES, SAYING "KISSING FRIEND" IS A BAD IDEA.
KIDDER, BUT STILL A HARD-WORKING CAREER WOMAN.
I GUESS IT RUNS IN YOUR FAMILY, THEN...
BUT SHE SEEMS A BIT TOO FAMILIAR IN THIS PIC, DON'T YOU THINK?
HA HA HA...
EVEN IN FRANCE, YAGAMI CAN'T CATCH A BREAK...

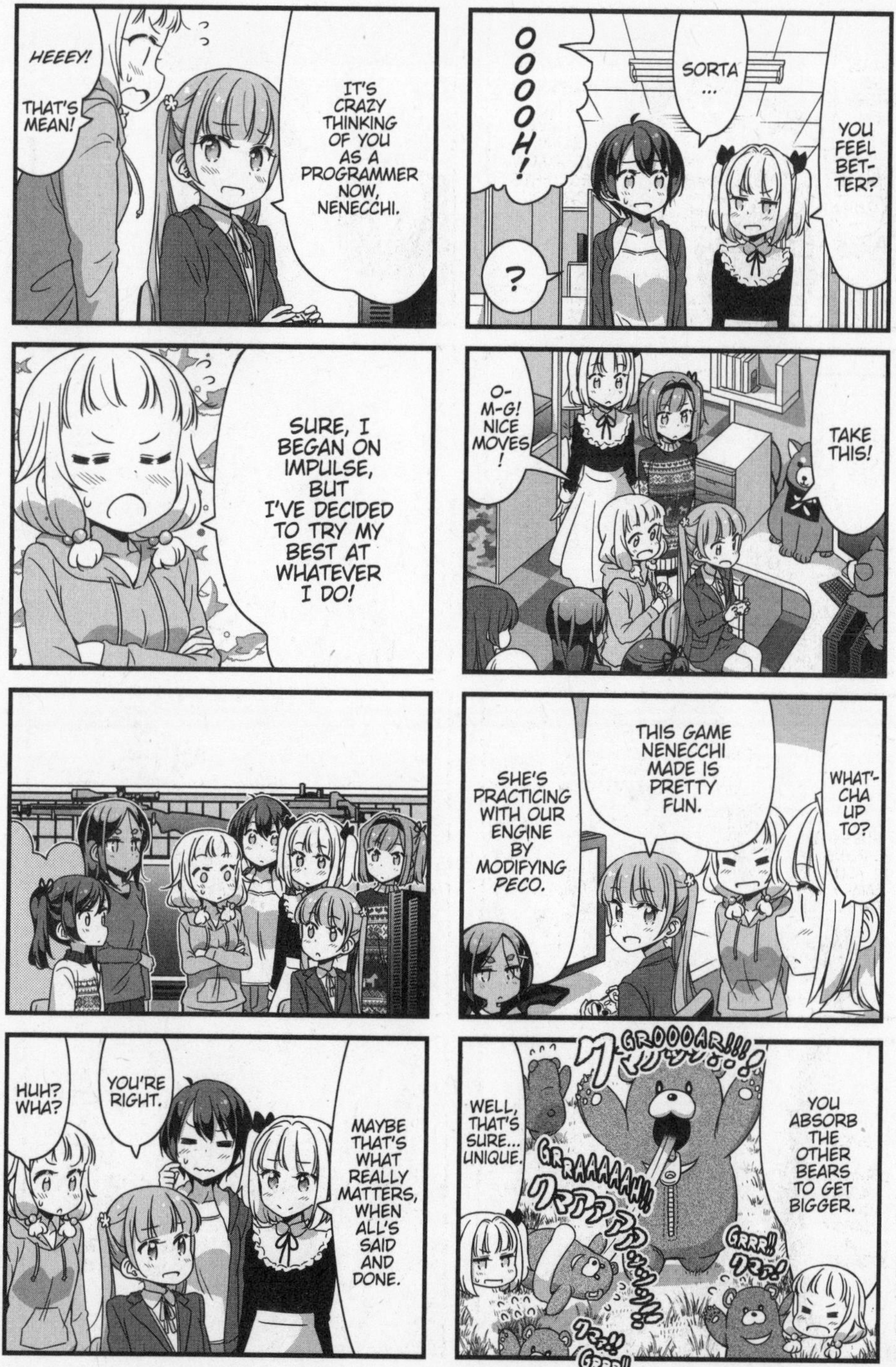
SORTA...
YOU FEEL BET-TER?
OOOOOH!
?
TAKE THIS!
O-M-G! NICE MOVES!
WHAT'-CHA UP TO?
THIS GAME NENECCHI MADE IS PRETTY FUN.
SHE'S PRACTICING WITH OUR ENGINE BY MODIFYING PECO.
YOU ABSORB THE OTHER BEARS TO GET BIGGER.
GROOOAR!!!
WELL, THAT'S SURE... UNIQUE.
GRRAAAAAAH!!
GRRR!!
GRRR!!
IT'S CRAZY THINKING OF YOU AS A PROGRAMMER NOW, NENECCHI.
HEEEY!
THAT'S MEAN!
SURE, I BEGAN ON IMPULSE, BUT I'VE DECIDED TO TRY MY BEST AT WHATEVER I DO!
MAYBE THAT'S WHAT REALLY MATTERS, WHEN ALL'S SAID AND DONE.
YOU'RE RIGHT.
HUH? WHA?

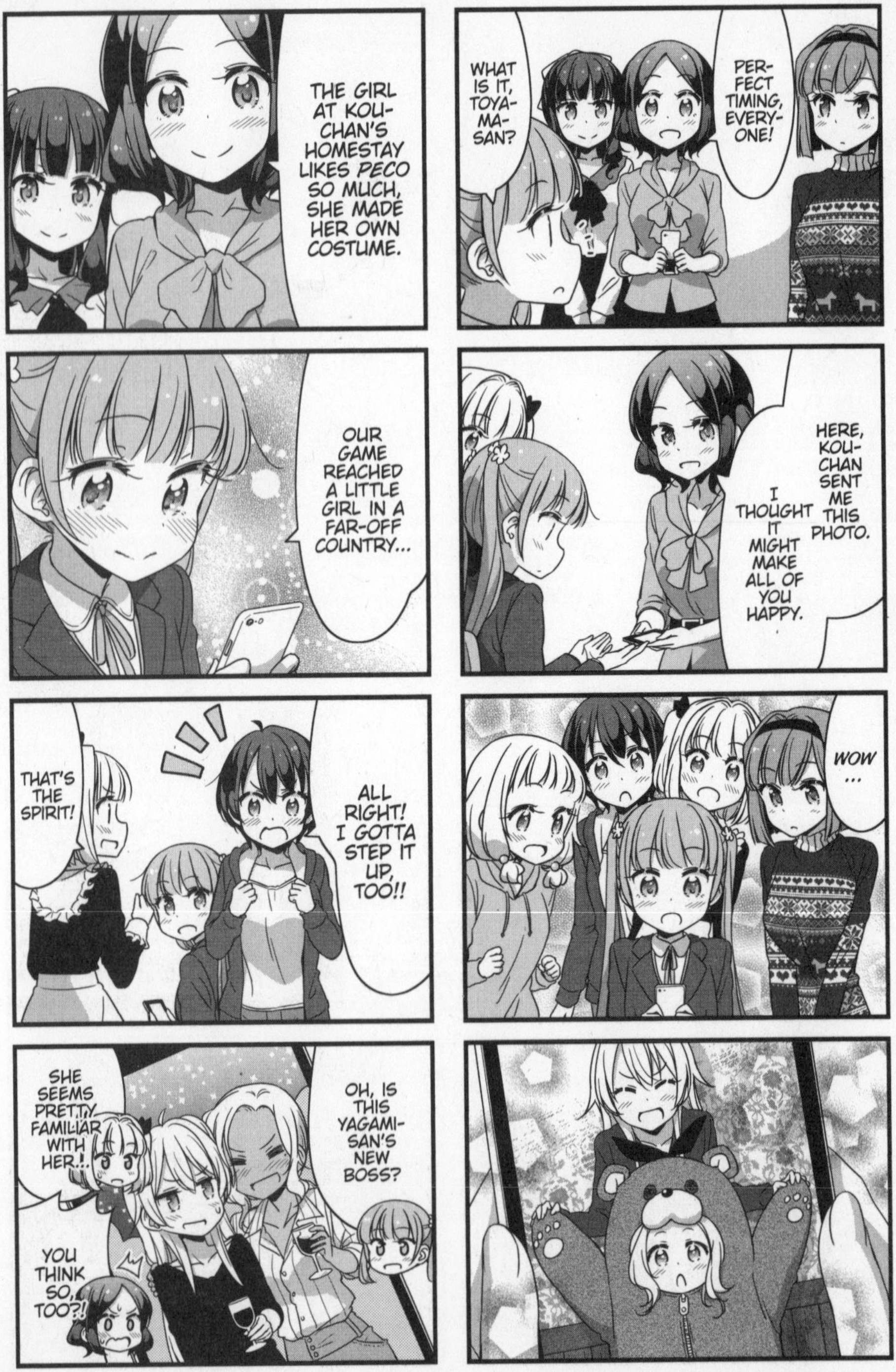
PERFECT TIMING, EVERYONE!
WHAT IS IT, TOYAMA-SAN?
THE GIRL AT KOU-CHAN'S HOMESTAY LIKES *PECO* SO MUCH, SHE MADE HER OWN COSTUME.
HERE, KOU-CHAN SENT ME THIS PHOTO.
I THOUGHT IT MIGHT MAKE ALL OF YOU HAPPY.
OUR GAME REACHED A LITTLE GIRL IN A FAR-OFF COUNTRY...
WOW...
ALL RIGHT! I GOTTA STEP IT UP, TOO!!
THAT'S THE SPIRIT!
OH, IS THIS YAGAMI-SAN'S NEW BOSS?
SHE SEEMS PRETTY FAMILIAR WITH HER...!
YOU THINK SO, TOO?!

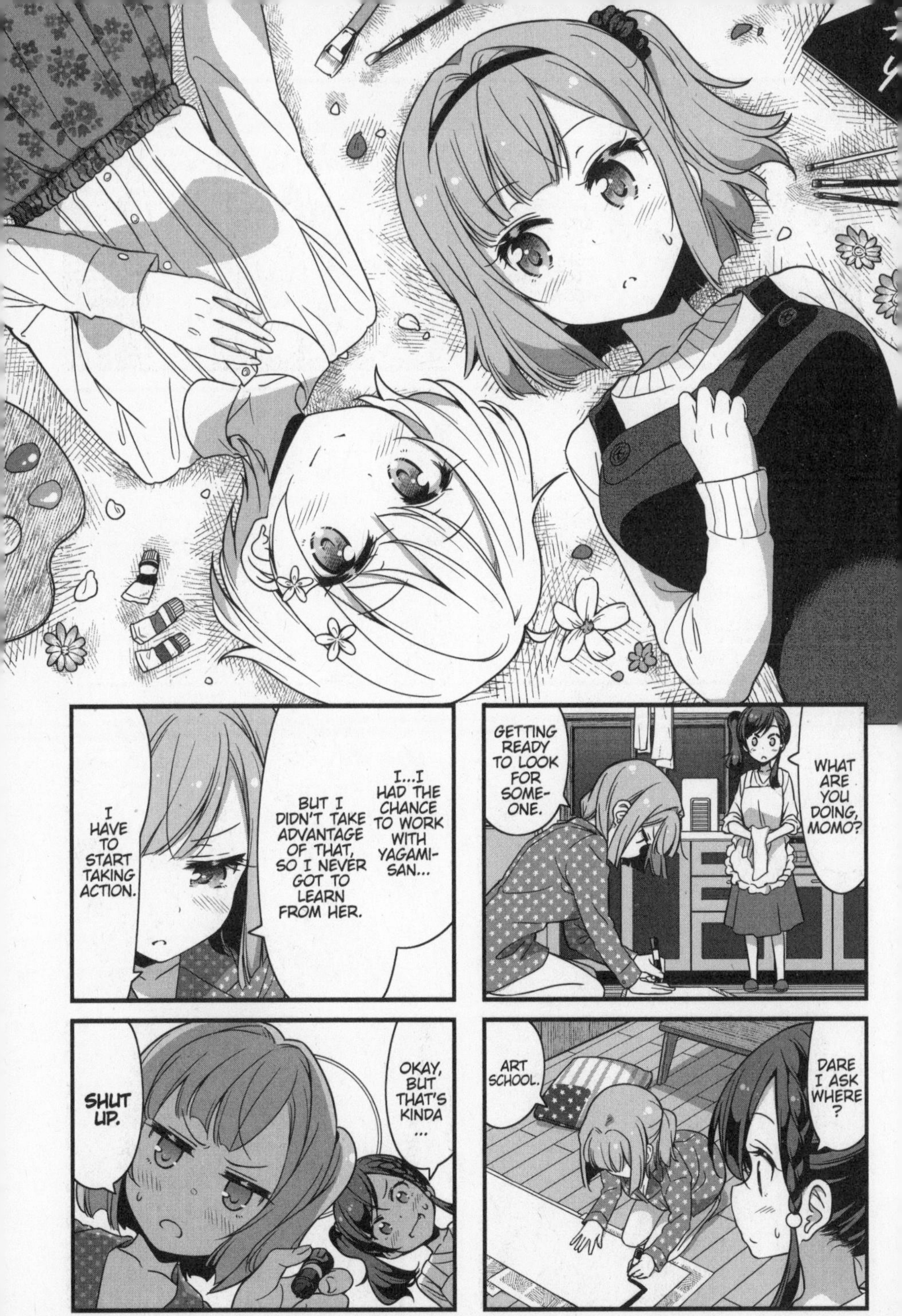
WHAT ARE YOU DOING, MOMO?
GETTING READY TO LOOK FOR SOME-ONE.
I...I HAD THE CHANCE TO WORK WITH YAGAMI-SAN...
BUT I DIDN'T TAKE ADVANTAGE OF THAT, SO I NEVER GOT TO LEARN FROM HER.
I HAVE TO START TAKING ACTION.
DARE I ASK WHERE?
ART SCHOOL.
OKAY, BUT THAT'S KINDA ...
SHUT UP.

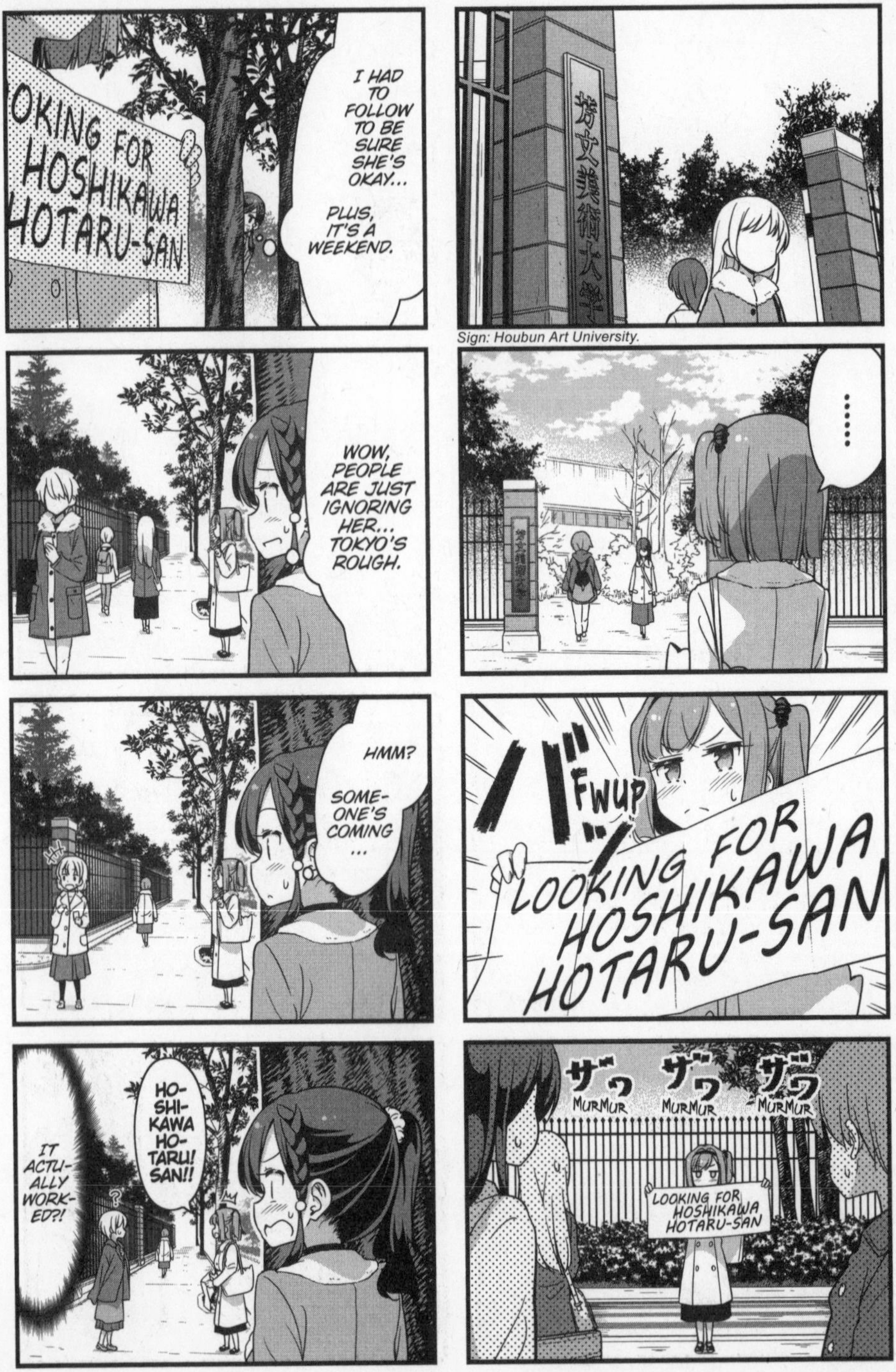
芳文美術大学
......
バ
FWUP
LOOKING FOR HOSHIKAWA HOTARU-SAN
ザワ ザワ ザワ
MURMUR MURMUR MURMUR
LOOKING FOR HOSHIKAWA HOTARU-SAN
OKING FOR HOSHIKAWA HOTARU-SAN
I HAD TO FOLLOW TO BE SURE SHE'S OKAY...
PLUS, IT'S A WEEKEND.
WOW, PEOPLE ARE JUST IGNORING HER... TOKYO'S ROUGH.
HMM?
SOMEONE'S COMING...
HO-SHI-KAWA HOTARU! SAN!!
?
IT ACTUALLY WORKED?!
Sign: Houbun Art University.

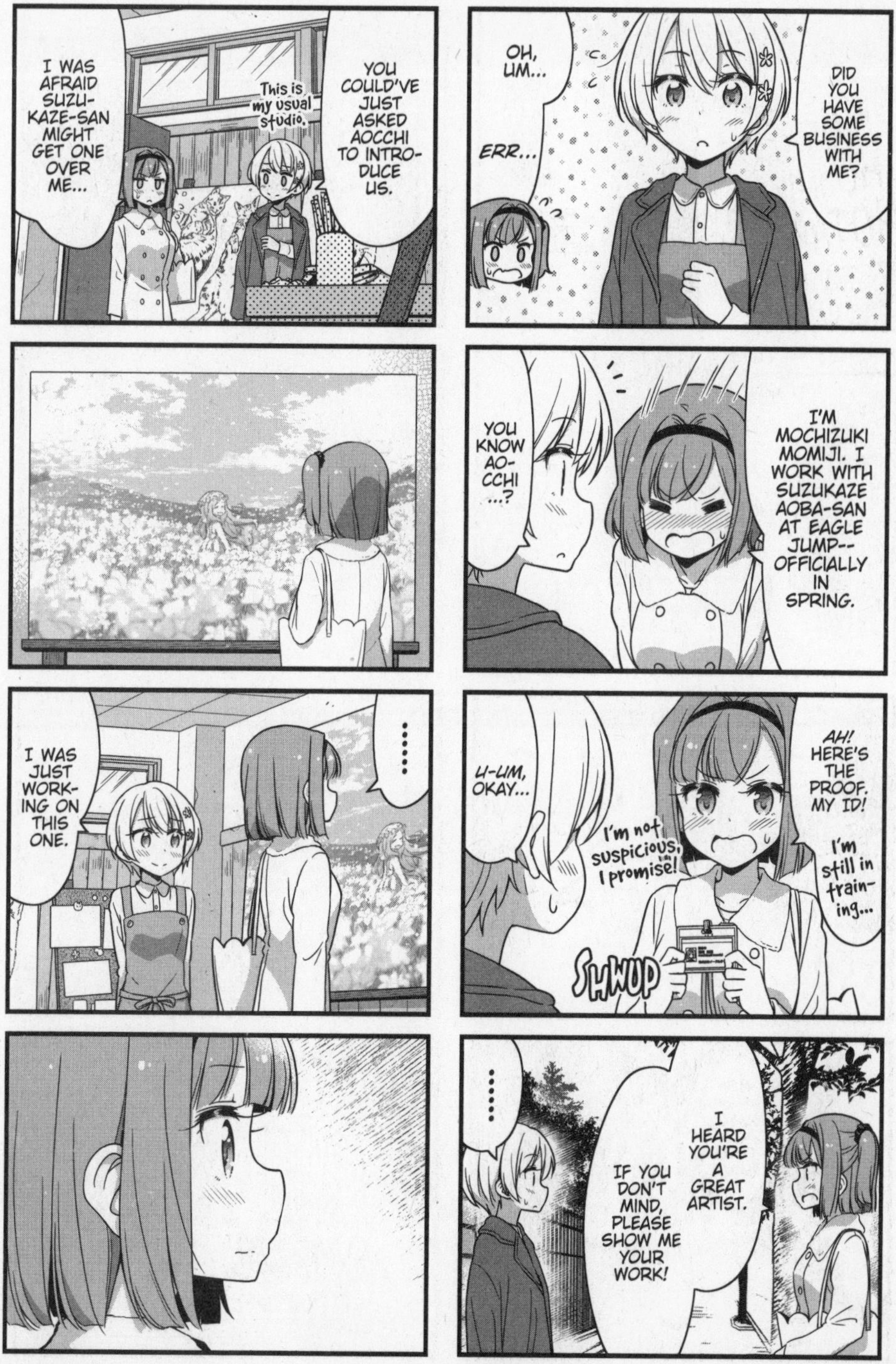
DID YOU HAVE SOME BUSINESS WITH ME?
OH, UM...
ERR...
YOU COULD'VE JUST ASKED AOCCHI TO INTRODUCE US.
This is my usual studio.
I WAS AFRAID SUZUKAZE-SAN MIGHT GET ONE OVER ME...
I'M MOCHIZUKI MOMIJI. I WORK WITH SUZUKAZE AOBA-SAN AT EAGLE JUMP--OFFICIALLY IN SPRING.
YOU KNOW AOCCHI...?
AH! HERE'S THE PROOF. MY ID!
I'm still in training...
I'm not suspicious, I promise!
U-UM, OKAY...
SHWUP
......
I WAS JUST WORKING ON THIS ONE.
I HEARD YOU'RE A GREAT ARTIST.
IF YOU DON'T MIND, PLEASE SHOW ME YOUR WORK!
......

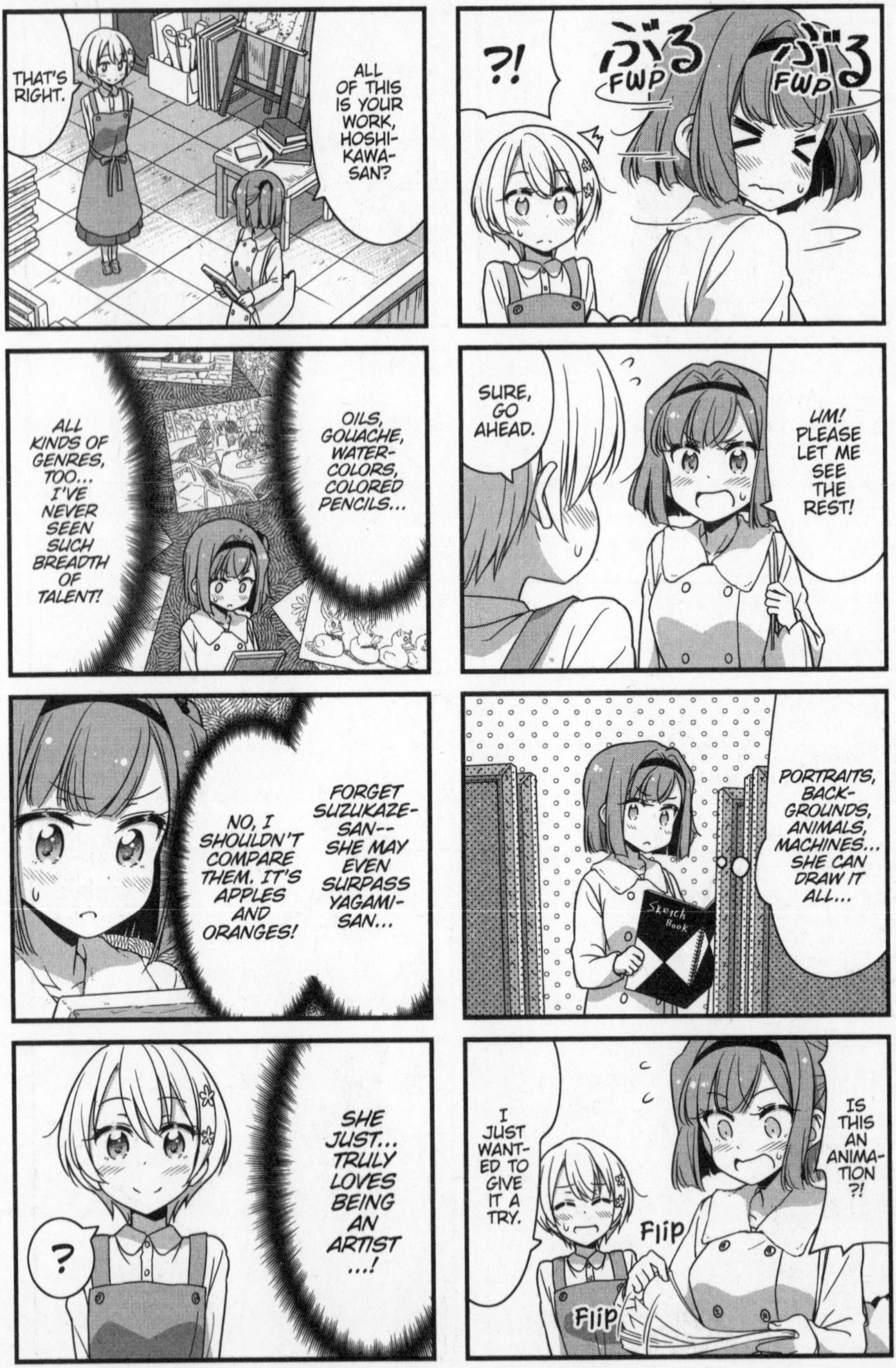
?!
ぶる FWP
ぶる FWP
ALL OF THIS IS YOUR WORK, HOSHIKAWA-SAN?
THAT'S RIGHT.
UM! PLEASE LET ME SEE THE REST!
SURE, GO AHEAD.
OILS, GOUACHE, WATER-COLORS, COLORED PENCILS...
ALL KINDS OF GENRES, TOO... I'VE NEVER SEEN SUCH BREADTH OF TALENT!
PORTRAITS, BACK-GROUNDS, ANIMALS, MACHINES... SHE CAN DRAW IT ALL...
Sketch Book
FORGET SUZUKAZE-SAN-- SHE MAY EVEN SURPASS YAGAMI-SAN...
NO, I SHOULDN'T COMPARE THEM. IT'S APPLES AND ORANGES!
IS THIS AN ANIMA-TION ?!
Flip
I JUST WANT-ED TO GIVE IT A TRY.
Flip
SHE JUST... TRULY LOVES BEING AN ARTIST ...!
?

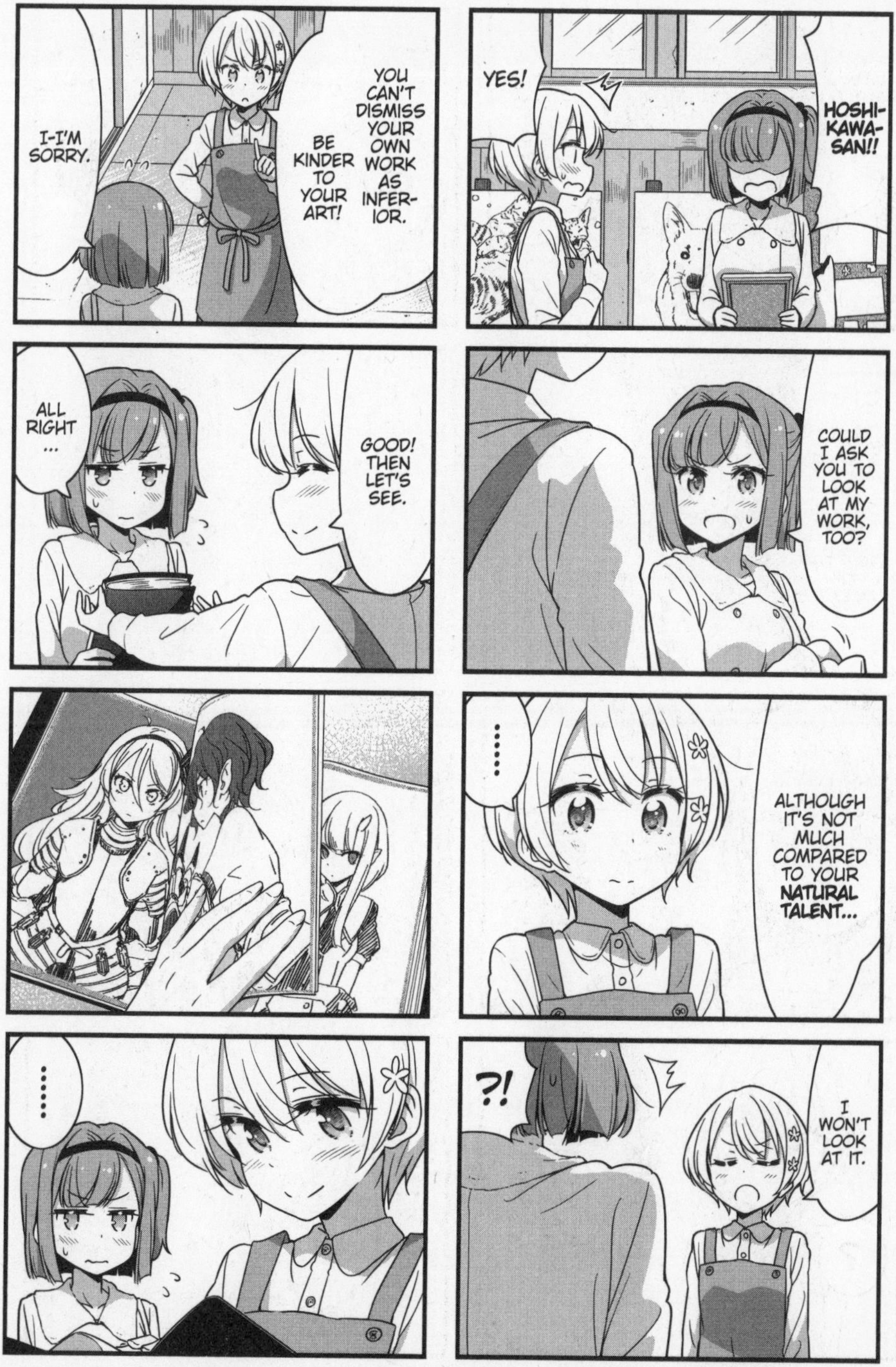
HOSHI-KAWA-SAN!!
YES!
YOU CAN'T DISMISS YOUR OWN WORK AS INFER-IOR.
BE KINDER TO YOUR ART!
I-I'M SORRY.
COULD I ASK YOU TO LOOK AT MY WORK, TOO?
GOOD! THEN LET'S SEE.
ALL RIGHT ...
ALTHOUGH IT'S NOT MUCH COMPARED TO YOUR **NATURAL TALENT**...
......
I WON'T LOOK AT IT.
?!
......

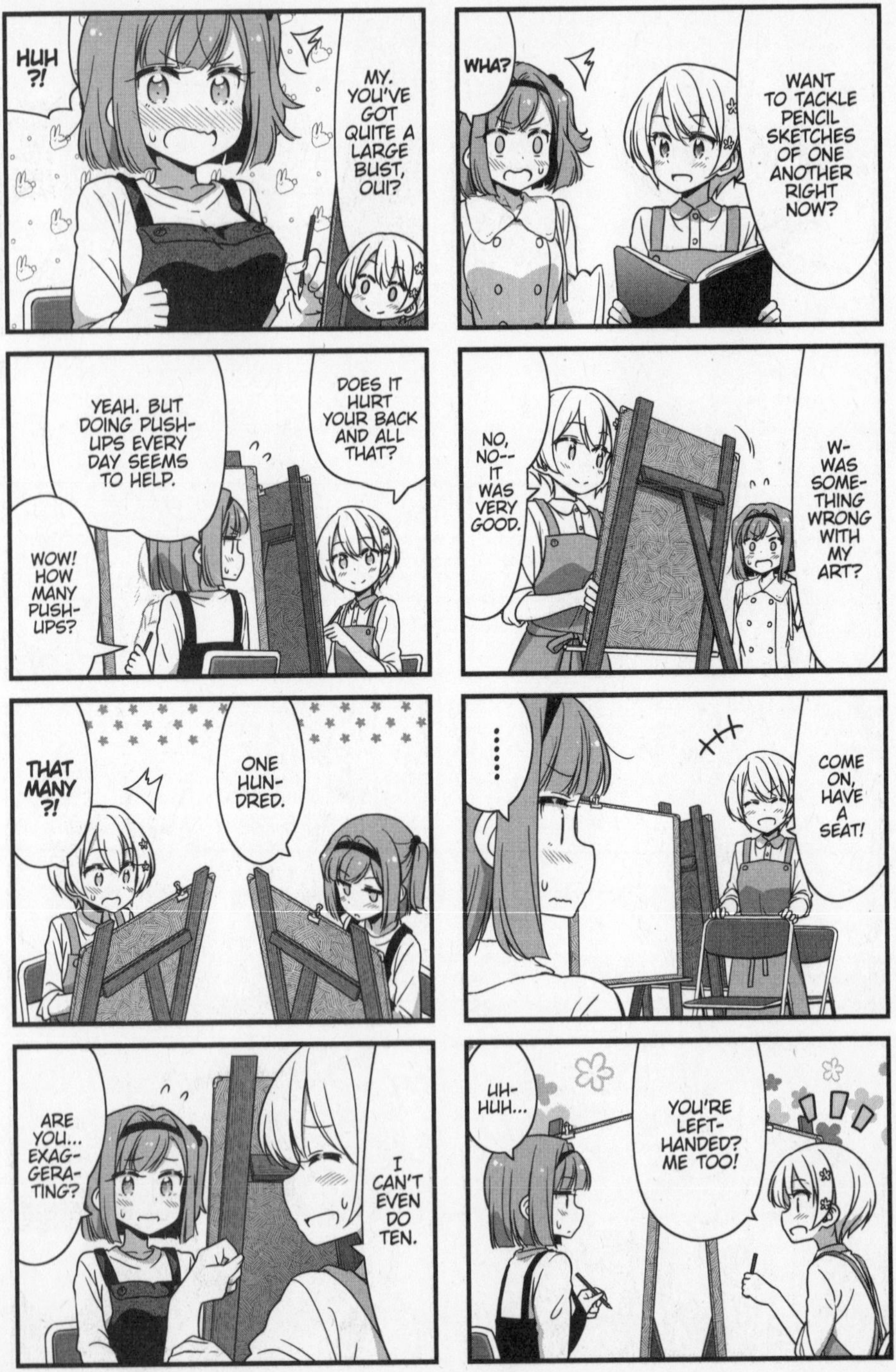
WANT TO TACKLE PENCIL SKETCHES OF ONE ANOTHER RIGHT NOW?
WHA?
W-WAS SOMETHING WRONG WITH MY ART?
NO, NO-- IT WAS VERY GOOD.
COME ON, HAVE A SEAT!
......
YOU'RE LEFT-HANDED? ME TOO!
UH-HUH...
MY. YOU'VE GOT QUITE A LARGE BUST, OUI?
HUH ?!
DOES IT HURT YOUR BACK AND ALL THAT?
YEAH. BUT DOING PUSH-UPS EVERY DAY SEEMS TO HELP.
WOW! HOW MANY PUSH-UPS?
ONE HUN-DRED.
THAT MANY ?!
I CAN'T EVEN DO TEN.
ARE YOU... EXAG-GERA-TING?

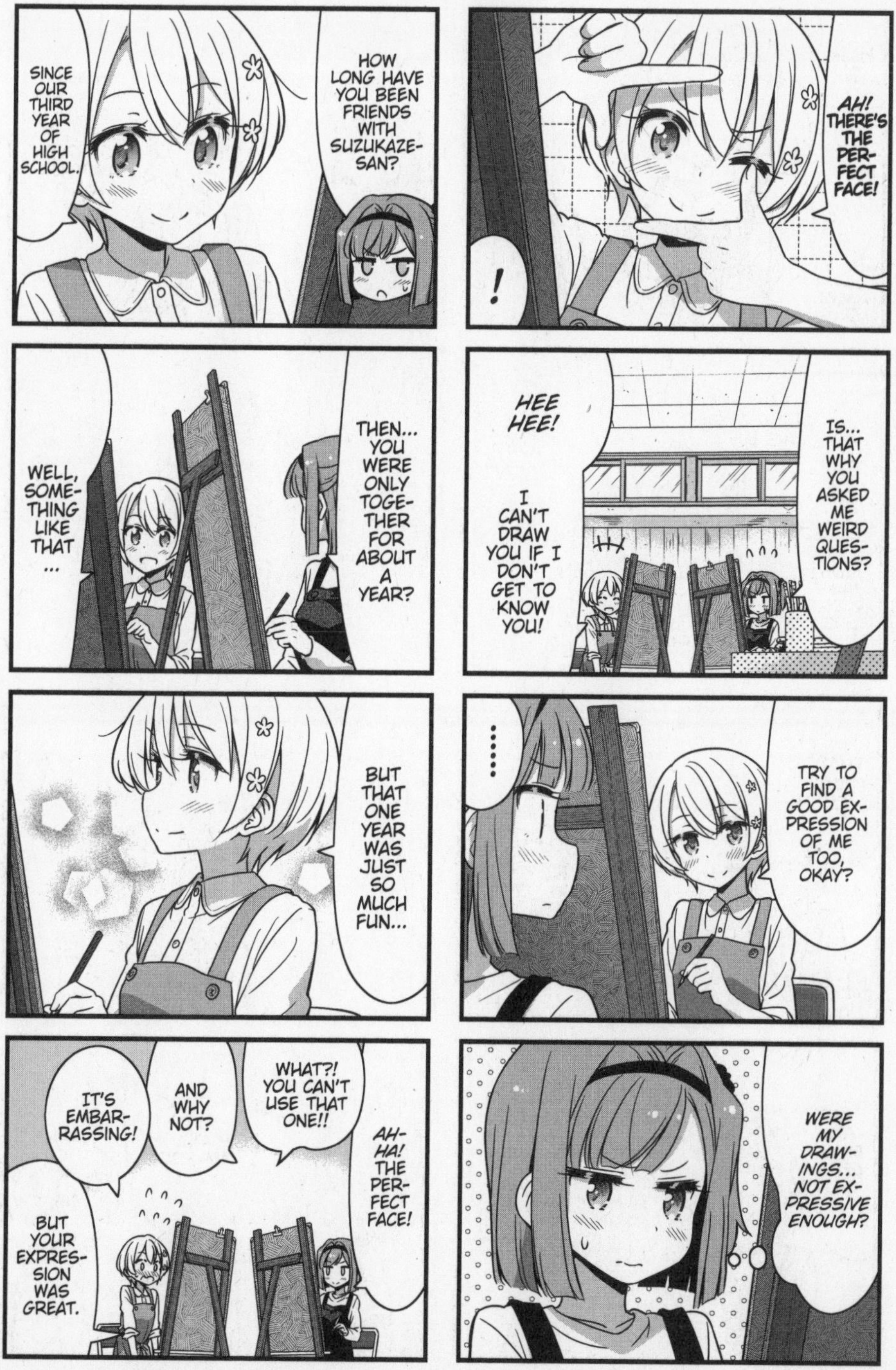
AH! THERE'S THE PERFECT FACE!
!
IS... THAT WHY YOU ASKED ME WEIRD QUESTIONS?
HEE HEE!
I CAN'T DRAW YOU IF I DON'T GET TO KNOW YOU!
TRY TO FIND A GOOD EX-PRESSION OF ME TOO, OKAY?
......
WERE MY DRAW-INGS... NOT EX-PRESSIVE ENOUGH?
HOW LONG HAVE YOU BEEN FRIENDS WITH SUZUKAZE-SAN?
SINCE OUR THIRD YEAR OF HIGH SCHOOL.
THEN... YOU WERE ONLY TOGE-THER FOR ABOUT A YEAR?
WELL, SOME-THING LIKE THAT ...
BUT THAT ONE YEAR WAS JUST SO MUCH FUN...
AH-HA! THE PER-FECT FACE!
WHAT?! YOU CAN'T USE THAT ONE!!
AND WHY NOT?
IT'S EMBAR-RASSING!
BUT YOUR EXPRES-SION WAS GREAT.

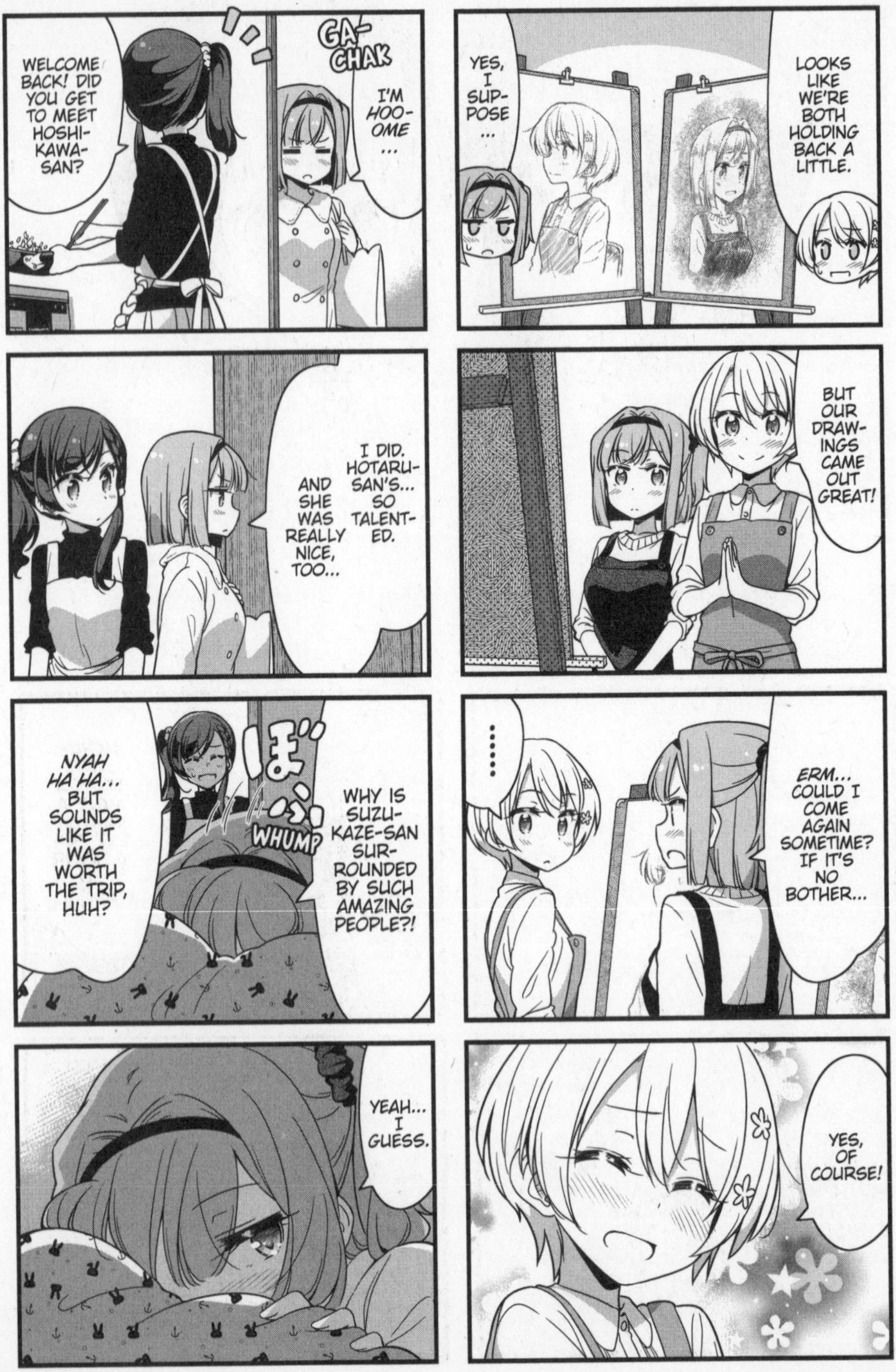
LOOKS LIKE WE'RE BOTH HOLDING BACK A LITTLE.
YES, I SUP-POSE ...
BUT OUR DRAW-INGS CAME OUT GREAT!
ERM... COULD I COME AGAIN SOMETIME? IF IT'S NO BOTHER...
......
YES, OF COURSE!
GA-CHAK
I'M HOO-OME ...
WELCOME BACK! DID YOU GET TO MEET HOSHI-KAWA-SAN?
I DID. HOTARU-SAN'S... SO TALENT-ED.
AND SHE WAS REALLY NICE, TOO...
WHY IS SUZU-KAZE-SAN SUR-ROUNDED BY SUCH AMAZING PEOPLE?!
WHUMP
NYAH HA HA... BUT SOUNDS LIKE IT WAS WORTH THE TRIP, HUH?
YEAH... I GUESS.

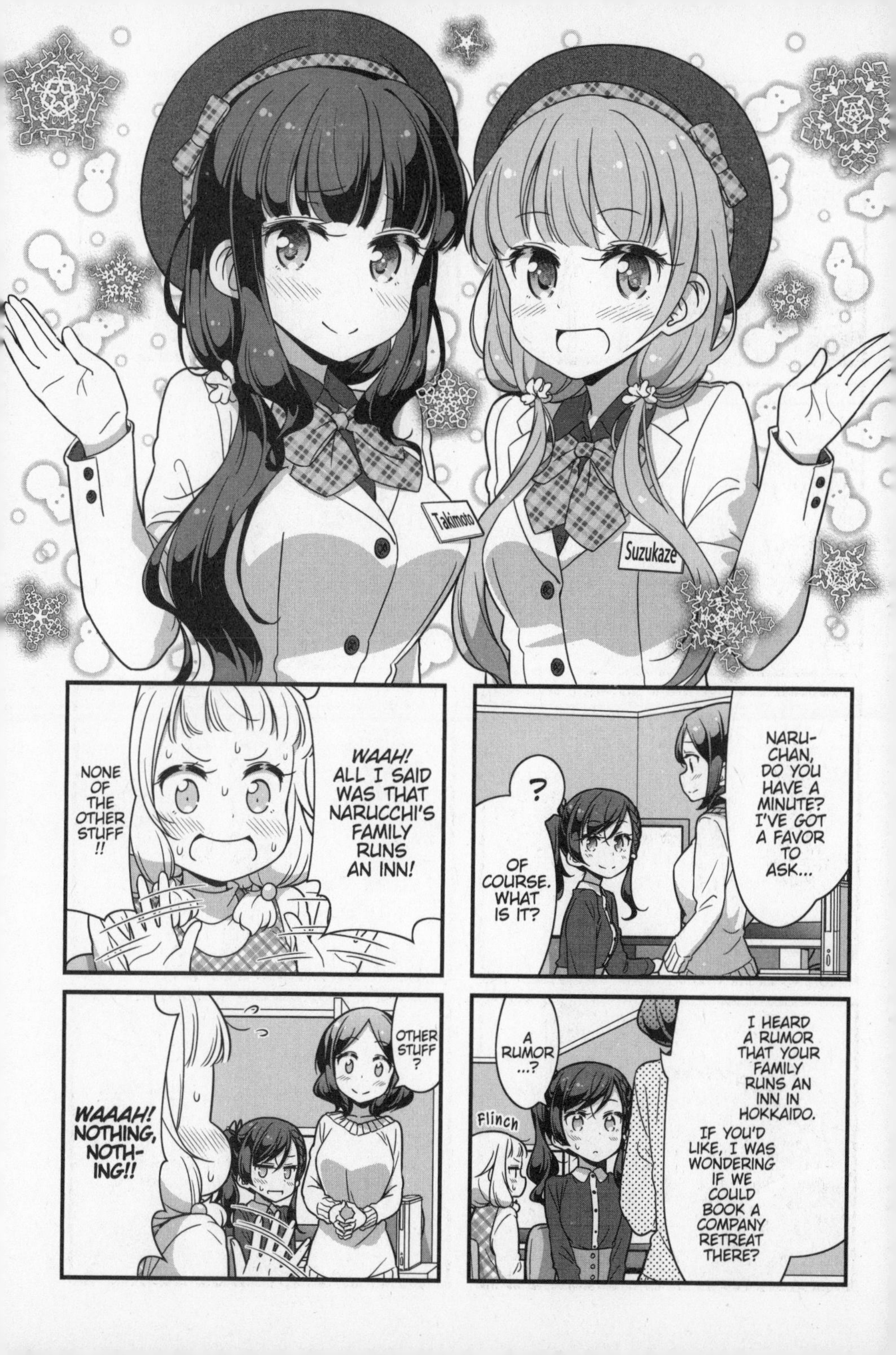
Takimoto
Suzukaze
NARU-CHAN, DO YOU HAVE A MINUTE? I'VE GOT A FAVOR TO ASK...
?
OF COURSE. WHAT IS IT?
I HEARD A RUMOR THAT YOUR FAMILY RUNS AN INN IN HOKKAIDO.
IF YOU'D LIKE, I WAS WONDERING IF WE COULD BOOK A COMPANY RETREAT THERE?
A RUMOR ...?
Flinch
WAAH! ALL I SAID WAS THAT NARUCCHI'S FAMILY RUNS AN INN!
NONE OF THE OTHER STUFF!!
OTHER STUFF?
WAAAH! NOTHING, NOTHING!!

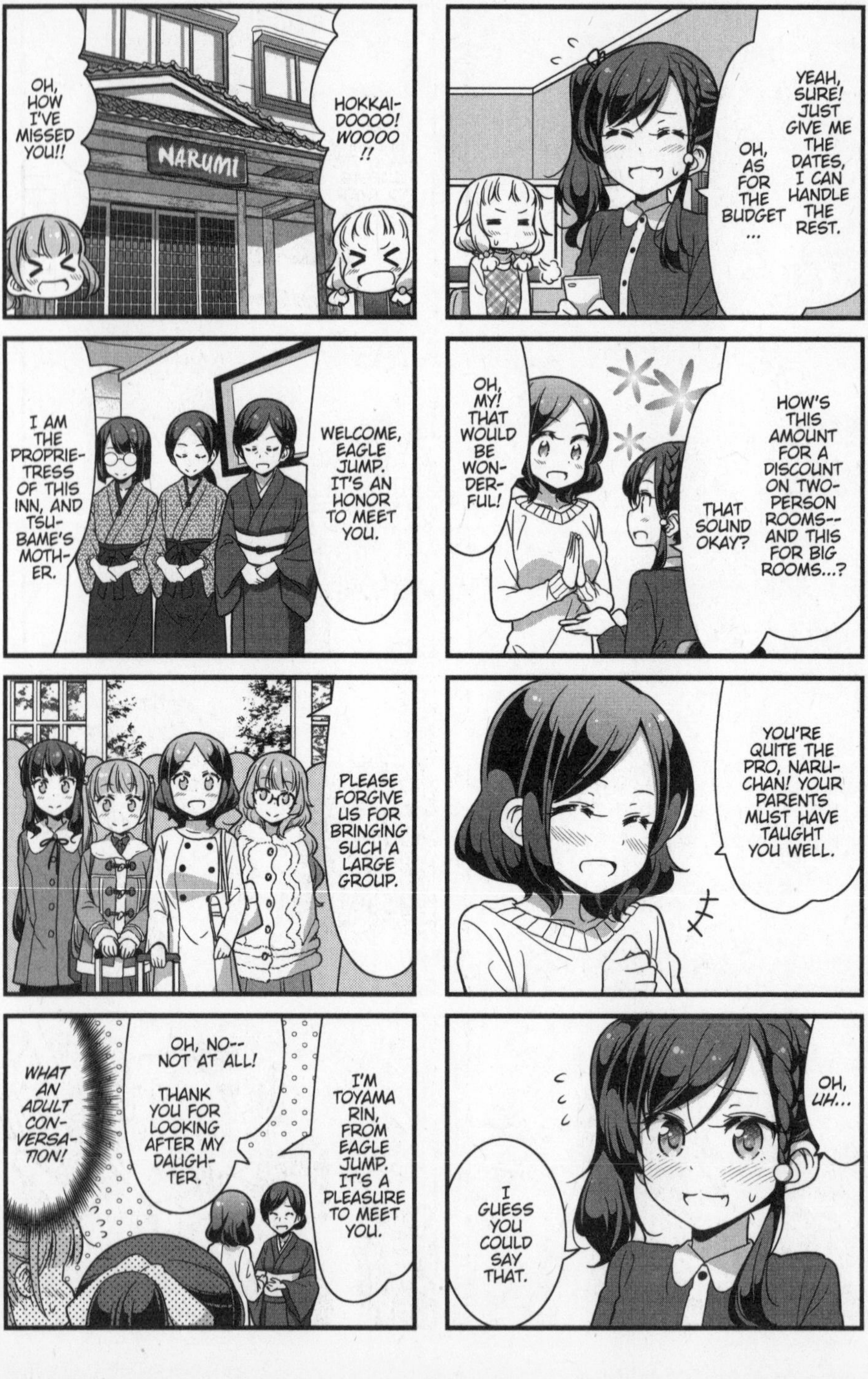
YEAH, SURE! JUST GIVE ME THE DATES, I CAN HANDLE THE REST.
OH, AS FOR THE BUDGET...
HOW'S THIS AMOUNT FOR A DISCOUNT ON TWO-PERSON ROOMS--AND THIS FOR BIG ROOMS...?
THAT SOUND OKAY?
OH, MY! THAT WOULD BE WONDERFUL!
YOU'RE QUITE THE PRO, NARU-CHAN! YOUR PARENTS MUST HAVE TAUGHT YOU WELL.
OH, UH...
I GUESS YOU COULD SAY THAT.
HOKKAIDOOOO! WOOOO!!
NARUMI
OH, HOW I'VE MISSED YOU!!
WELCOME, EAGLE JUMP. IT'S AN HONOR TO MEET YOU.
I AM THE PROPRIETRESS OF THIS INN, AND TSUBAME'S MOTHER.
PLEASE FORGIVE US FOR BRINGING SUCH A LARGE GROUP.
I'M TOYAMA RIN, FROM EAGLE JUMP. IT'S A PLEASURE TO MEET YOU.
OH, NO--NOT AT ALL! THANK YOU FOR LOOKING AFTER MY DAUGHTER.
WHAT AN ADULT CONVERSATION!

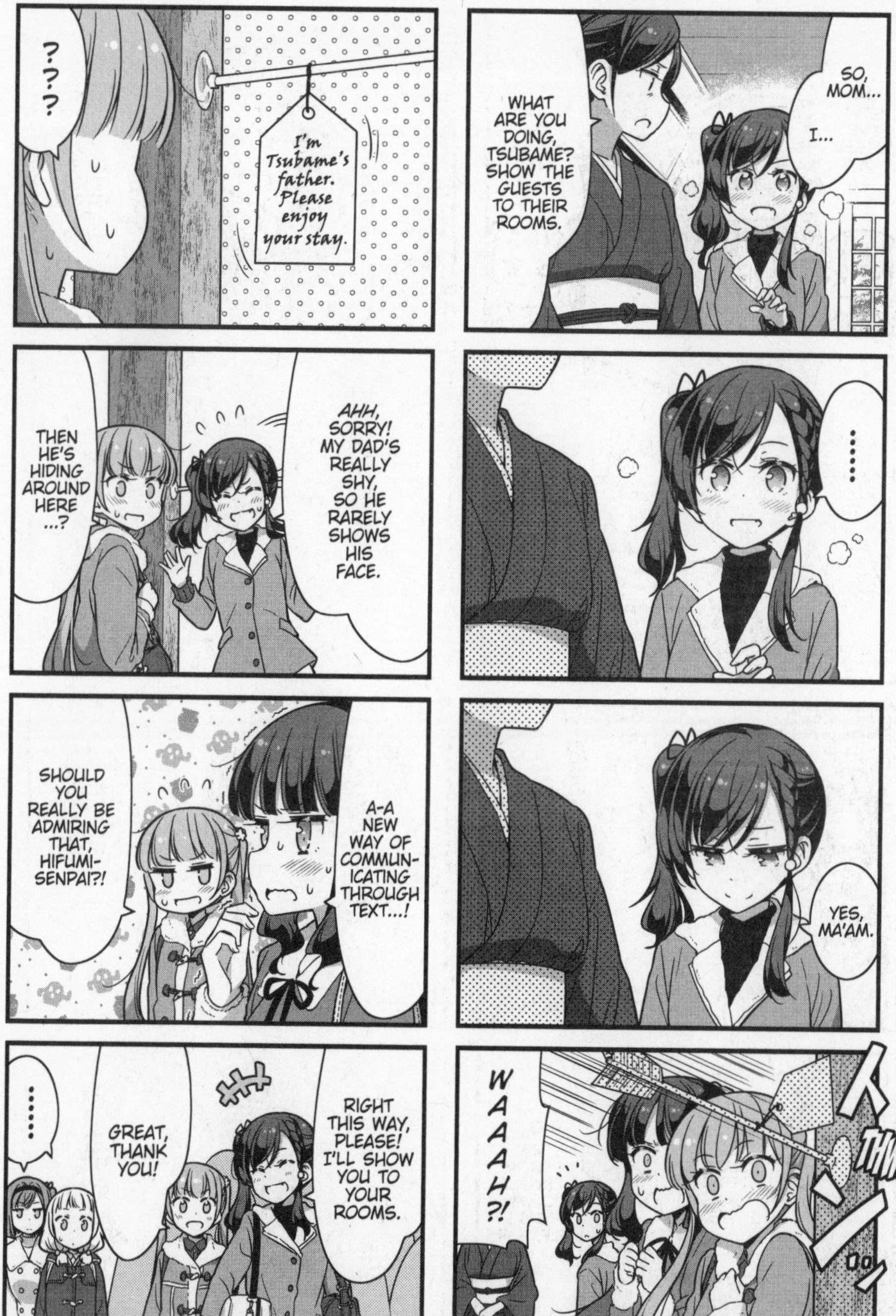
SO, MOM...
I...
WHAT ARE YOU DOING, TSUBAME? SHOW THE GUESTS TO THEIR ROOMS.
?.?.?
I'm Tsubame's father. Please enjoy your stay.
......
AHH, SORRY! MY DAD'S REALLY SHY, SO HE RARELY SHOWS HIS FACE.
THEN HE'S HIDING AROUND HERE ...?
YES, MA'AM.
A-A NEW WAY OF COMMUNICATING THROUGH TEXT...!
SHOULD YOU REALLY BE ADMIRING THAT, HIFUMI-SENPAI?!
THWOP
WAAAAH?!
RIGHT THIS WAY, PLEASE! I'LL SHOW YOU TO YOUR ROOMS.
GREAT, THANK YOU!
......

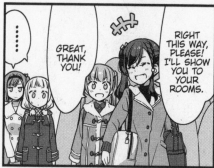

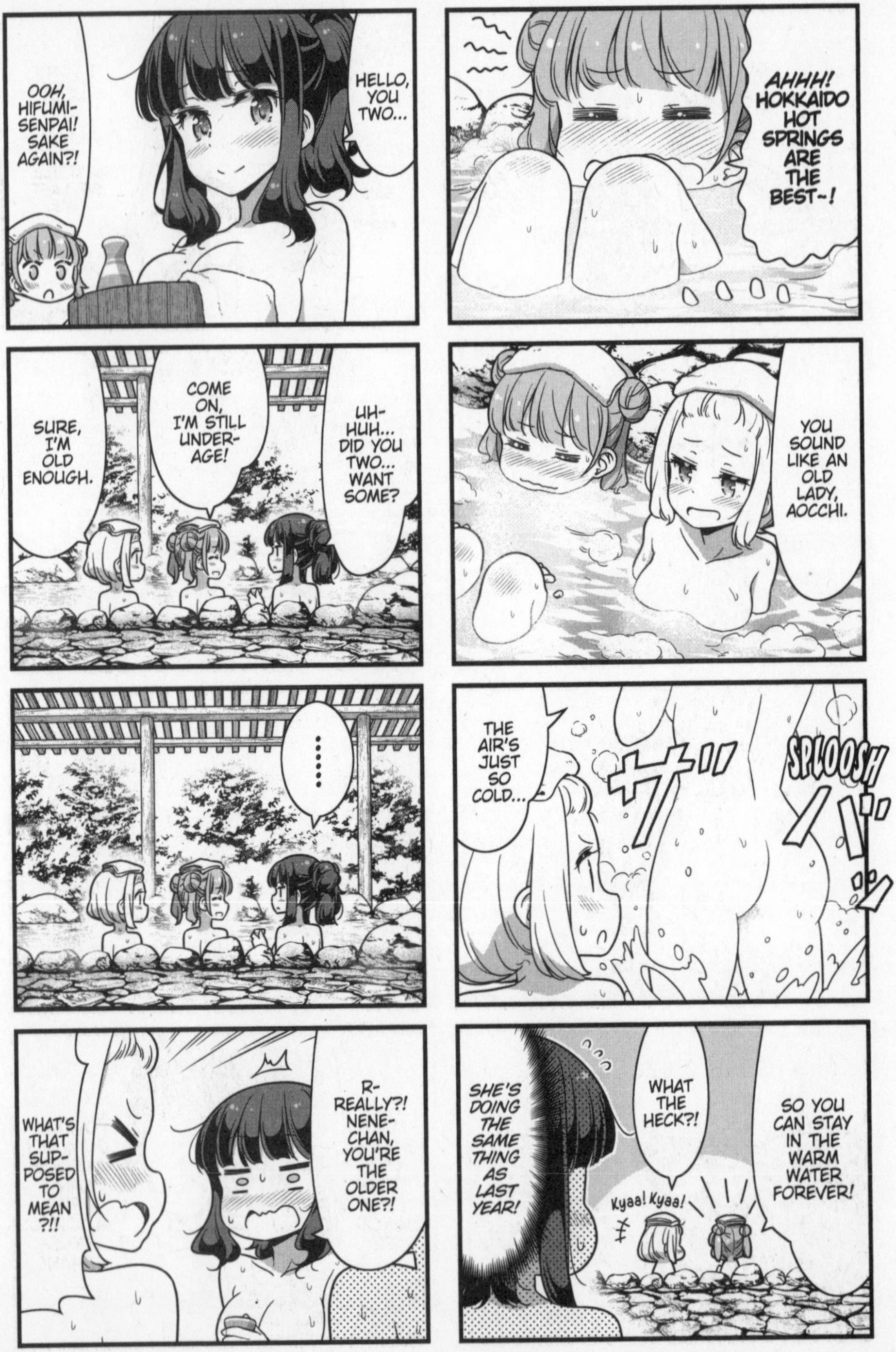
AHHH! HOKKAIDO HOT SPRINGS ARE THE BEST~!
HELLO, YOU TWO...
OOH, HIFUMI-SENPAI! SAKE AGAIN?!
YOU SOUND LIKE AN OLD LADY, AOCCHI.
UH-HUH... DID YOU TWO... WANT SOME?
COME ON, I'M STILL UNDER-AGE!
SURE, I'M OLD ENOUGH.
SPLOOSH
THE AIR'S JUST SO COLD...
......
SO YOU CAN STAY IN THE WARM WATER FOREVER!
WHAT THE HECK?!
SHE'S DOING THE SAME THING AS LAST YEAR!
Kyaa! Kyaa!
R-REALLY?! NENE-CHAN, YOU'RE THE OLDER ONE?!
WHAT'S THAT SUP-POSED TO MEAN?!!

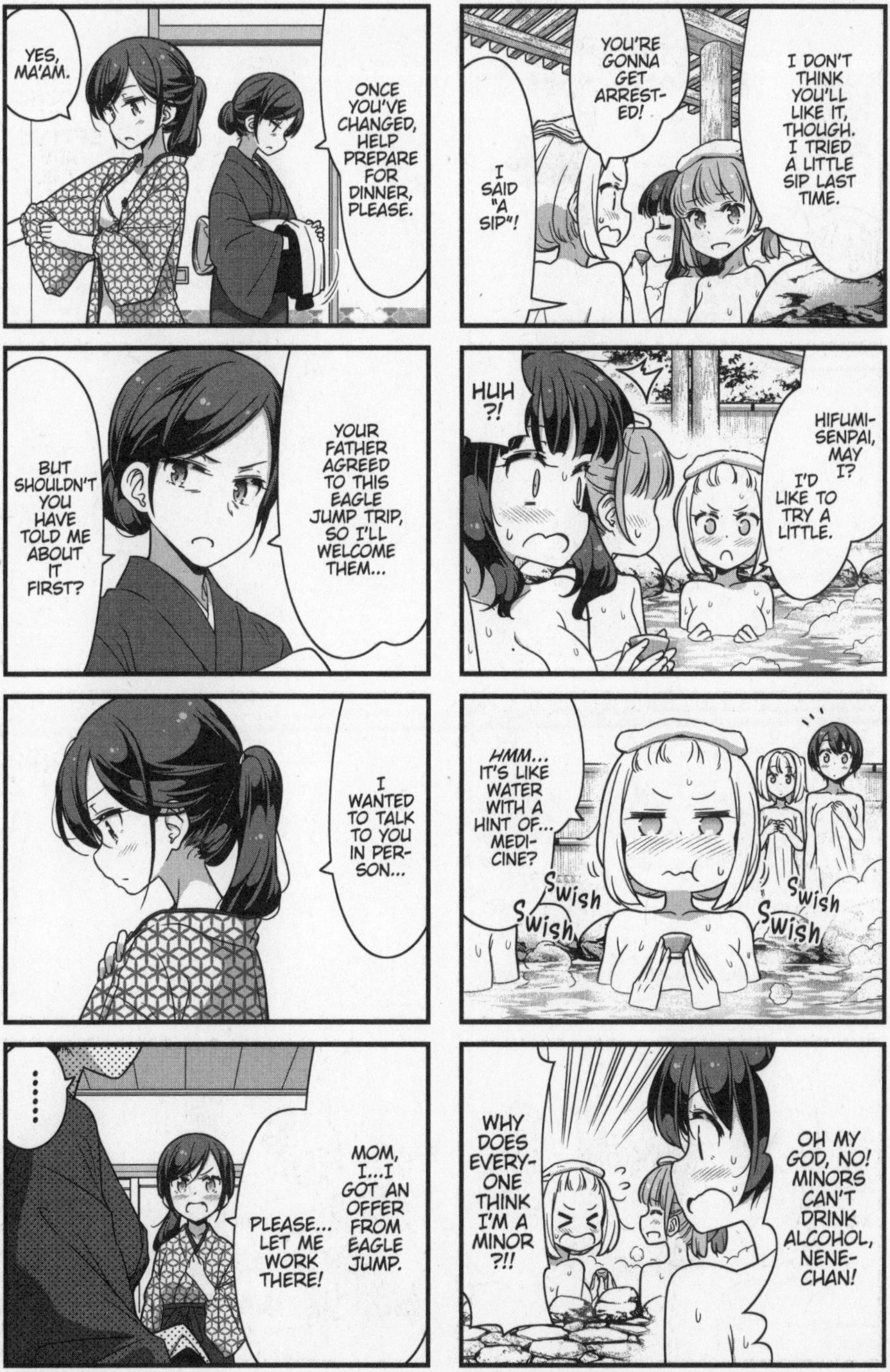
I DON'T THINK YOU'LL LIKE IT, THOUGH. I TRIED A LITTLE SIP LAST TIME.
YOU'RE GONNA GET ARREST-ED!
I SAID "A SIP"!
HIFUMI-SENPAI, MAY I?
I'D LIKE TO TRY A LITTLE.
HUH ?!
HMM... IT'S LIKE WATER WITH A HINT OF... MEDI-CINE?
Swish
Swish
Swish
Swish
OH MY GOD, NO! MINORS CAN'T DRINK ALCOHOL, NENE-CHAN!
WHY DOES EVERY-ONE THINK I'M A MINOR ?!!
ONCE YOU'VE CHANGED, HELP PREPARE FOR DINNER, PLEASE.
YES, MA'AM.
YOUR FATHER AGREED TO THIS EAGLE JUMP TRIP, SO I'LL WELCOME THEM...
BUT SHOULDN'T YOU HAVE TOLD ME ABOUT IT FIRST?
I WANTED TO TALK TO YOU IN PER-SON...
MOM, I...I GOT AN OFFER FROM EAGLE JUMP.
PLEASE... LET ME WORK THERE!
......

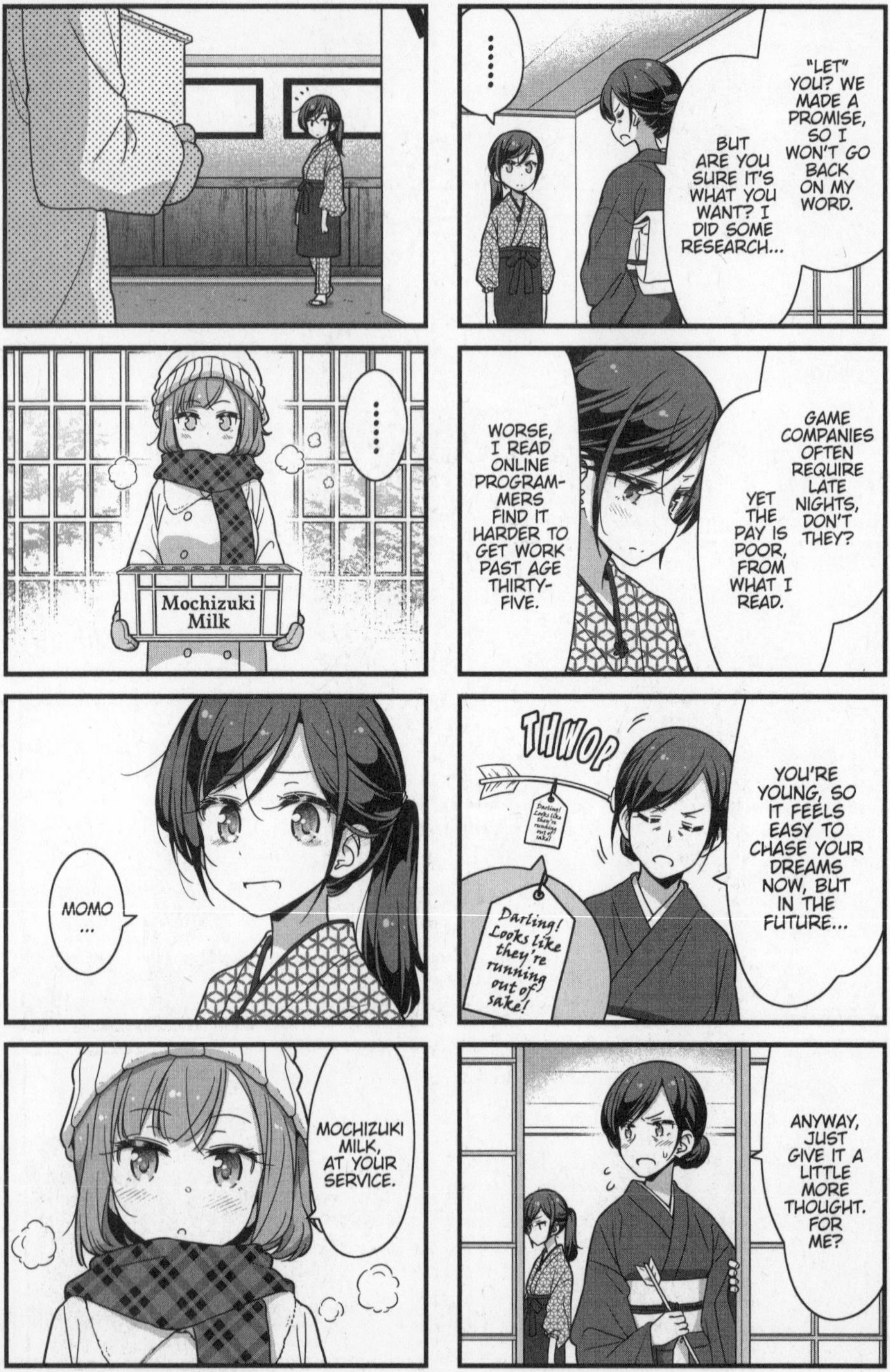

"LET" YOU? WE MADE A PROMISE, SO I WON'T GO BACK ON MY WORD.
BUT ARE YOU SURE IT'S WHAT YOU WANT? I DID SOME RESEARCH...
……
GAME COMPANIES OFTEN REQUIRE LATE NIGHTS, DON'T THEY?
YET THE PAY IS POOR, FROM WHAT I READ.
WORSE, I READ ONLINE PROGRAM-MERS FIND IT HARDER TO GET WORK PAST AGE THIRTY-FIVE.
……
Mochizuki Milk
THWOP
YOU'RE YOUNG, SO IT FEELS EASY TO CHASE YOUR DREAMS NOW, BUT IN THE FUTURE...
Darling! Looks like they're running out of sake!
MOMO ...
ANYWAY, JUST GIVE IT A LITTLE MORE THOUGHT. FOR ME?
MOCHIZUKI MILK, AT YOUR SERVICE.

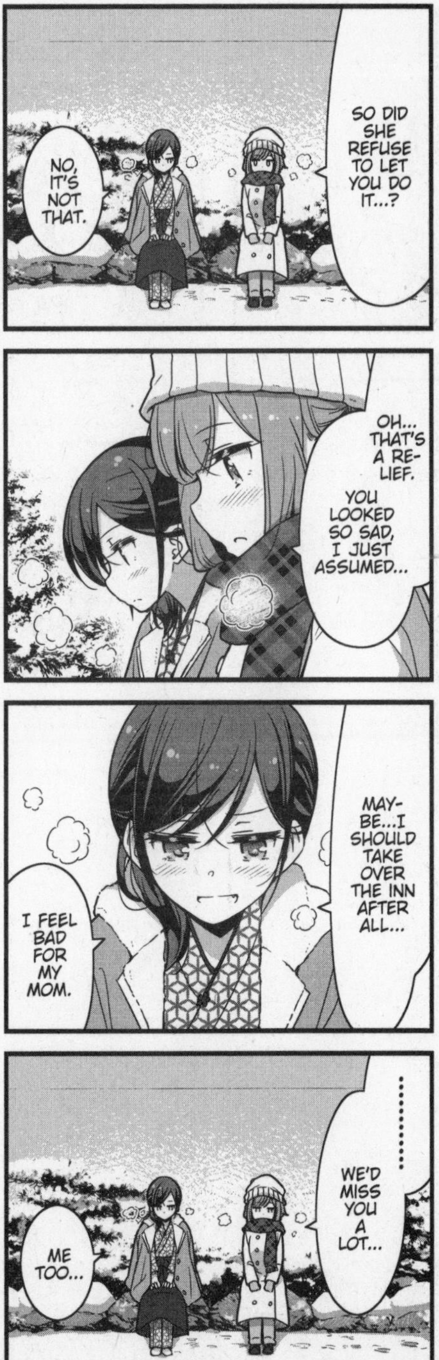
SO DID SHE REFUSE TO LET YOU DO IT...?
NO, IT'S NOT THAT.
OH... THAT'S A RE-LIEF.
YOU LOOKED SO SAD, I JUST ASSUMED...
MAY-BE...I SHOULD TAKE OVER THE INN AFTER ALL...
I FEEL BAD FOR MY MOM.
........
WE'D MISS YOU A LOT...
ME TOO...
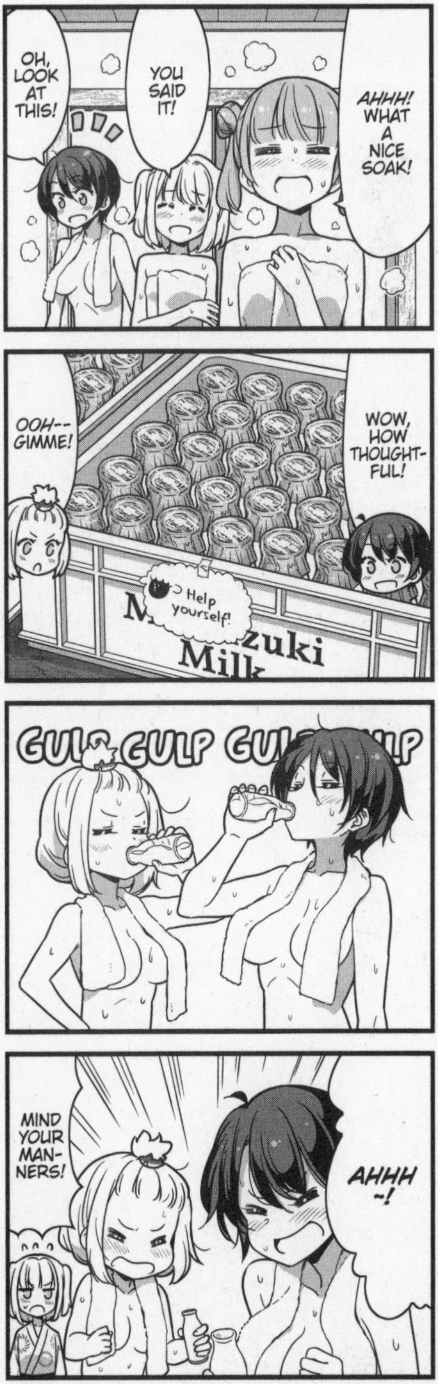
AHHH! WHAT A NICE SOAK!
YOU SAID IT!
OH, LOOK AT THIS!
WOW, HOW THOUGHT-FUL!
OOH-- GIMME!
Help yourself!
GULP
GULP
AHHH~!
MIND YOUR MAN-NERS!

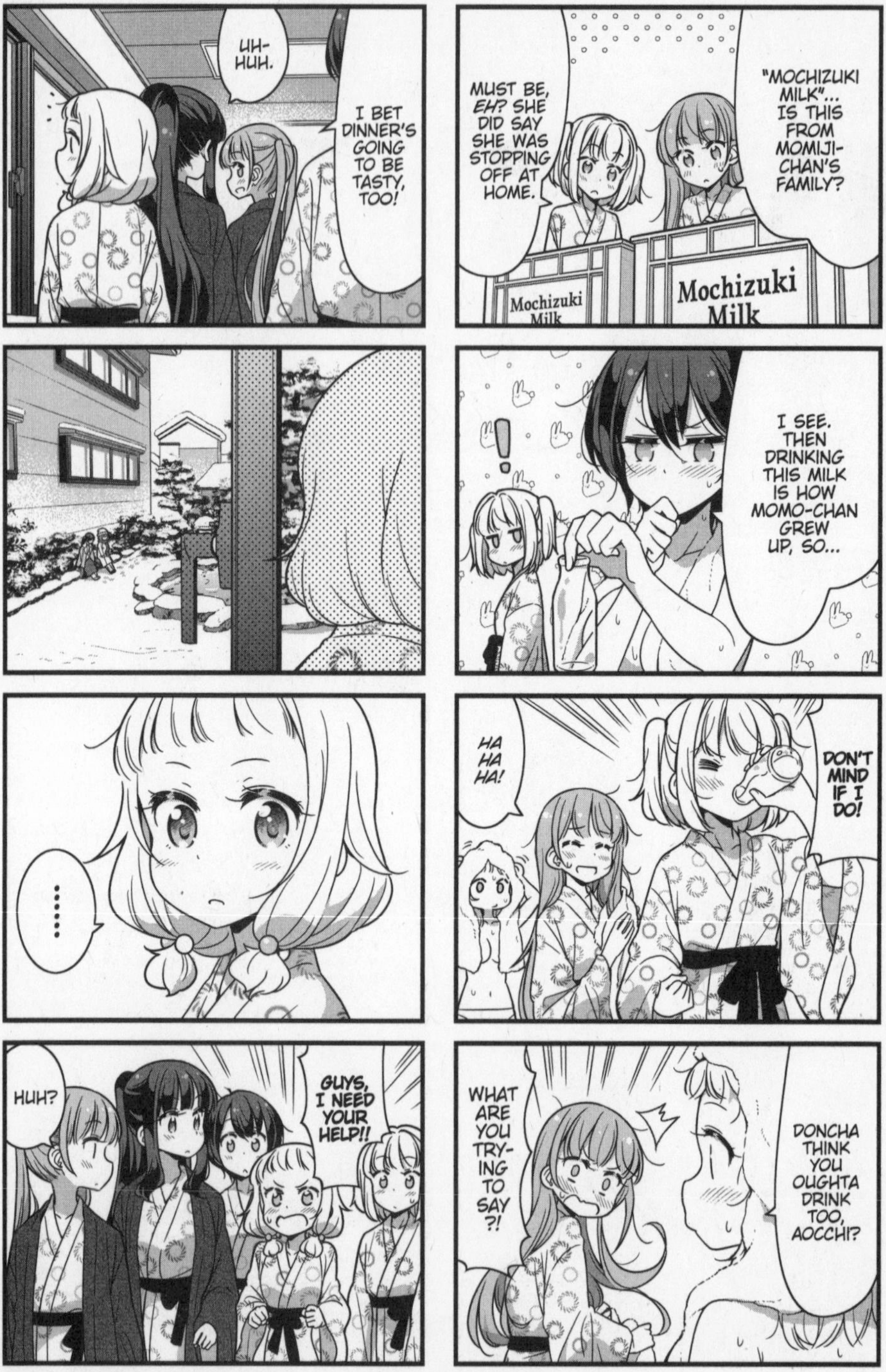
"MOCHIZUKI MILK"... IS THIS FROM MOMIJI-CHAN'S FAMILY?
Mochizuki Milk
MUST BE, EH? SHE DID SAY SHE WAS STOPPING OFF AT HOME.
Mochizuki Milk
I BET DINNER'S GOING TO BE TASTY, TOO!
UH-HUH.
I SEE. THEN DRINKING THIS MILK IS HOW MOMO-CHAN GREW UP, SO...
DON'T MIND IF I DO!
HA HA HA!
......
DONCHA THINK YOU OUGHTA DRINK TOO, AOCCHI?
WHAT ARE YOU TRYING TO SAY?!
GUYS, I NEED YOUR HELP!!
HUH?

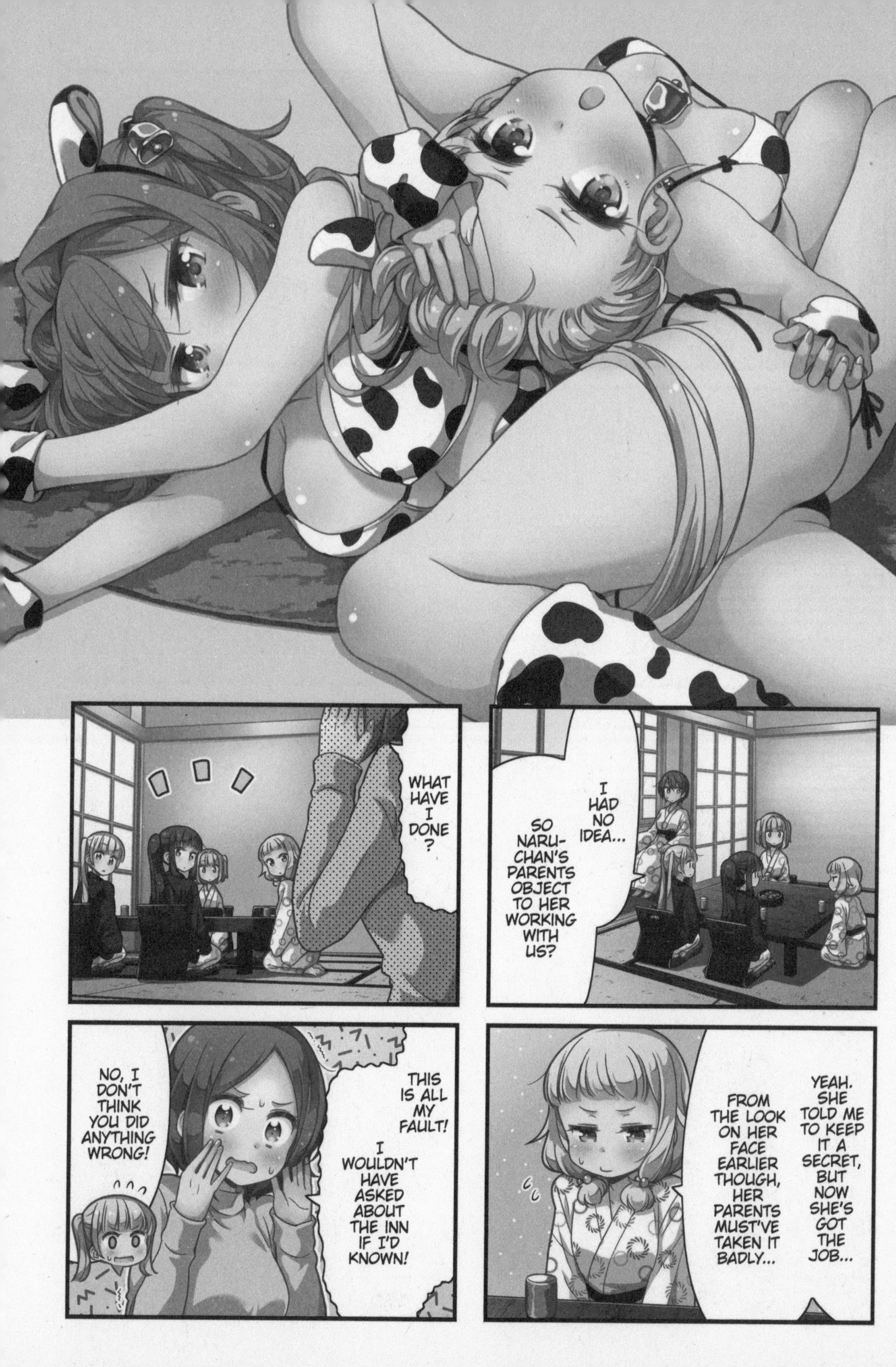
I HAD NO IDEA...
SO NARU-CHAN'S PARENTS OBJECT TO HER WORKING WITH US?
WHAT HAVE I DONE?
YEAH. SHE TOLD ME TO KEEP IT A SECRET, BUT NOW SHE'S GOT THE JOB...
FROM THE LOOK ON HER FACE EARLIER THOUGH, HER PARENTS MUST'VE TAKEN IT BADLY...
THIS IS ALL MY FAULT!
I WOULDN'T HAVE ASKED ABOUT THE INN IF I'D KNOWN!
NO, I DON'T THINK YOU DID ANYTHING WRONG!

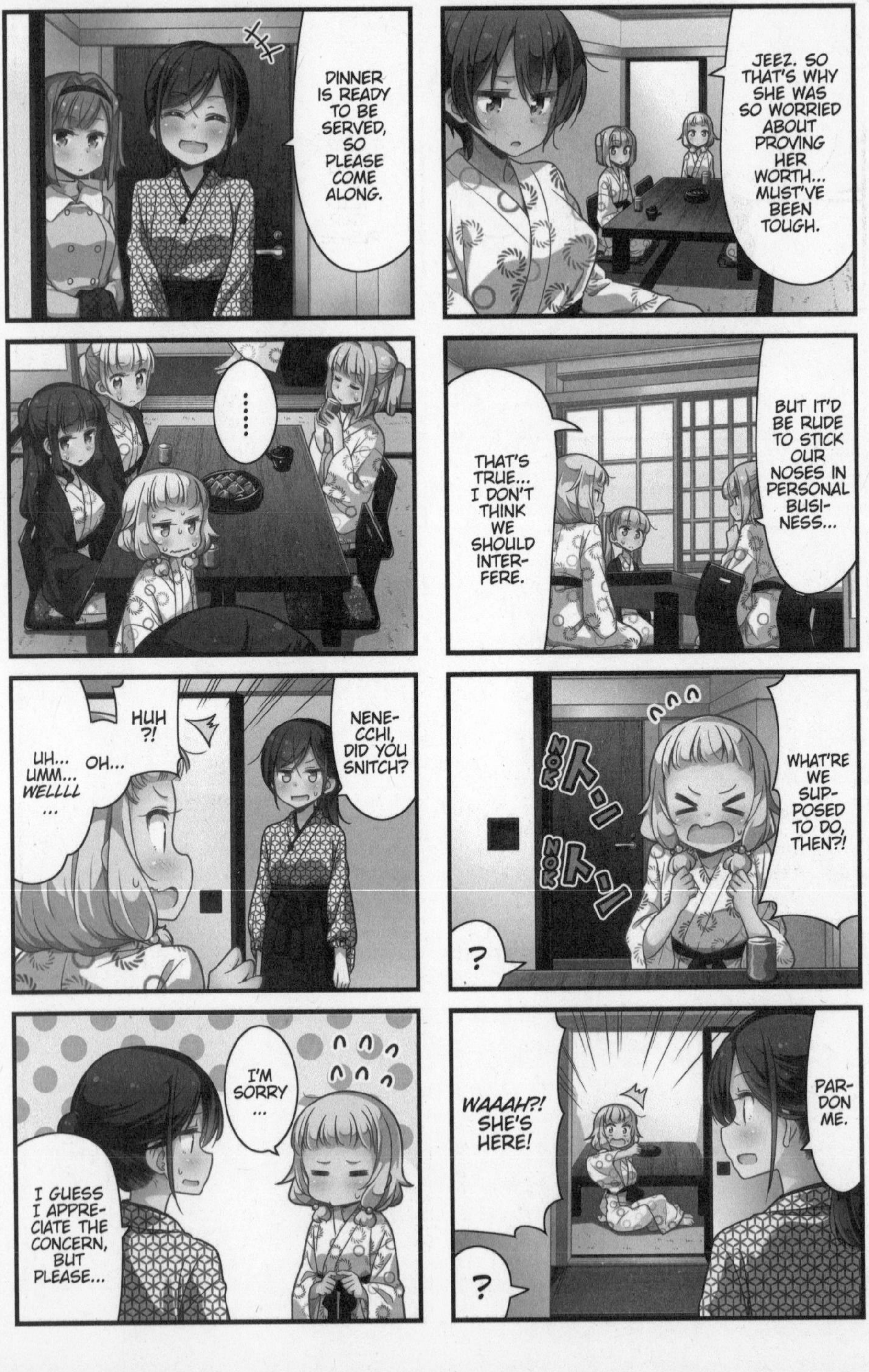
JEEZ. SO THAT'S WHY SHE WAS SO WORRIED ABOUT PROVING HER WORTH... MUST'VE BEEN TOUGH.
BUT IT'D BE RUDE TO STICK OUR NOSES IN PERSONAL BUSI-NESS...
THAT'S TRUE... I DON'T THINK WE SHOULD INTER-FERE.
WHAT'RE WE SUP-POSED TO DO, THEN?!
NOK
NOK
?
PAR-DON ME.
WAAAH?! SHE'S HERE!
?
DINNER IS READY TO BE SERVED, SO PLEASE COME ALONG.
......
NENE-CCHI, DID YOU SNITCH?
HUH ?!
OH...
UH... UMM... WELLLL ...
I'M SORRY ...
I GUESS I APPRE-CIATE THE CONCERN, BUT PLEASE...

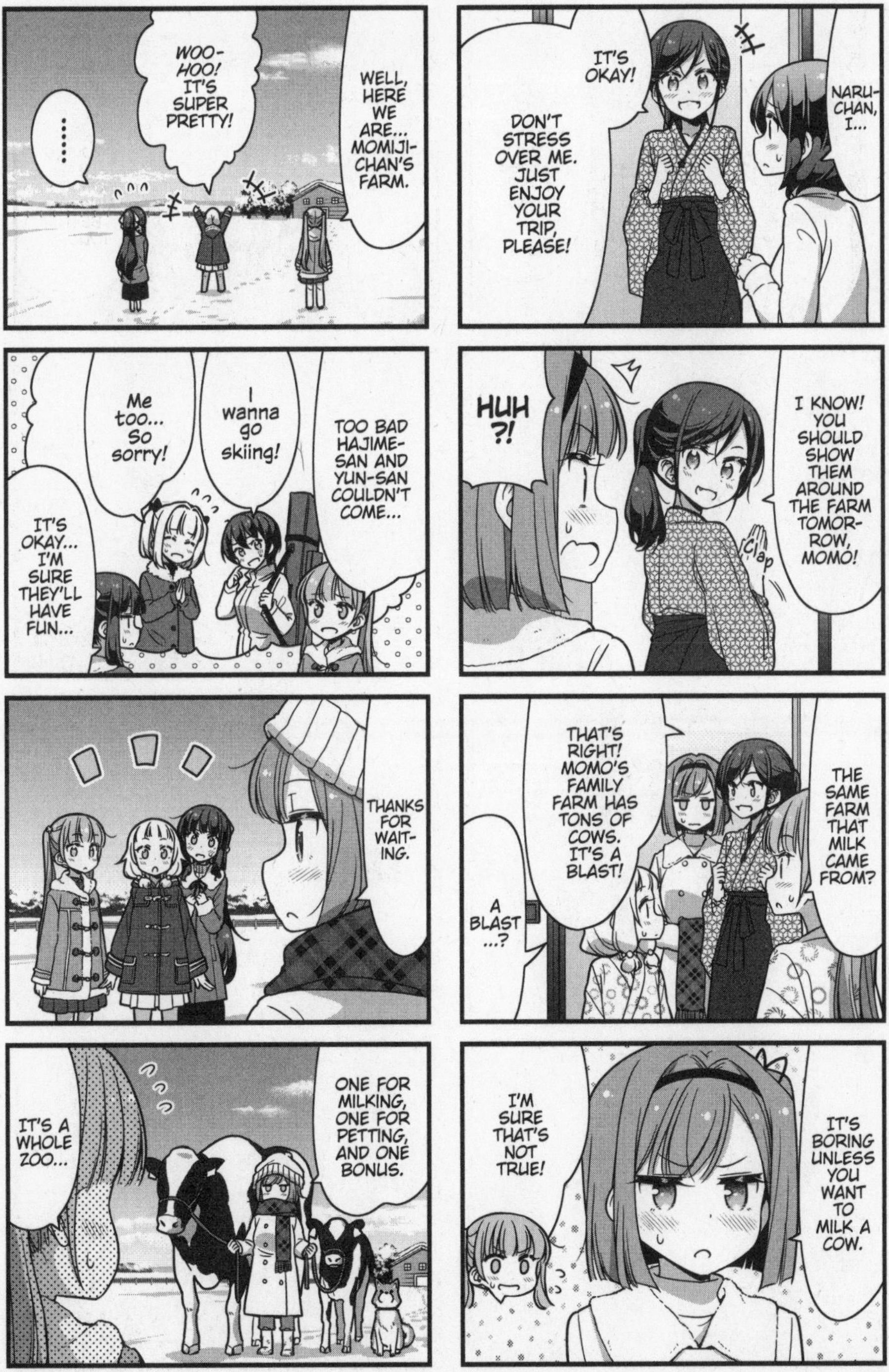
NARU-CHAN, I...
IT'S OKAY!
DON'T STRESS OVER ME. JUST ENJOY YOUR TRIP, PLEASE!
I KNOW! YOU SHOULD SHOW THEM AROUND THE FARM TOMOR-ROW, MOMO!
Clap
HUH?!
THE SAME FARM THAT MILK CAME FROM?
THAT'S RIGHT! MOMO'S FAMILY FARM HAS TONS OF COWS. IT'S A BLAST!
A BLAST...?
IT'S BORING UNLESS YOU WANT TO MILK A COW.
I'M SURE THAT'S NOT TRUE!
WELL, HERE WE ARE... MOMIJI-CHAN'S FARM.
WOO-HOO! IT'S SUPER PRETTY!
......
TOO BAD HAJIME-SAN AND YUN-SAN COULDN'T COME...
I wanna go skiing!
Me too... So sorry!
IT'S OKAY... I'M SURE THEY'LL HAVE FUN...
THANKS FOR WAIT-ING.
ONE FOR MILKING, ONE FOR PETTING, AND ONE BONUS.
IT'S A WHOLE ZOO...

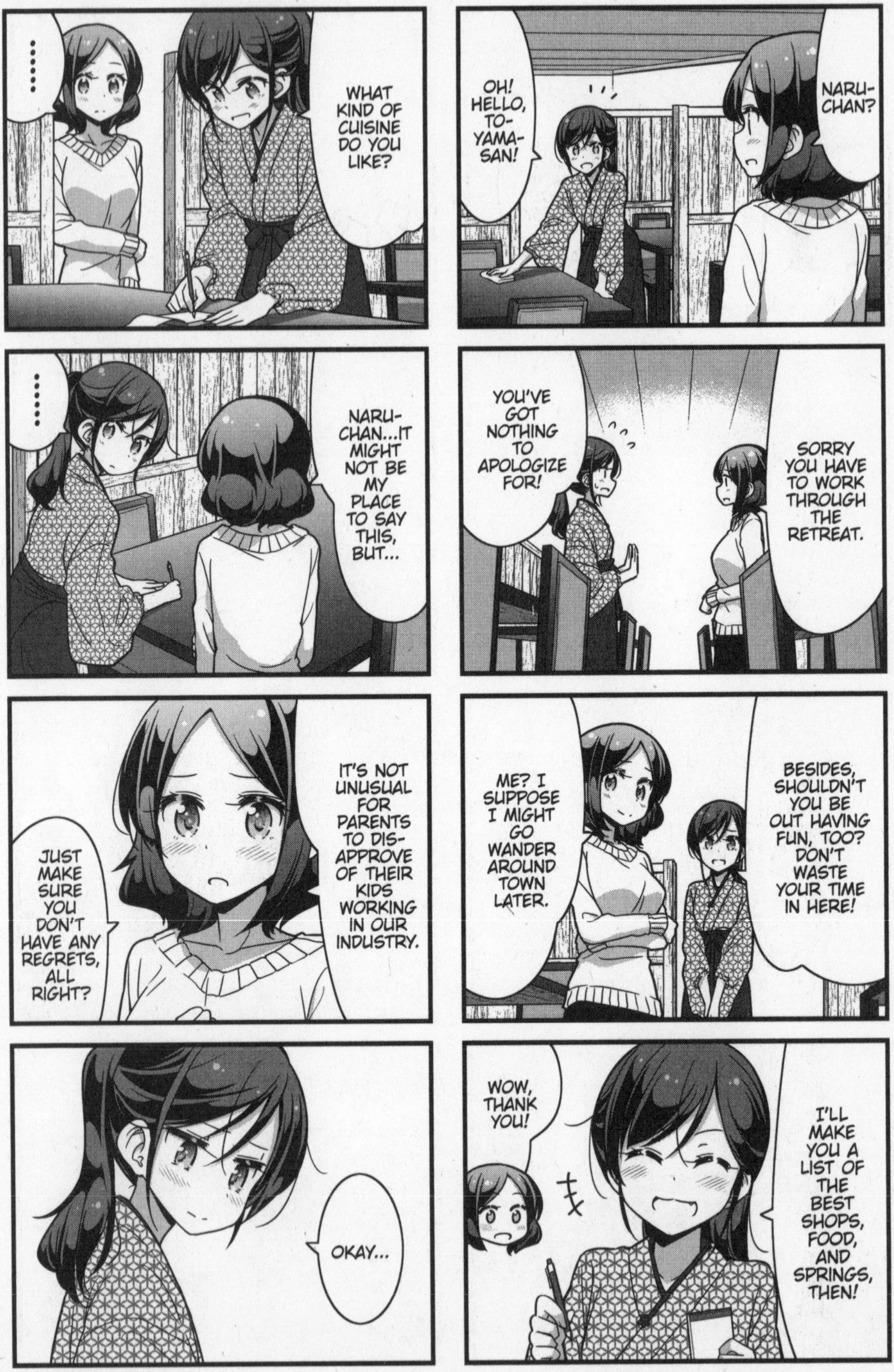
NARU-CHAN?
OH! HELLO, TO-YAMA-SAN!
WHAT KIND OF CUISINE DO YOU LIKE?
......
SORRY YOU HAVE TO WORK THROUGH THE RETREAT.
YOU'VE GOT NOTHING TO APOLOGIZE FOR!
NARU-CHAN...IT MIGHT NOT BE MY PLACE TO SAY THIS, BUT...
......
BESIDES, SHOULDN'T YOU BE OUT HAVING FUN, TOO? DON'T WASTE YOUR TIME IN HERE!
ME? I SUPPOSE I MIGHT GO WANDER AROUND TOWN LATER.
IT'S NOT UNUSUAL FOR PARENTS TO DIS-APPROVE OF THEIR KIDS WORKING IN OUR INDUSTRY.
JUST MAKE SURE YOU DON'T HAVE ANY REGRETS, ALL RIGHT?
I'LL MAKE YOU A LIST OF THE BEST SHOPS, FOOD, AND SPRINGS, THEN!
WOW, THANK YOU!
OKAY...

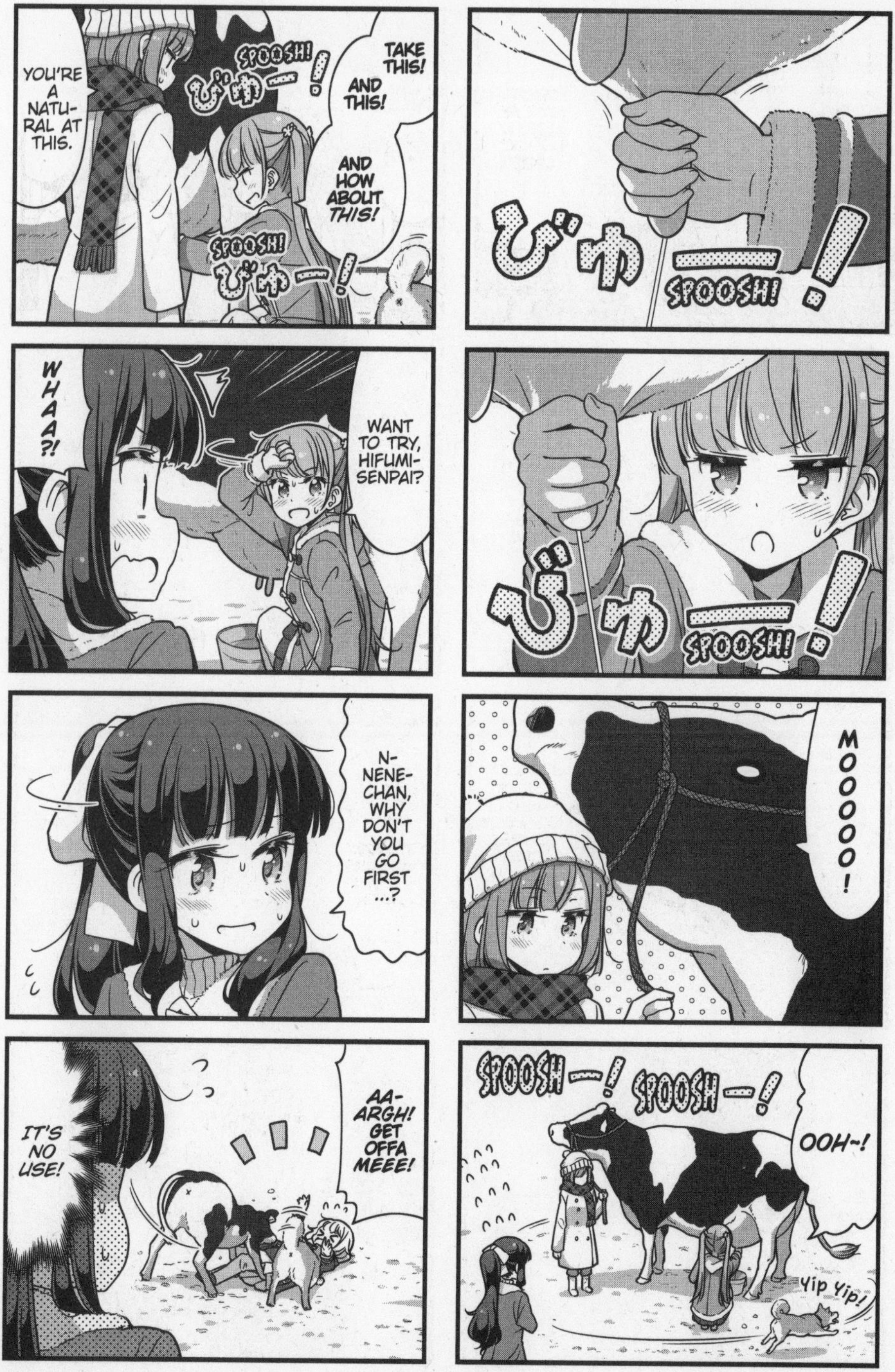
びゅー!
SPOOSH!
TAKE THIS! AND THIS!
AND HOW ABOUT THIS!
SPOOSH! びゅー!
SPOOSH! びゅー!
YOU'RE A NATURAL AT THIS.
びゅー!
SPOOSH!
WANT TO TRY, HIFUMI-SENPAI?
WHAAA?!
MOOOOOO!
N-NENE-CHAN, WHY DON'T YOU GO FIRST ...?
OOH~!
SPOOSH—! SPOOSH—!
Yip Yip!
AA-ARGH! GET OFFA MEEE!
IT'S NO USE!

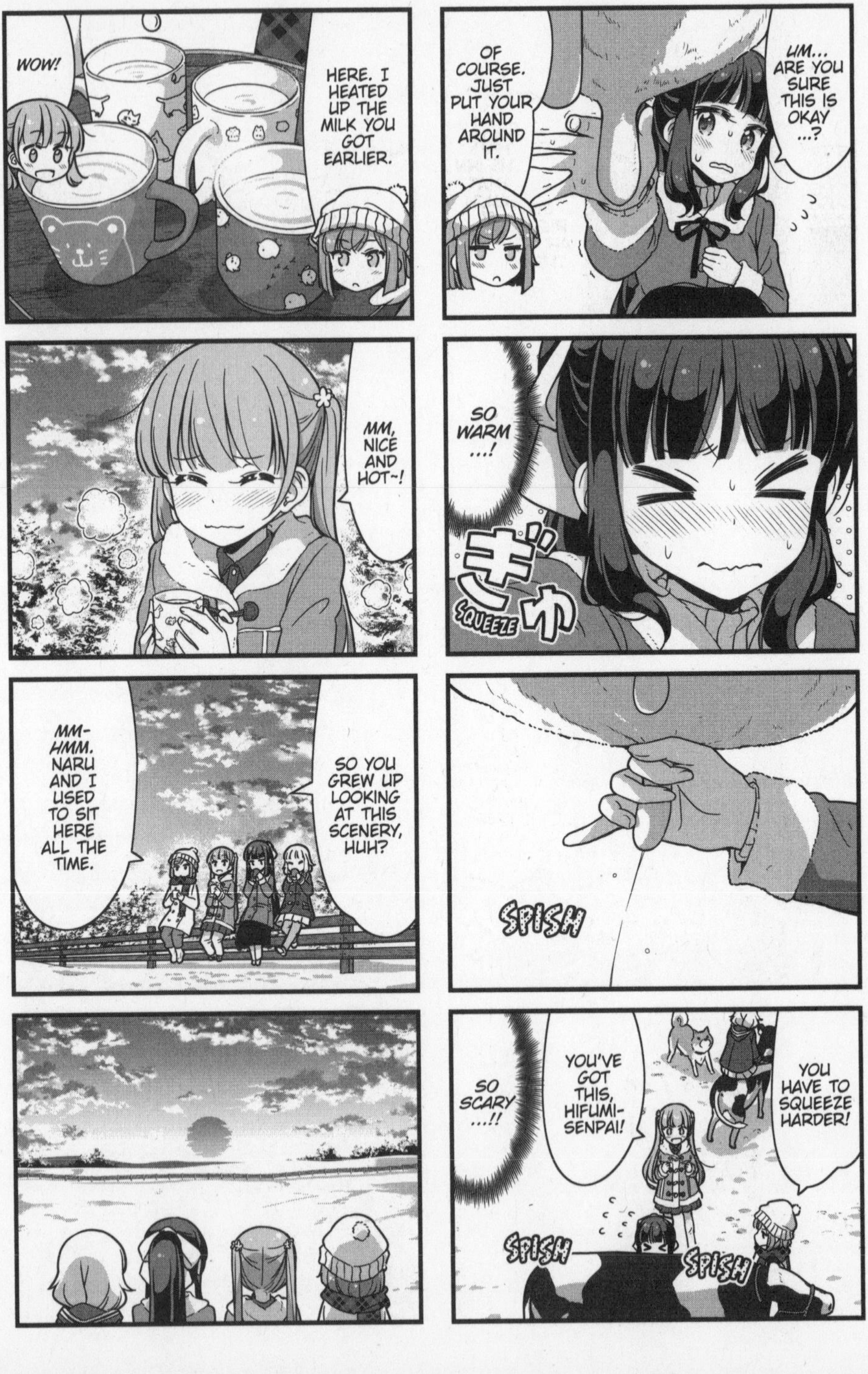
UM... ARE YOU SURE THIS IS OKAY ...?
OF COURSE. JUST PUT YOUR HAND AROUND IT.
HERE. I HEATED UP THE MILK YOU GOT EARLIER.
WOW!
SO WARM ...!
ぎゅ
SQUEEZE
MM, NICE AND HOT~!
SPISH
SO YOU GREW UP LOOKING AT THIS SCENERY, HUH?
MM-HMM. NARU AND I USED TO SIT HERE ALL THE TIME.
YOU HAVE TO SQUEEZE HARDER!
YOU'VE GOT THIS, HIFUMI-SENPAI!
SO SCARY ...!!
SPISH
SPISH

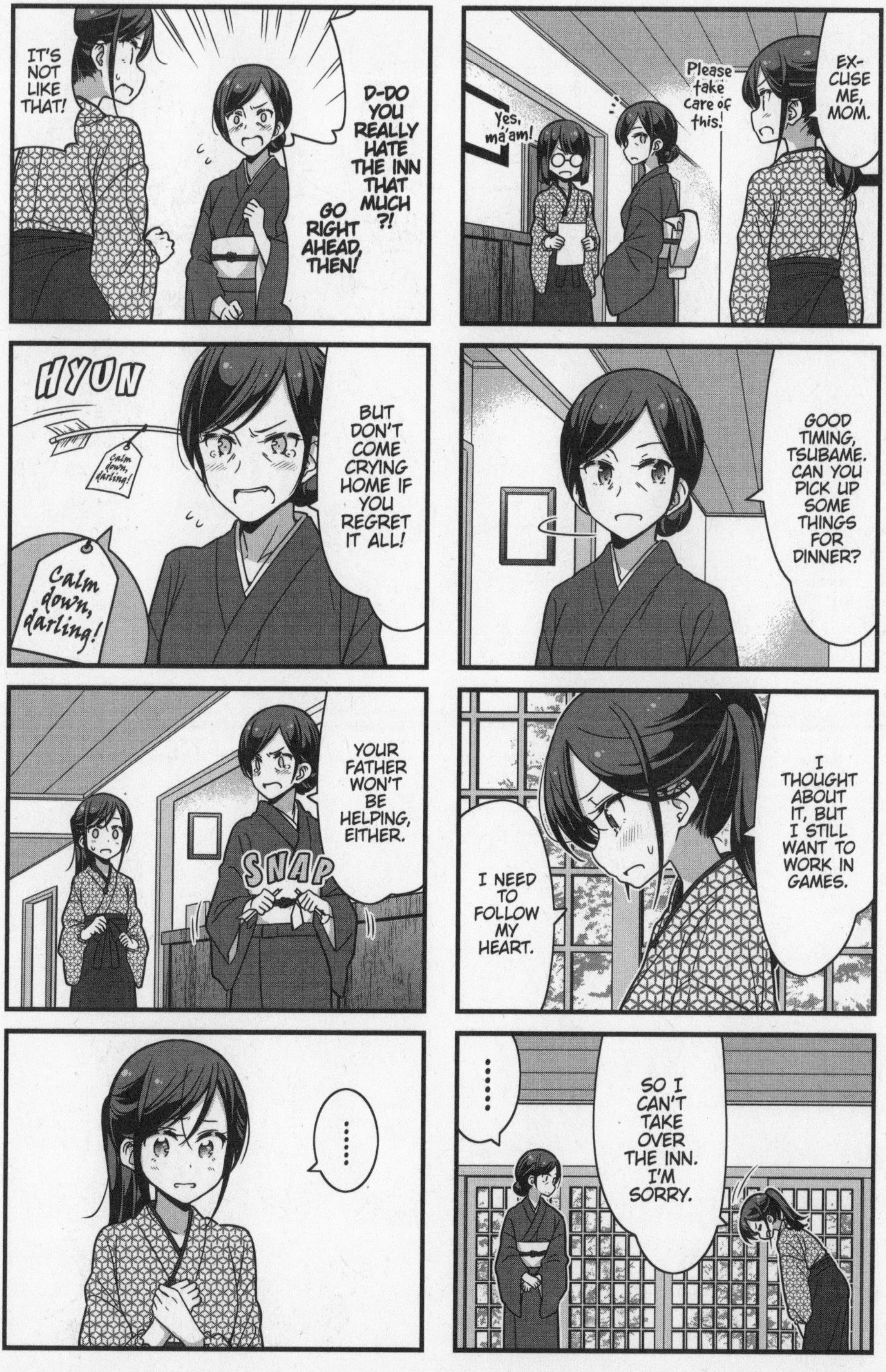
EX-CUSE ME, MOM.
Please take care of this!
Yes, ma'am!
GOOD TIMING, TSUBAME. CAN YOU PICK UP SOME THINGS FOR DINNER?
I THOUGHT ABOUT IT, BUT I STILL WANT TO WORK IN GAMES.
I NEED TO FOLLOW MY HEART.
......
SO I CAN'T TAKE OVER THE INN. I'M SORRY.
D-DO YOU REALLY HATE THE INN THAT MUCH?!
GO RIGHT AHEAD, THEN!
IT'S NOT LIKE THAT!
HYUN
BUT DON'T COME CRYING HOME IF YOU REGRET IT ALL!
Calm down, darling!
Calm down, darling!
YOUR FATHER WON'T BE HELPING, EITHER.
SNAP
......

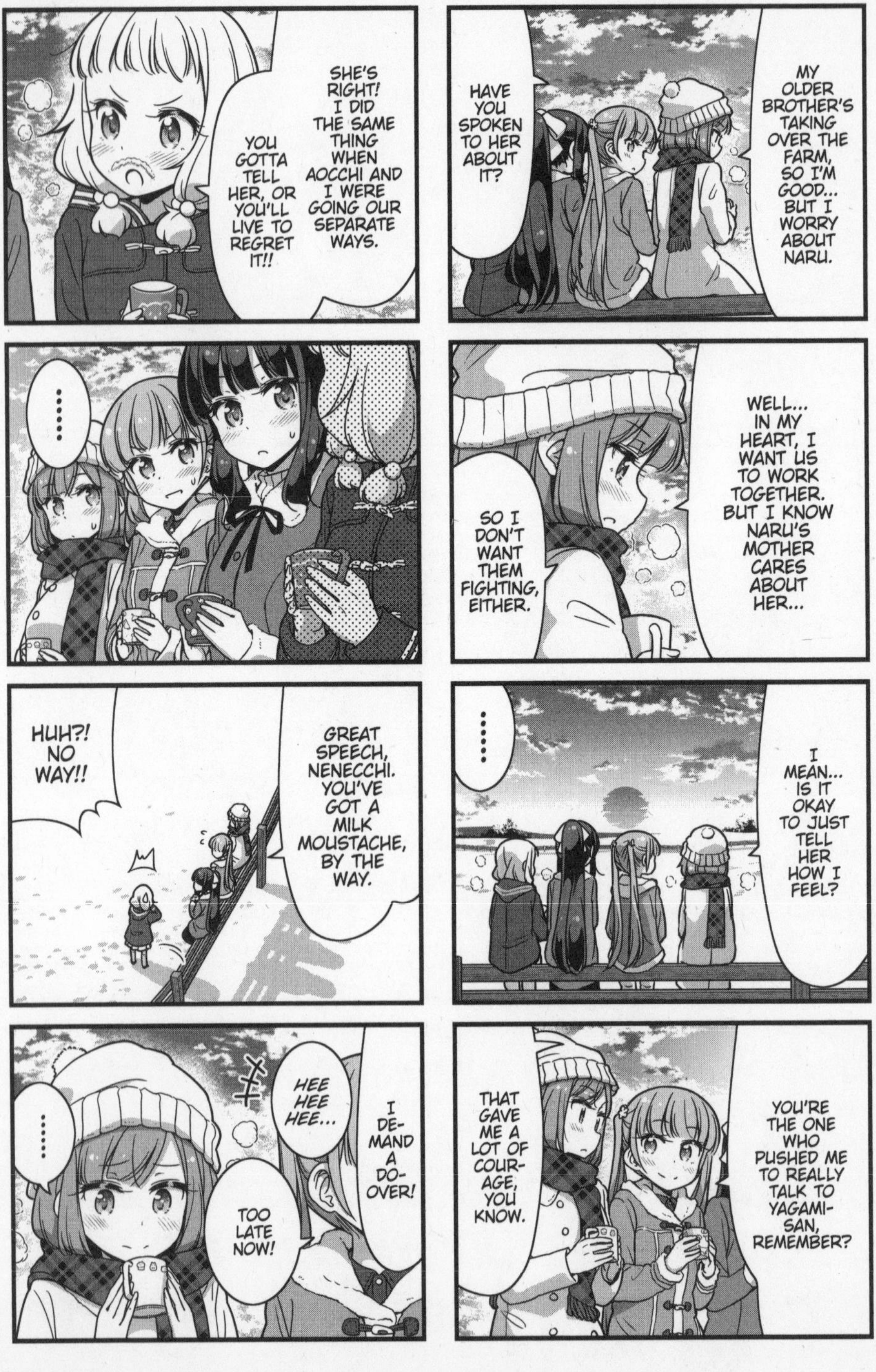

MY OLDER BROTHER'S TAKING OVER THE FARM, SO I'M GOOD... BUT I WORRY ABOUT NARU.
HAVE YOU SPOKEN TO HER ABOUT IT?
SHE'S RIGHT! I DID THE SAME THING WHEN AOCCHI AND I WERE GOING OUR SEPARATE WAYS.
YOU GOTTA TELL HER, OR YOU'LL LIVE TO REGRET IT!!
WELL... IN MY HEART, I WANT US TO WORK TOGETHER. BUT I KNOW NARU'S MOTHER CARES ABOUT HER...
SO I DON'T WANT THEM FIGHTING, EITHER.
......
I MEAN... IS IT OKAY TO JUST TELL HER HOW I FEEL?
......
GREAT SPEECH, NENECCHI. YOU'VE GOT A MILK MOUSTACHE, BY THE WAY.
HUH?! NO WAY!!
YOU'RE THE ONE WHO PUSHED ME TO REALLY TALK TO YAGAMI-SAN, REMEMBER?
THAT GAVE ME A LOT OF COURAGE, YOU KNOW.
I DE-MAND A DO-OVER!
HEE HEE HEE...
TOO LATE NOW!
......

nEW GAME!

NEW GAME!

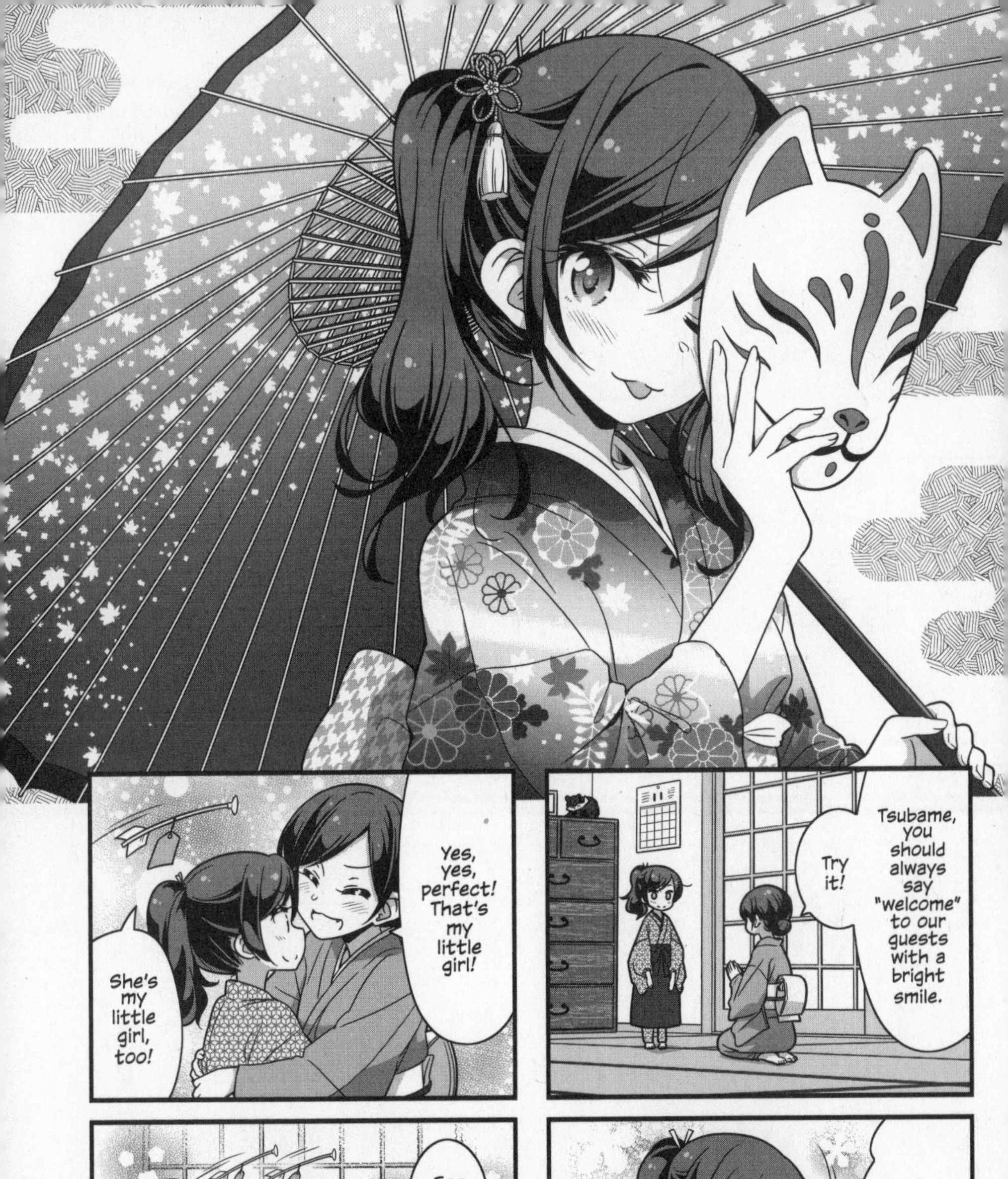
Tsubame, you should always say "welcome" to our guests with a bright smile.
Try it!
Yes, yes, perfect! That's my little girl!
She's my little girl, too!
Welcome, guests!
Eee hee hee!
I love you, Mommy!

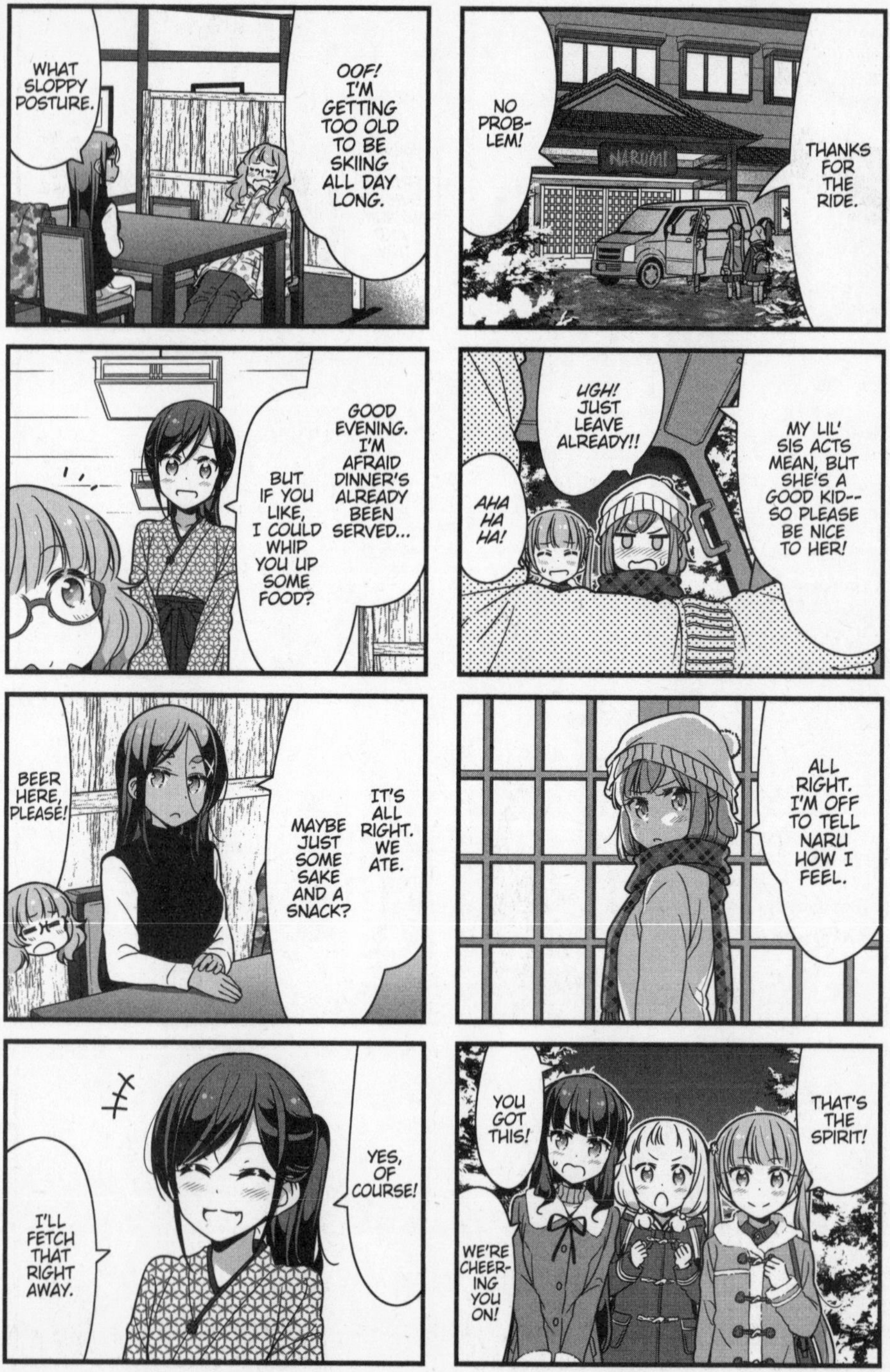
THANKS FOR THE RIDE.
NO PROB-LEM!
NARUMI
MY LIL' SIS ACTS MEAN, BUT SHE'S A GOOD KID-- SO PLEASE BE NICE TO HER!
UGH! JUST LEAVE ALREADY!!
AHA HA HA!
ALL RIGHT. I'M OFF TO TELL NARU HOW I FEEL.
THAT'S THE SPIRIT!
YOU GOT THIS!
WE'RE CHEER-ING YOU ON!
OOF! I'M GETTING TOO OLD TO BE SKIING ALL DAY LONG.
WHAT SLOPPY POSTURE.
GOOD EVENING. I'M AFRAID DINNER'S ALREADY BEEN SERVED...
BUT IF YOU LIKE, I COULD WHIP YOU UP SOME FOOD?
IT'S ALL RIGHT. WE ATE.
MAYBE JUST SOME SAKE AND A SNACK?
BEER HERE, PLEASE!
YES, OF COURSE!
I'LL FETCH THAT RIGHT AWAY.

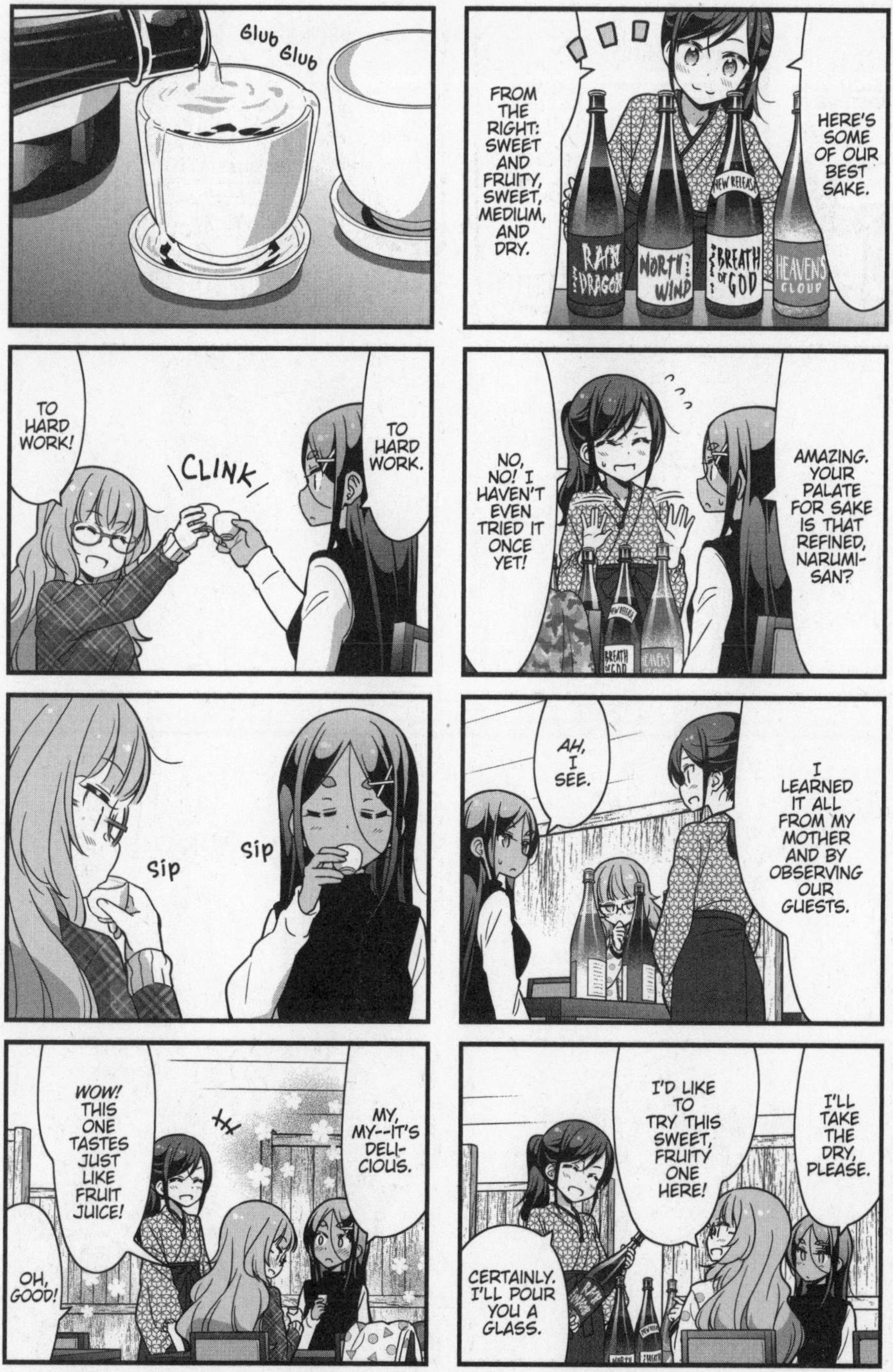
HERE'S SOME OF OUR BEST SAKE.
FROM THE RIGHT: SWEET AND FRUITY, SWEET, MEDIUM, AND DRY.
HEAVENS CLOUD
NEW RELEASE
BREATH OF GOD
NORTH WIND
RAIN DRAGON
Glub Glub
AMAZING. YOUR PALATE FOR SAKE IS THAT REFINED, NARUMI-SAN?
NO, NO! I HAVEN'T EVEN TRIED IT ONCE YET!
TO HARD WORK.
CLINK
TO HARD WORK!
I LEARNED IT ALL FROM MY MOTHER AND BY OBSERVING OUR GUESTS.
AH, I SEE.
Sip
Sip
I'LL TAKE THE DRY, PLEASE.
I'D LIKE TO TRY THIS SWEET, FRUITY ONE HERE!
CERTAINLY. I'LL POUR YOU A GLASS.
MY, MY--IT'S DELICIOUS.
WOW! THIS ONE TASTES JUST LIKE FRUIT JUICE!
OH, GOOD!

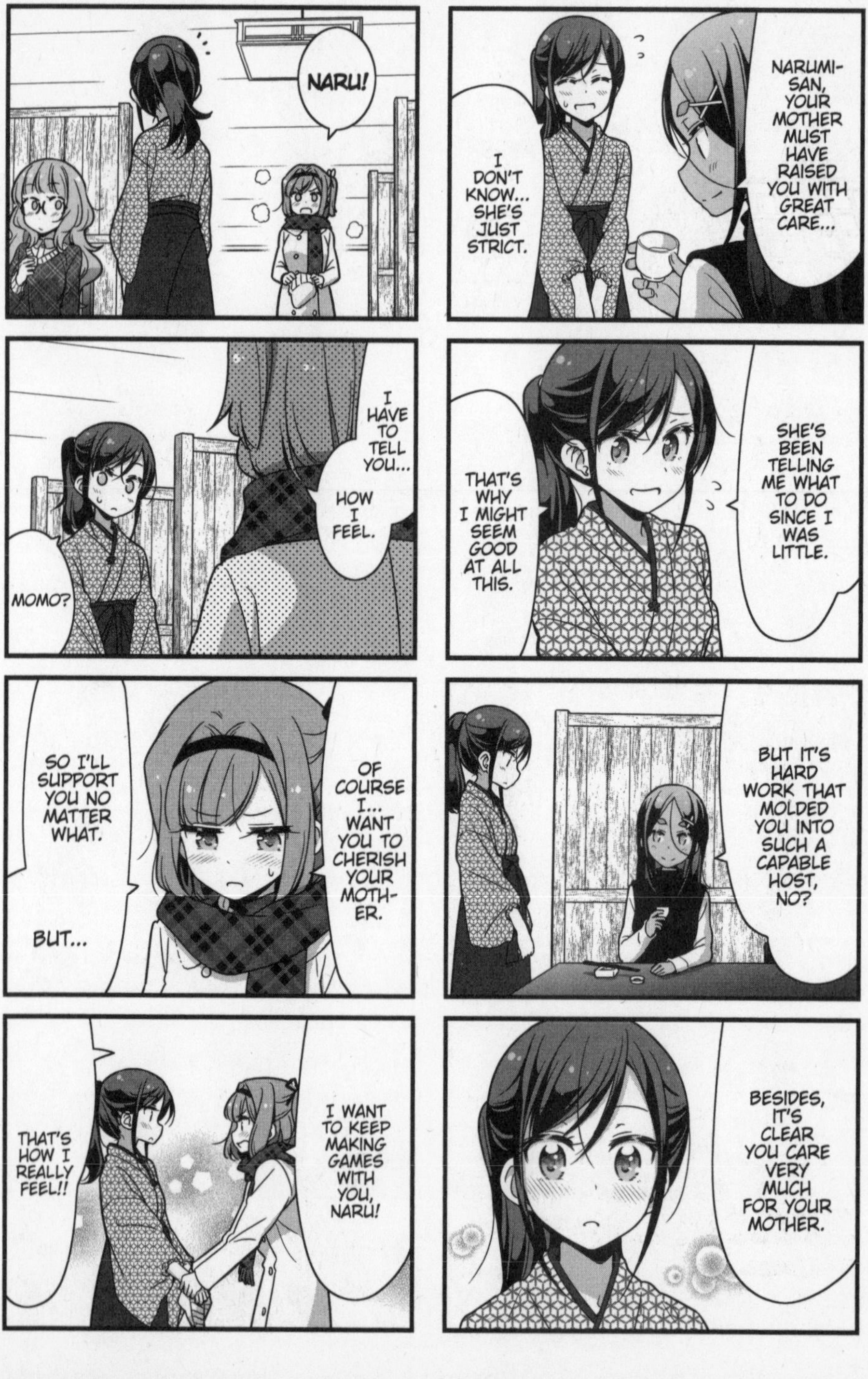
NARUMI-SAN, YOUR MOTHER MUST HAVE RAISED YOU WITH GREAT CARE...
I DON'T KNOW... SHE'S JUST STRICT.
NARU!
SHE'S BEEN TELLING ME WHAT TO DO SINCE I WAS LITTLE.
THAT'S WHY I MIGHT SEEM GOOD AT ALL THIS.
I HAVE TO TELL YOU...
HOW I FEEL.
MOMO?
BUT IT'S HARD WORK THAT MOLDED YOU INTO SUCH A CAPABLE HOST, NO?
OF COURSE I... WANT YOU TO CHERISH YOUR MOTH-ER.
SO I'LL SUPPORT YOU NO MATTER WHAT.
BUT...
BESIDES, IT'S CLEAR YOU CARE VERY MUCH FOR YOUR MOTHER.
I WANT TO KEEP MAKING GAMES WITH YOU, NARU!
THAT'S HOW I REALLY FEEL!!

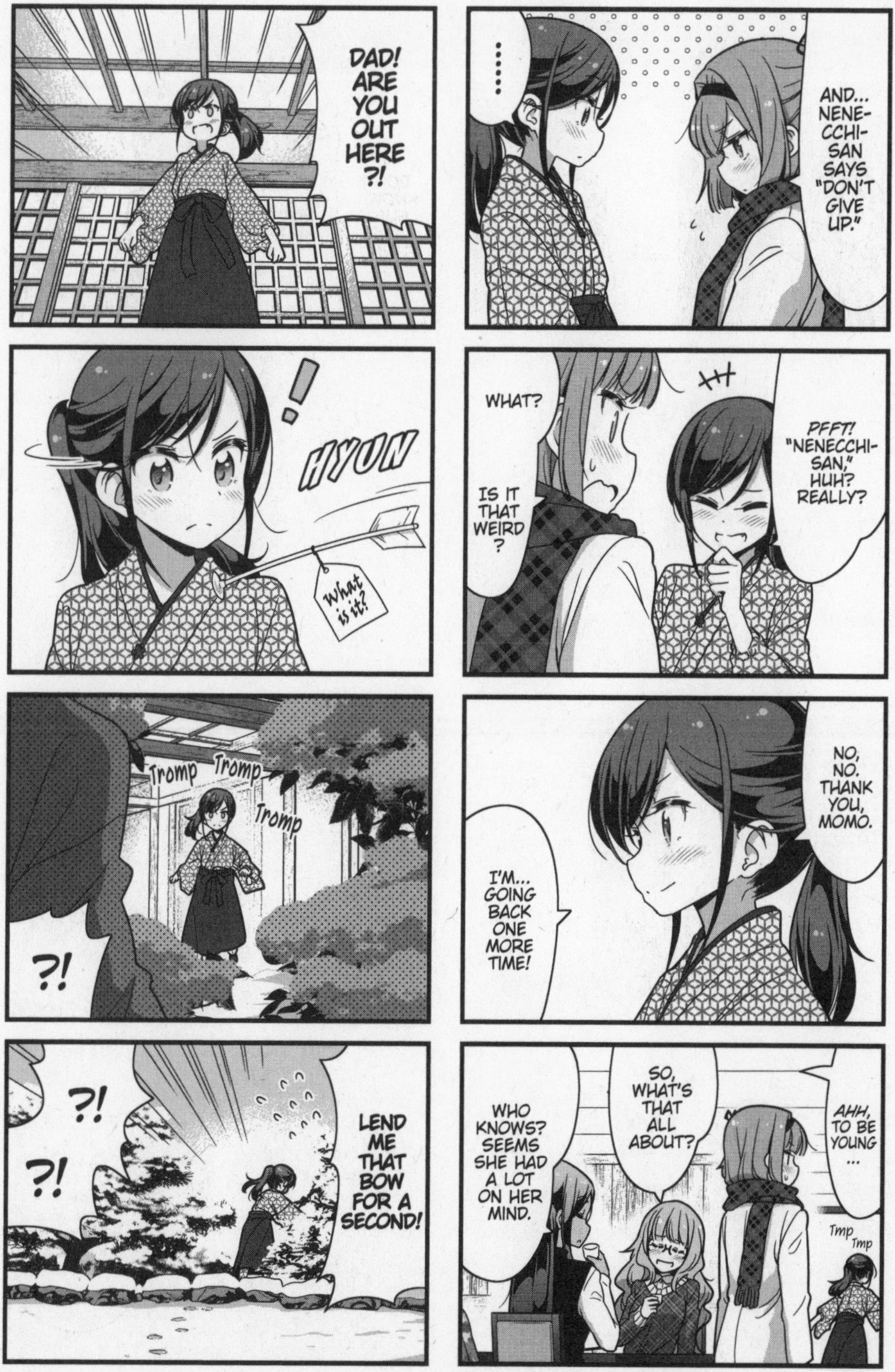
AND... NENECCHI-SAN SAYS "DON'T GIVE UP."
......
PFFT! "NENECCHI-SAN," HUH? REALLY?
WHAT?
IS IT THAT WEIRD?
NO, NO. THANK YOU, MOMO.
I'M... GOING BACK ONE MORE TIME!
AHH, TO BE YOUNG...
SO, WHAT'S THAT ALL ABOUT?
WHO KNOWS? SEEMS SHE HAD A LOT ON HER MIND.
Tmp Tmp
DAD! ARE YOU OUT HERE?!
!
HYUN
What is it?
Tromp Tromp Tromp
?!
LEND ME THAT BOW FOR A SECOND!
?!
?!

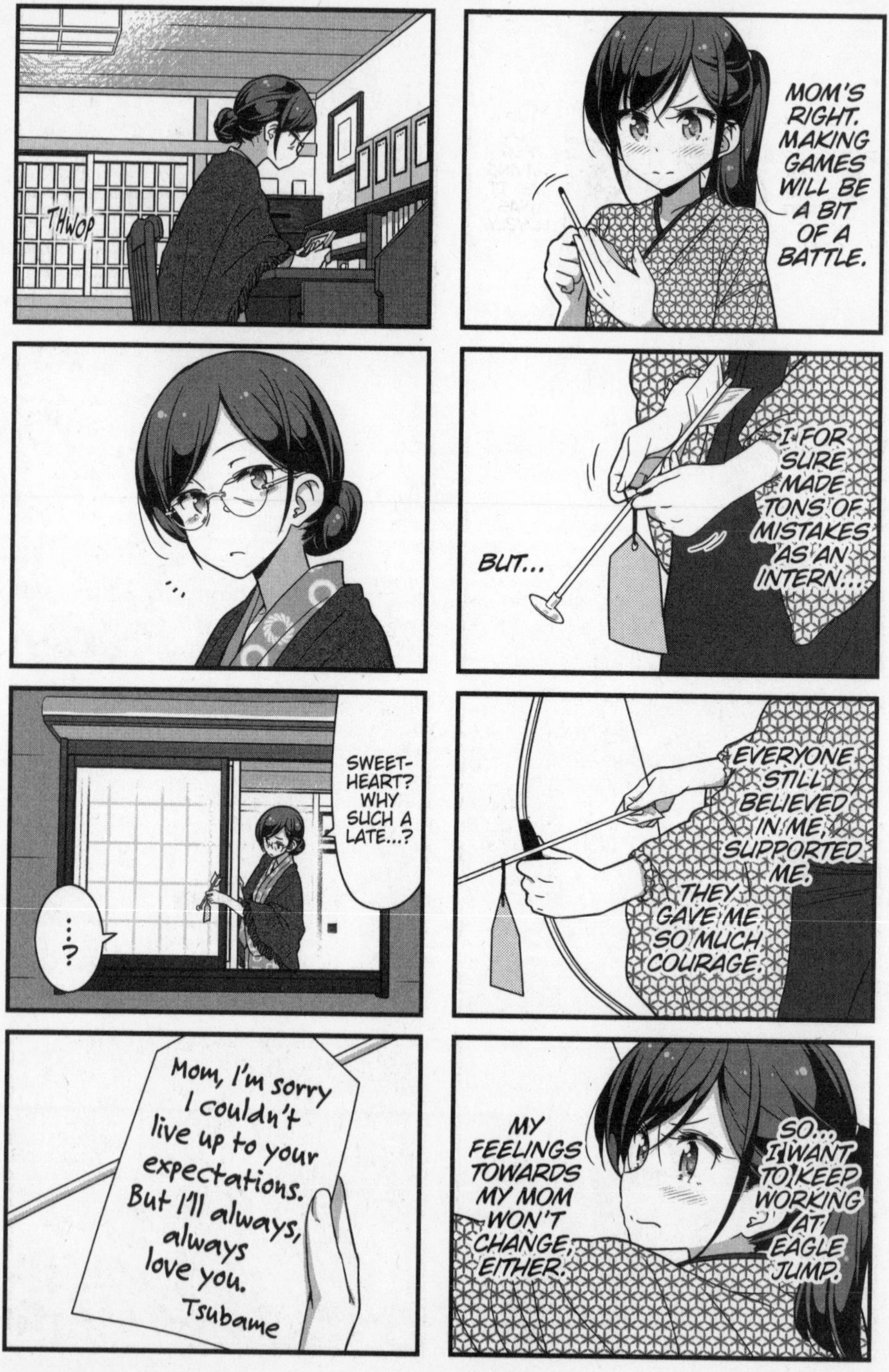
MOM'S RIGHT. MAKING GAMES WILL BE A BIT OF A BATTLE.
THWOP
I FOR SURE MADE TONS OF MISTAKES AS AN INTERN...
BUT...
...
EVERYONE STILL BELIEVED IN ME, SUPPORTED ME.
THEY GAVE ME SO MUCH COURAGE.
SWEET-HEART? WHY SUCH A LATE...?
...?
SO... I WANT TO KEEP WORKING AT EAGLE JUMP.
MY FEELINGS TOWARDS MY MOM WON'T CHANGE, EITHER.
Mom, I'm sorry I couldn't live up to your expectations. But I'll always, always love you.
Tsubame

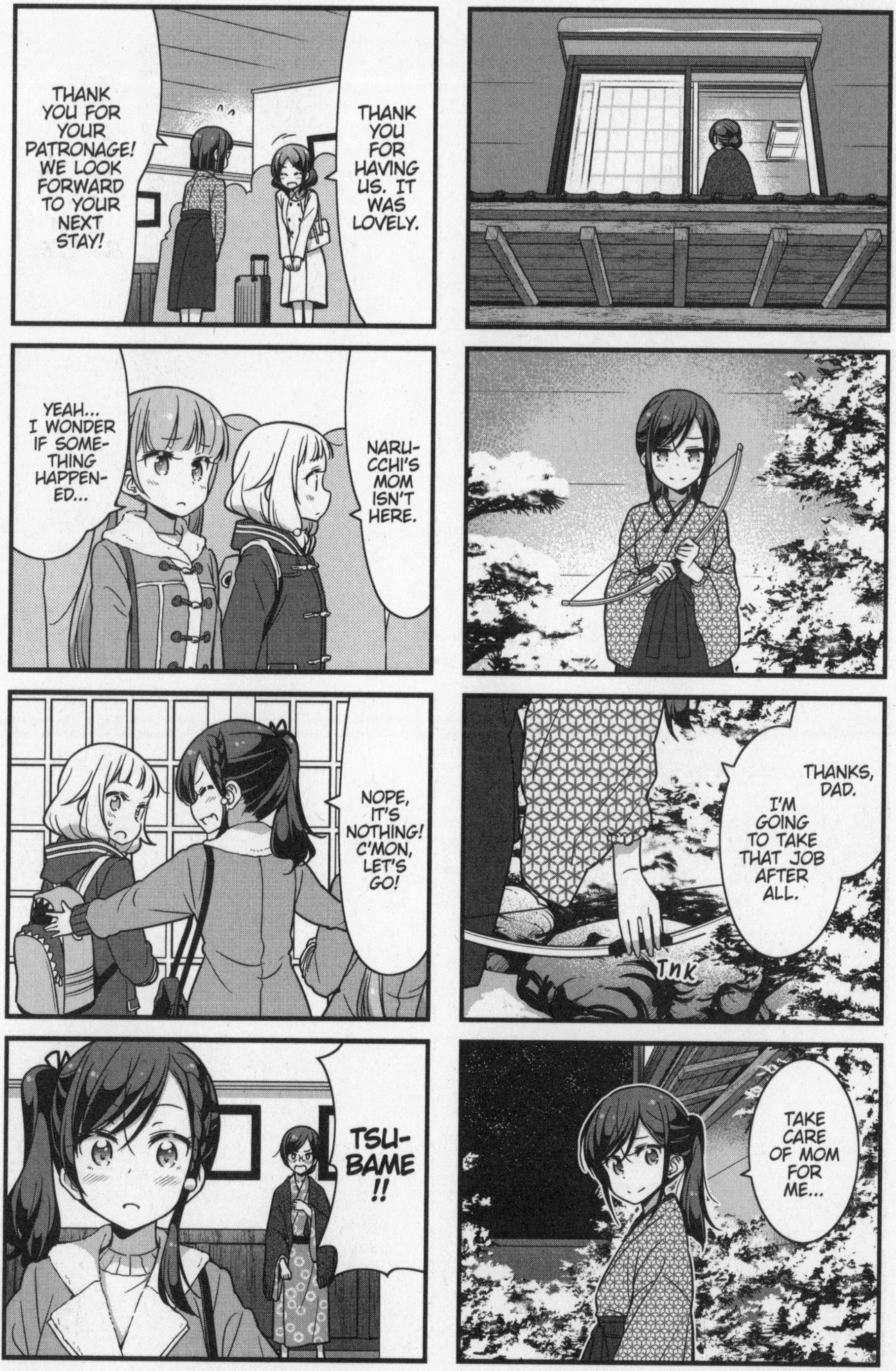
THANKS, DAD. I'M GOING TO TAKE THAT JOB AFTER ALL.
Tnk
TAKE CARE OF MOM FOR ME...
THANK YOU FOR HAVING US. IT WAS LOVELY.
THANK YOU FOR YOUR PATRONAGE! WE LOOK FORWARD TO YOUR NEXT STAY!
NARU-CCHI'S MOM ISN'T HERE.
YEAH... I WONDER IF SOME-THING HAPPEN-ED...
NOPE, IT'S NOTHING! C'MON, LET'S GO!
TSU-BAME !!

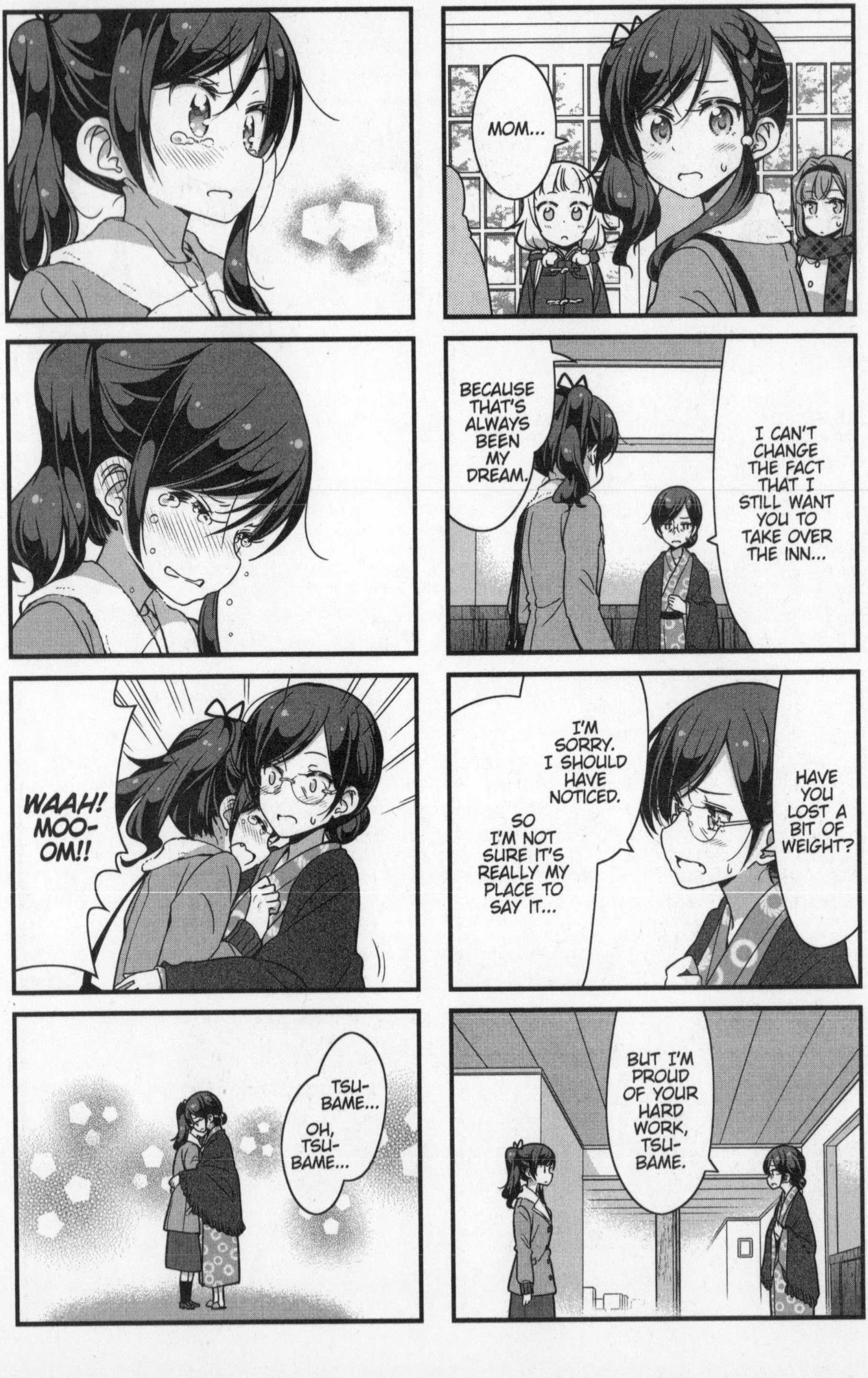
MOM...
I CAN'T CHANGE THE FACT THAT I STILL WANT YOU TO TAKE OVER THE INN...
BECAUSE THAT'S ALWAYS BEEN MY DREAM.
HAVE YOU LOST A BIT OF WEIGHT?
I'M SORRY. I SHOULD HAVE NOTICED.
SO I'M NOT SURE IT'S REALLY MY PLACE TO SAY IT...
BUT I'M PROUD OF YOUR HARD WORK, TSU-BAME.
WAAH! MOO-OM!!
TSU-BAME...
OH, TSU-BAME...

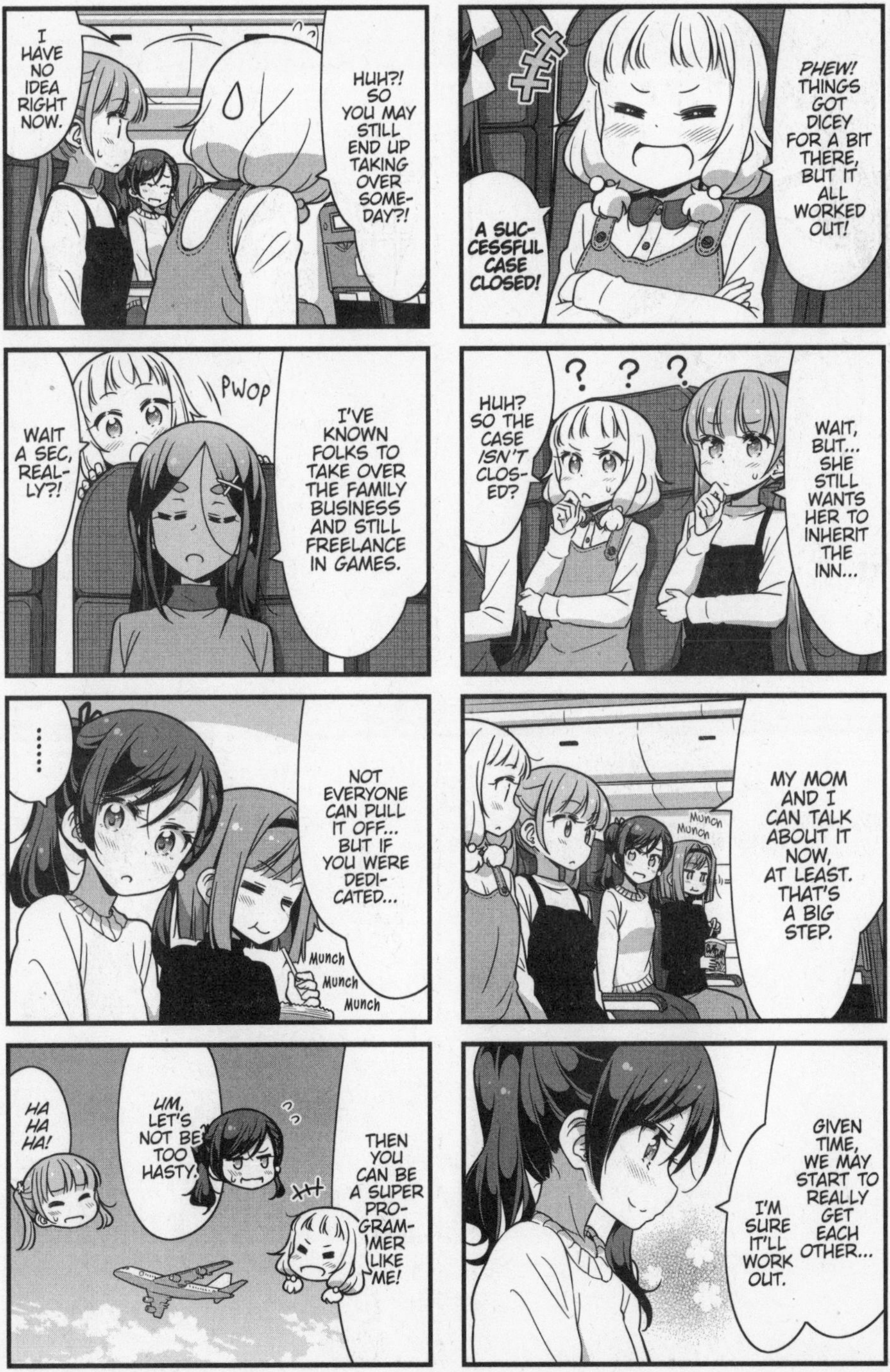
PHEW! THINGS GOT DICEY FOR A BIT THERE, BUT IT ALL WORKED OUT!
A SUCCESSFUL CASE CLOSED!
HUH?! SO YOU MAY STILL END UP TAKING OVER SOMEDAY?!
I HAVE NO IDEA RIGHT NOW.
WAIT, BUT... SHE STILL WANTS HER TO INHERIT THE INN...
HUH? SO THE CASE ISN'T CLOSED?
I'VE KNOWN FOLKS TO TAKE OVER THE FAMILY BUSINESS AND STILL FREELANCE IN GAMES.
PWOP
WAIT A SEC, REALLY?!
MY MOM AND I CAN TALK ABOUT IT NOW, AT LEAST. THAT'S A BIG STEP.
Munch Munch
NOT EVERYONE CAN PULL IT OFF... BUT IF YOU WERE DEDICATED...
Munch Munch Munch
......
GIVEN TIME, WE MAY START TO REALLY GET EACH OTHER...
I'M SURE IT'LL WORK OUT.
THEN YOU CAN BE A SUPER PROGRAMMER LIKE ME!
UM, LET'S NOT BE TOO HASTY.
HA HA HA!

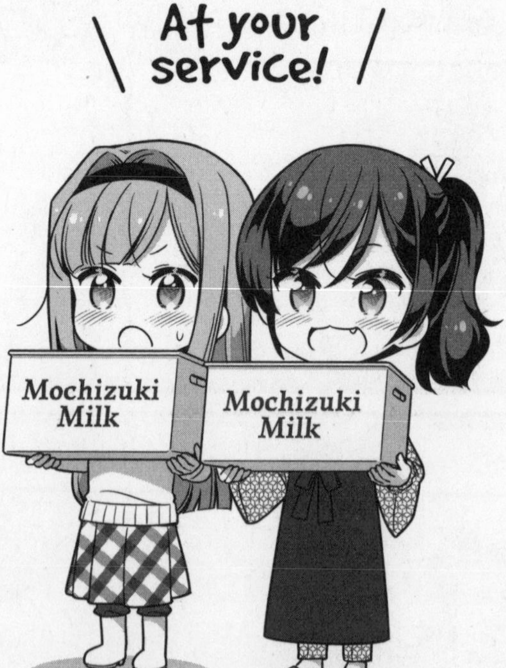
At your service!
Mochizuki Milk
Mochizuki Milk

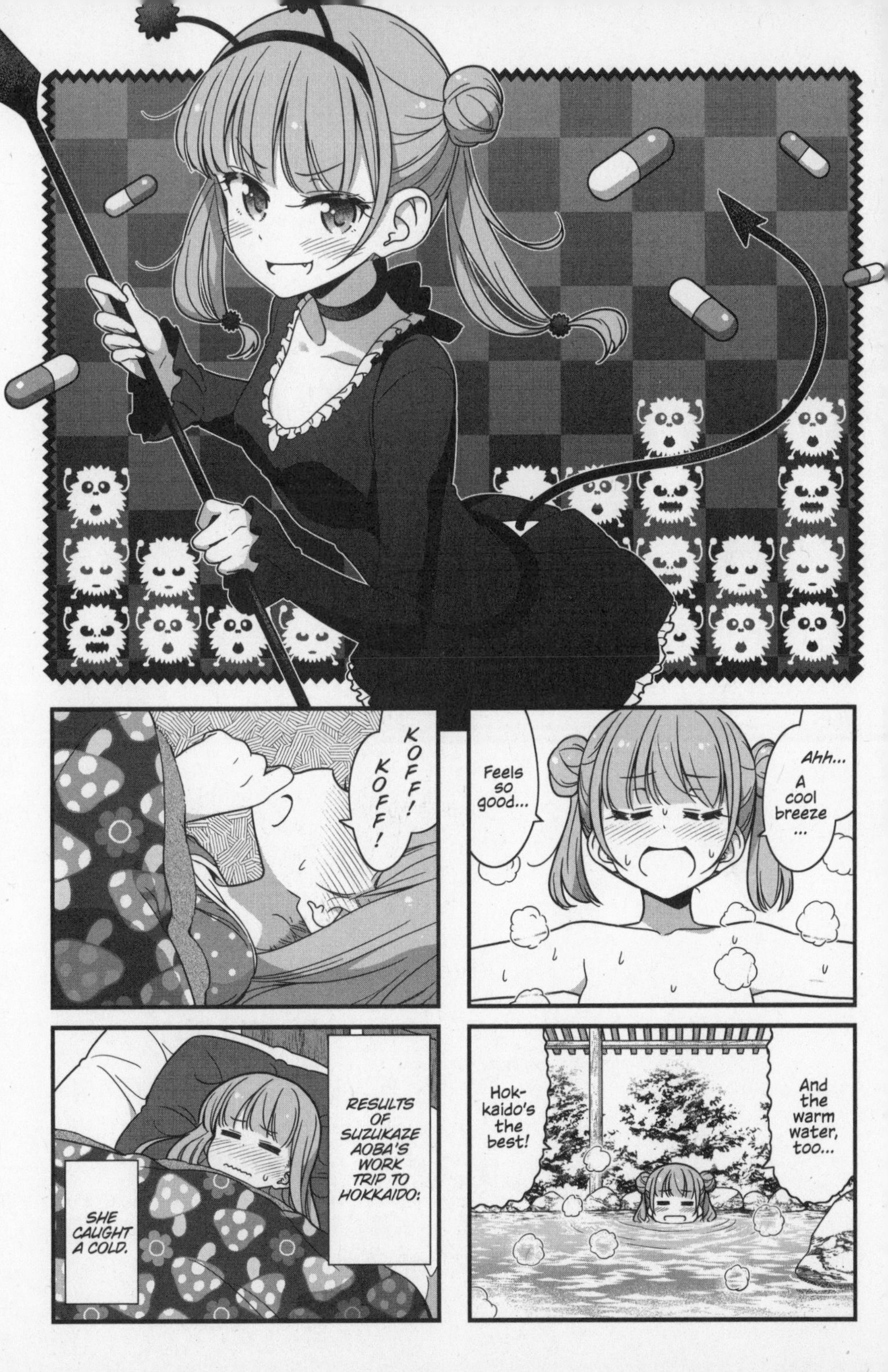
Ahh... A cool breeze ...
Feels so good...
KOFF! KOFF!
And the warm water, too...
Hok-kaido's the best!
RESULTS OF SUZUKAZE AOBA'S WORK TRIP TO HOKKAIDO:
SHE CAUGHT A COLD.

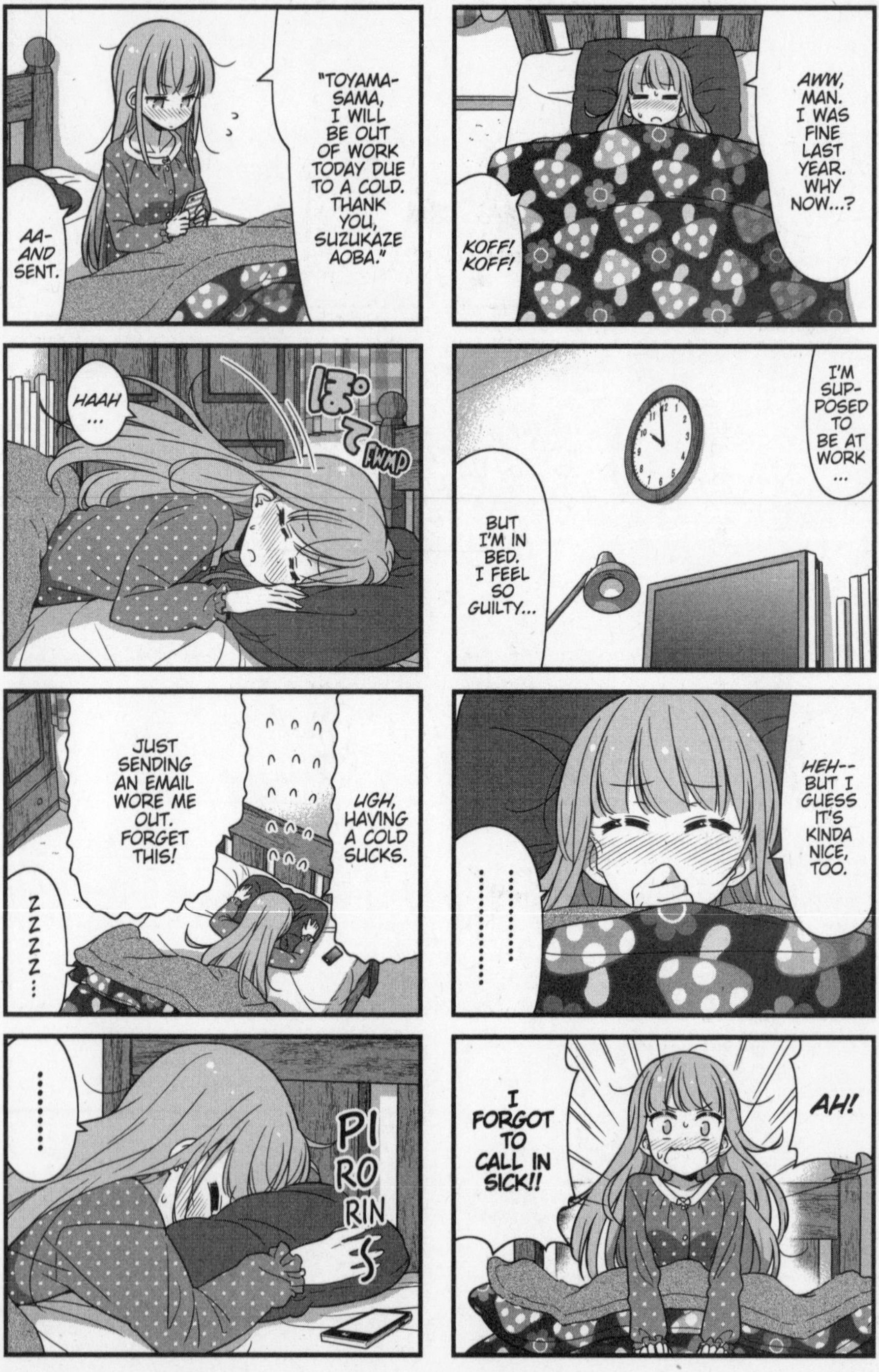
AWW, MAN. I WAS FINE LAST YEAR. WHY NOW...?
KOFF! KOFF!
I'M SUP-POSED TO BE AT WORK...
BUT I'M IN BED. I FEEL SO GUILTY...
HEH-- BUT I GUESS IT'S KINDA NICE, TOO.
........
AH!
I FORGOT TO CALL IN SICK!!
"TOYAMA-SAMA, I WILL BE OUT OF WORK TODAY DUE TO A COLD. THANK YOU, SUZUKAZE AOBA."
AA-AND SENT.
HAAH...
ぽて
FWMP
JUST SENDING AN EMAIL WORE ME OUT. FORGET THIS!
UGH, HAVING A COLD SUCKS.
ZZZZ...
........
PI RO RIN

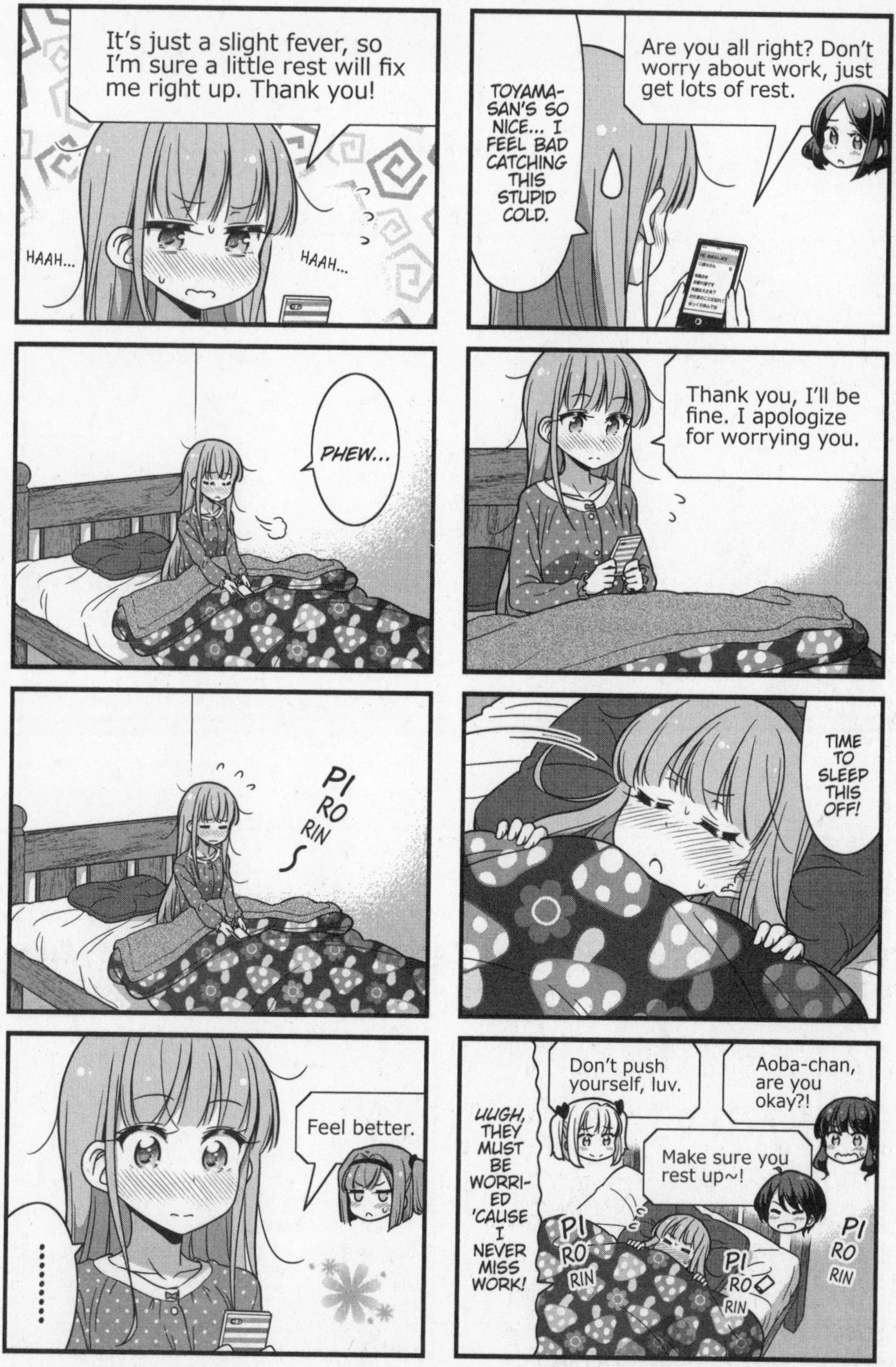
Are you all right? Don't worry about work, just get lots of rest.
TOYAMA-SAN'S SO NICE... I FEEL BAD CATCHING THIS STUPID COLD.
It's just a slight fever, so I'm sure a little rest will fix me right up. Thank you!
HAAH...
HAAH...
Thank you, I'll be fine. I apologize for worrying you.
PHEW...
TIME TO SLEEP THIS OFF!
PI RO RIN
Aoba-chan, are you okay?!
Don't push yourself, luv.
Make sure you rest up~!
UUGH, THEY MUST BE WORRIED 'CAUSE I NEVER MISS WORK!
PI RO RIN
PI RO RIN
PI RO RIN
Feel better.
........

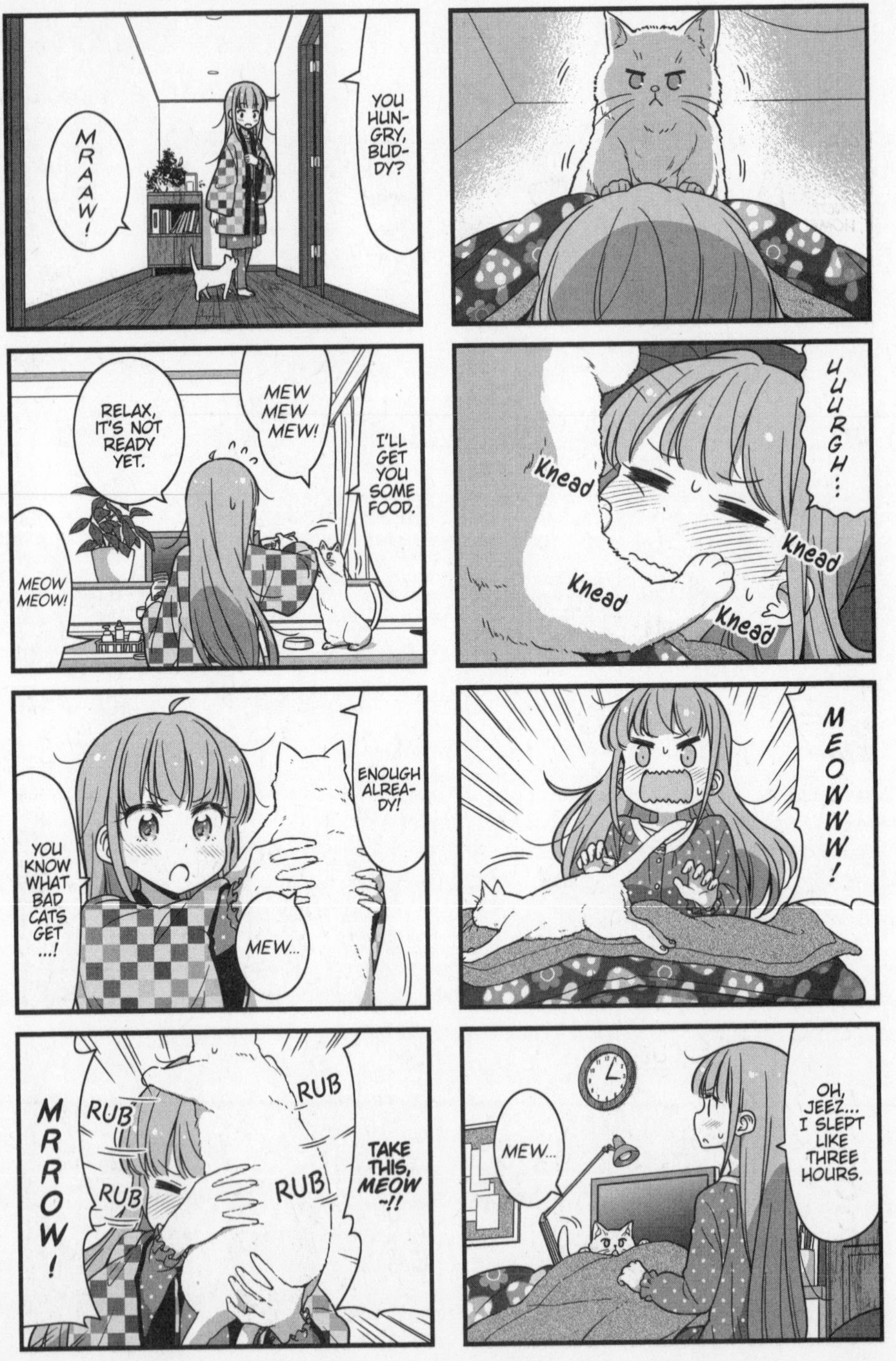
YOU HUNGRY, BUDDY?
MRAAW!
UUURGH...
Knead
Knead
Knead
Knead
I'LL GET YOU SOME FOOD.
MEW MEW MEW!
RELAX, IT'S NOT READY YET.
MEOW MEOW!
MEOWWW!
ENOUGH ALREADY!
YOU KNOW WHAT BAD CATS GET...!
MEW...
OH, JEEZ... I SLEPT LIKE THREE HOURS.
MEW...
TAKE THIS, MEOW~!!
RUB
RUB
RUB
RUB
MRROW!

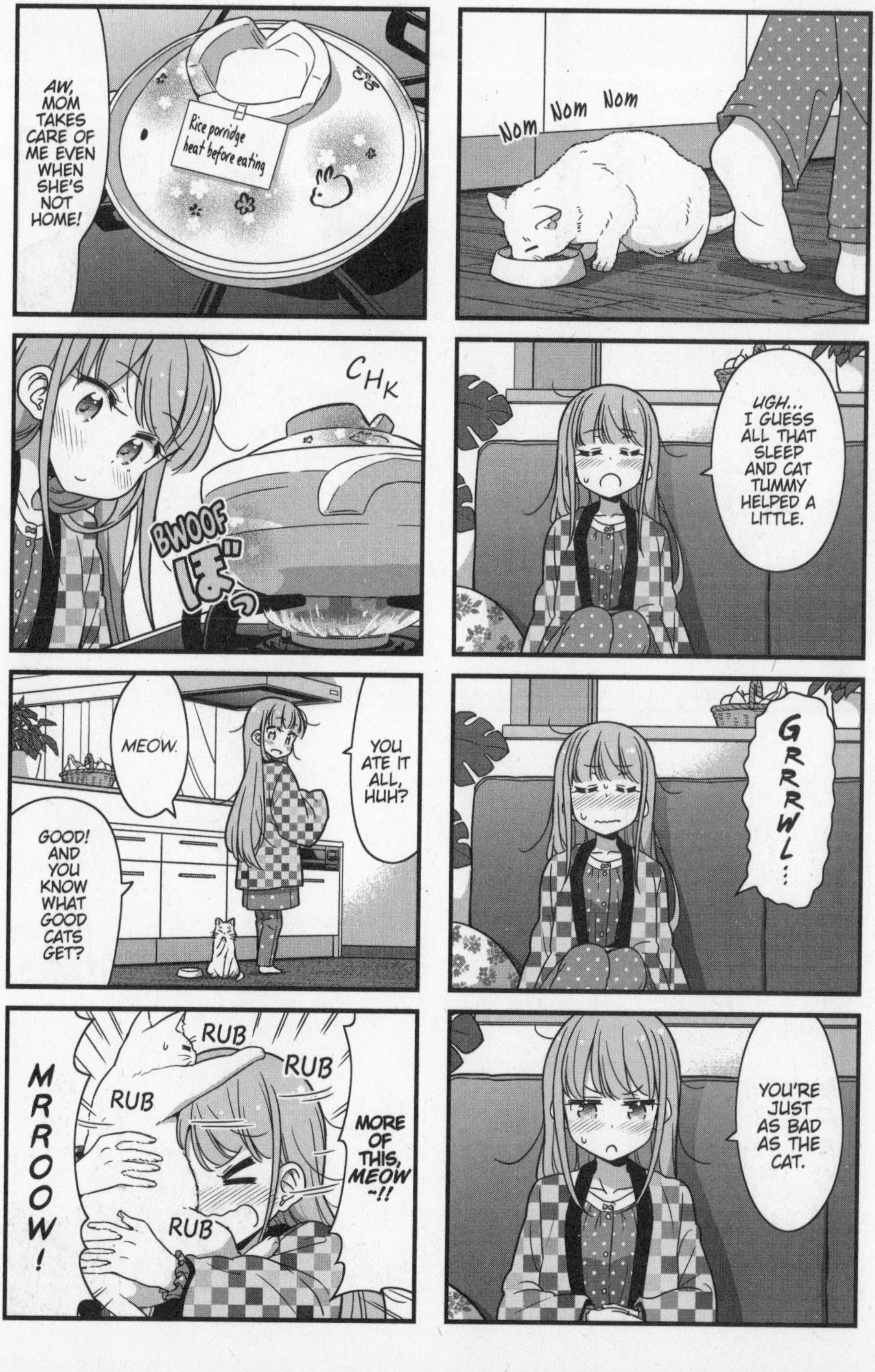
Nom Nom Nom
UGH... I GUESS ALL THAT SLEEP AND CAT TUMMY HELPED A LITTLE.
GRRRWL...
YOU'RE JUST AS BAD AS THE CAT.
AW, MOM TAKES CARE OF ME EVEN WHEN SHE'S NOT HOME!
Rice porridge heat before eating
CHK
BWOOF
ぼっ
YOU ATE IT ALL, HUH?
MEOW.
GOOD! AND YOU KNOW WHAT GOOD CATS GET?
RUB
RUB
RUB
MORE OF THIS, MEOW~!!
RUB
MRROOW!

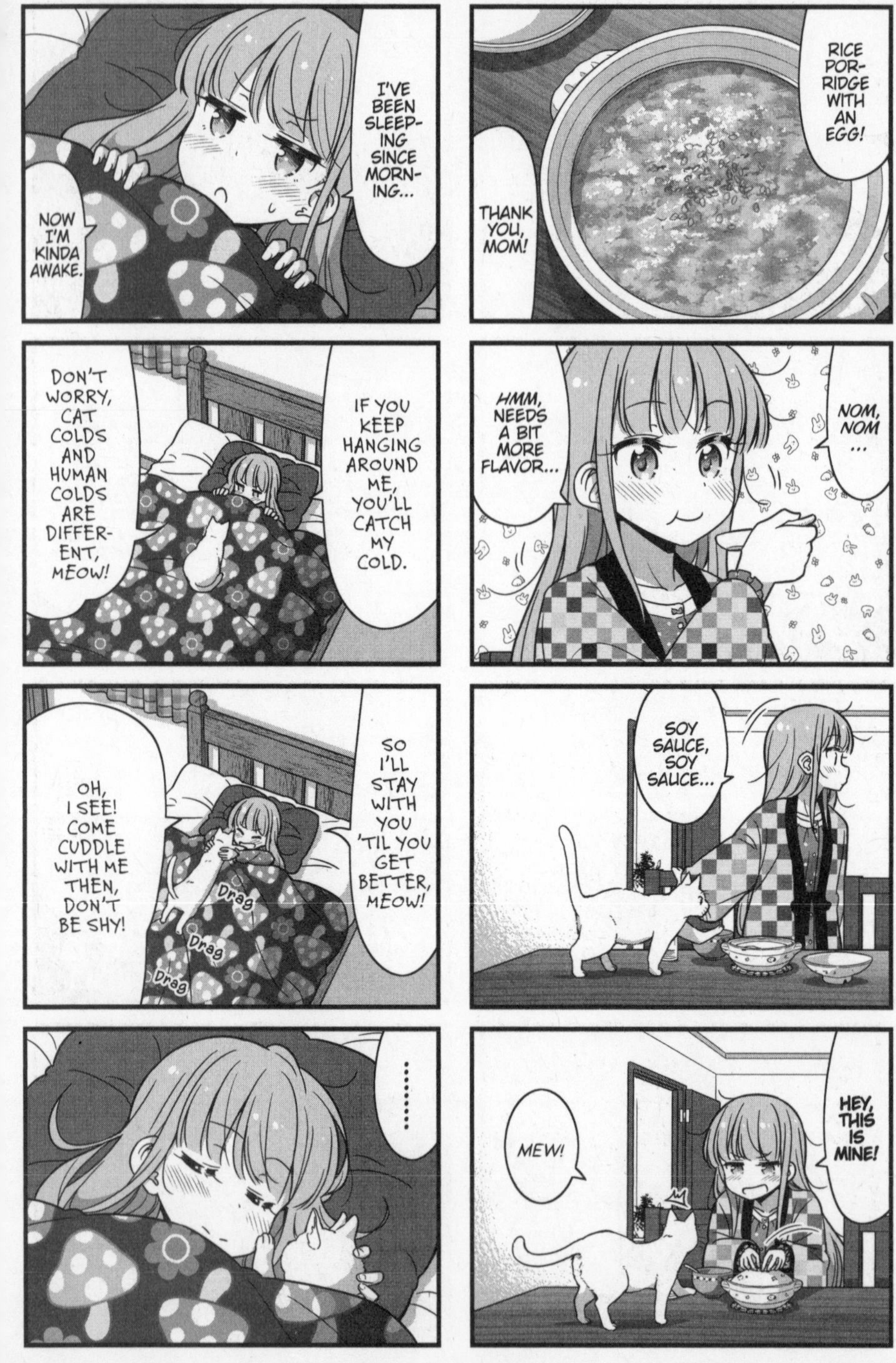
RICE PORRIDGE WITH AN EGG!
THANK YOU, MOM!
NOM, NOM ...
HMM, NEEDS A BIT MORE FLAVOR...
SOY SAUCE, SOY SAUCE...
HEY, THIS IS MINE!
MEW!
I'VE BEEN SLEEPING SINCE MORNING...
NOW I'M KINDA AWAKE.
IF YOU KEEP HANGING AROUND ME, YOU'LL CATCH MY COLD.
DON'T WORRY, CAT COLDS AND HUMAN COLDS ARE DIFFERENT, MEOW!
SO I'LL STAY WITH YOU 'TIL YOU GET BETTER, MEOW!
OH, I SEE! COME CUDDLE WITH ME THEN, DON'T BE SHY!
Drag
Drag
Drag
........

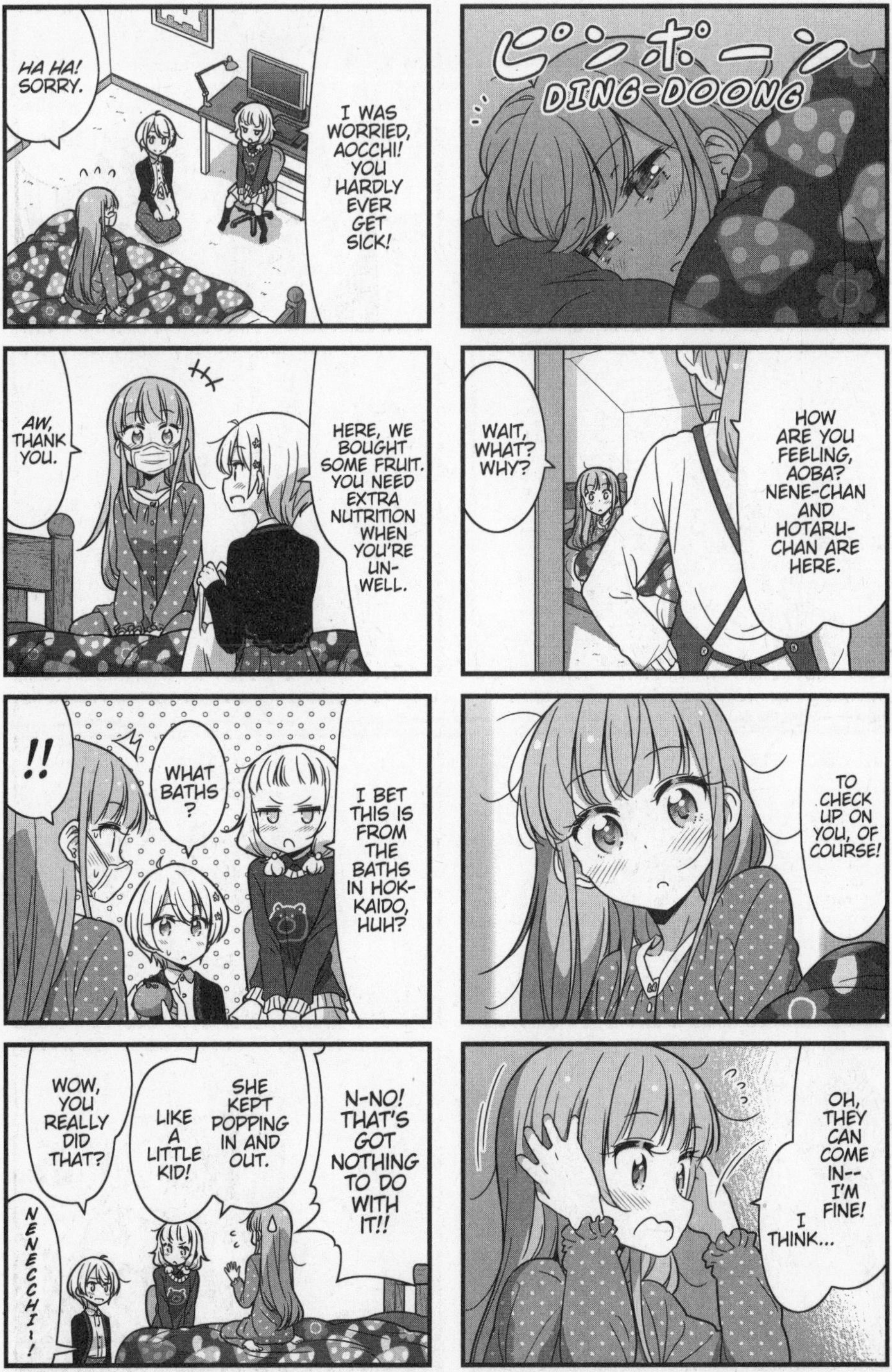
ピンポーン
DING-DOONG
HOW ARE YOU FEELING, AOBA? NENE-CHAN AND HOTARU-CHAN ARE HERE.
WAIT, WHAT? WHY?
TO CHECK UP ON YOU, OF COURSE!
OH, THEY CAN COME IN-- I'M FINE!
I THINK...
I WAS WORRIED, AOCCHI! YOU HARDLY EVER GET SICK!
HA HA! SORRY.
HERE, WE BOUGHT SOME FRUIT. YOU NEED EXTRA NUTRITION WHEN YOU'RE UN-WELL.
AW, THANK YOU.
I BET THIS IS FROM THE BATHS IN HOK-KAIDO, HUH?
WHAT BATHS?
!!
N-NO! THAT'S GOT NOTHING TO DO WITH IT!!
SHE KEPT POPPING IN AND OUT.
LIKE A LITTLE KID!
WOW, YOU REALLY DID THAT?
NENECCHI~!

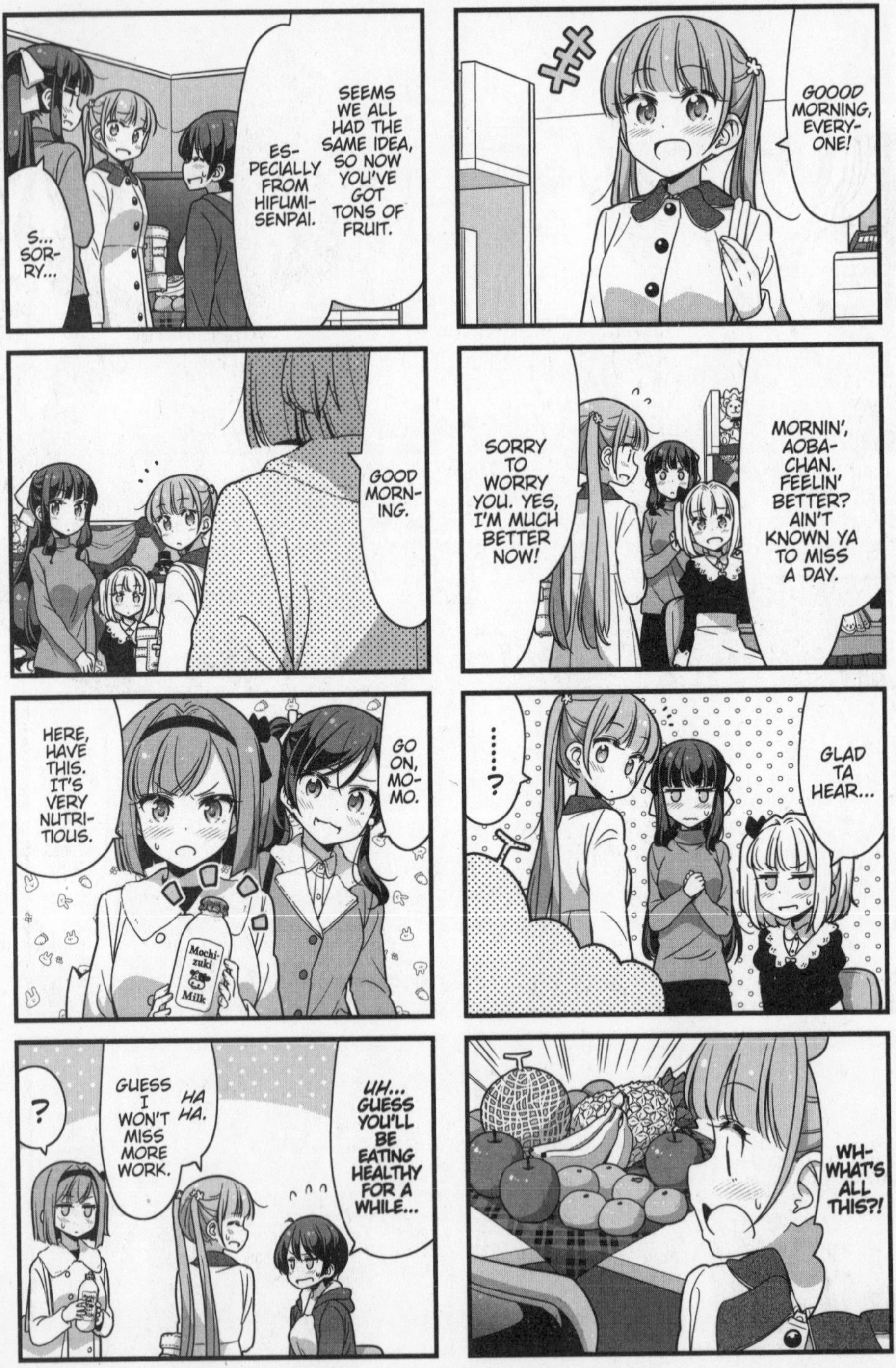
GOOOD MORNING, EVERY-ONE!
MORNIN', AOBA-CHAN. FEELIN' BETTER? AIN'T KNOWN YA TO MISS A DAY.
SORRY TO WORRY YOU. YES, I'M MUCH BETTER NOW!
GLAD TA HEAR...
......?
WH-WHAT'S ALL THIS?!
SEEMS WE ALL HAD THE SAME IDEA, SO NOW YOU'VE GOT TONS OF FRUIT.
ES-PECIALLY FROM HIFUMI-SENPAI.
S... SORRY...
GOOD MORN-ING.
GO ON, MO-MO.
HERE, HAVE THIS. IT'S VERY NUTRI-TIOUS.
Mochi-zuki Milk
UH... GUESS YOU'LL BE EATING HEALTHY FOR A WHILE...
HA HA.
GUESS I WON'T MISS MORE WORK.
?

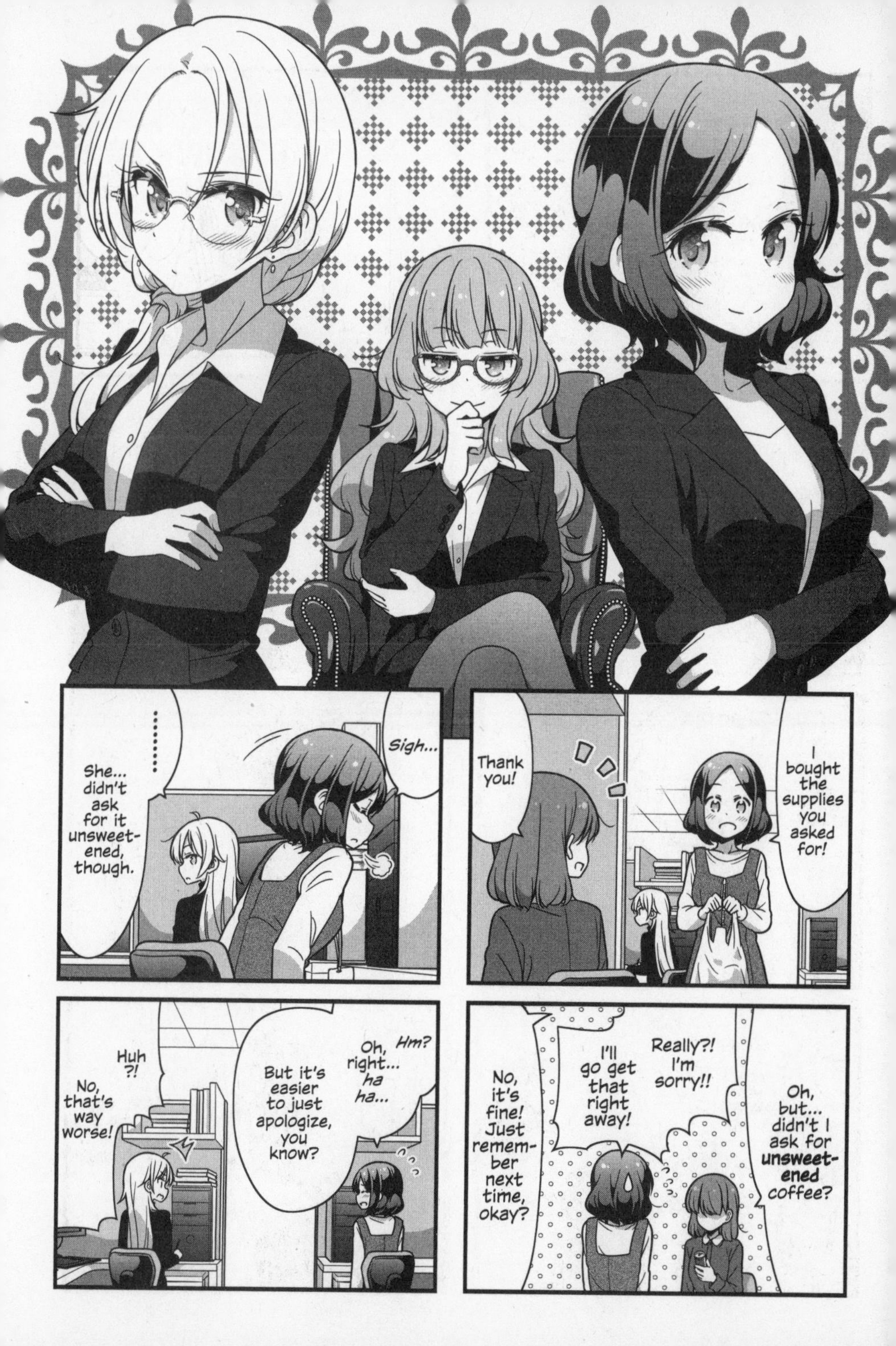
I bought the supplies you asked for!
Thank you!
Sigh...
......
She... didn't ask for it unsweetened, though.
Oh, but... didn't I ask for **unsweetened** coffee?
Really?! I'm sorry!!
I'll go get that right away!
No, it's fine! Just remember next time, okay?
Hm?
Oh, right... ha ha...
But it's easier to just apologize, you know?
Huh?!
No, that's way worse!

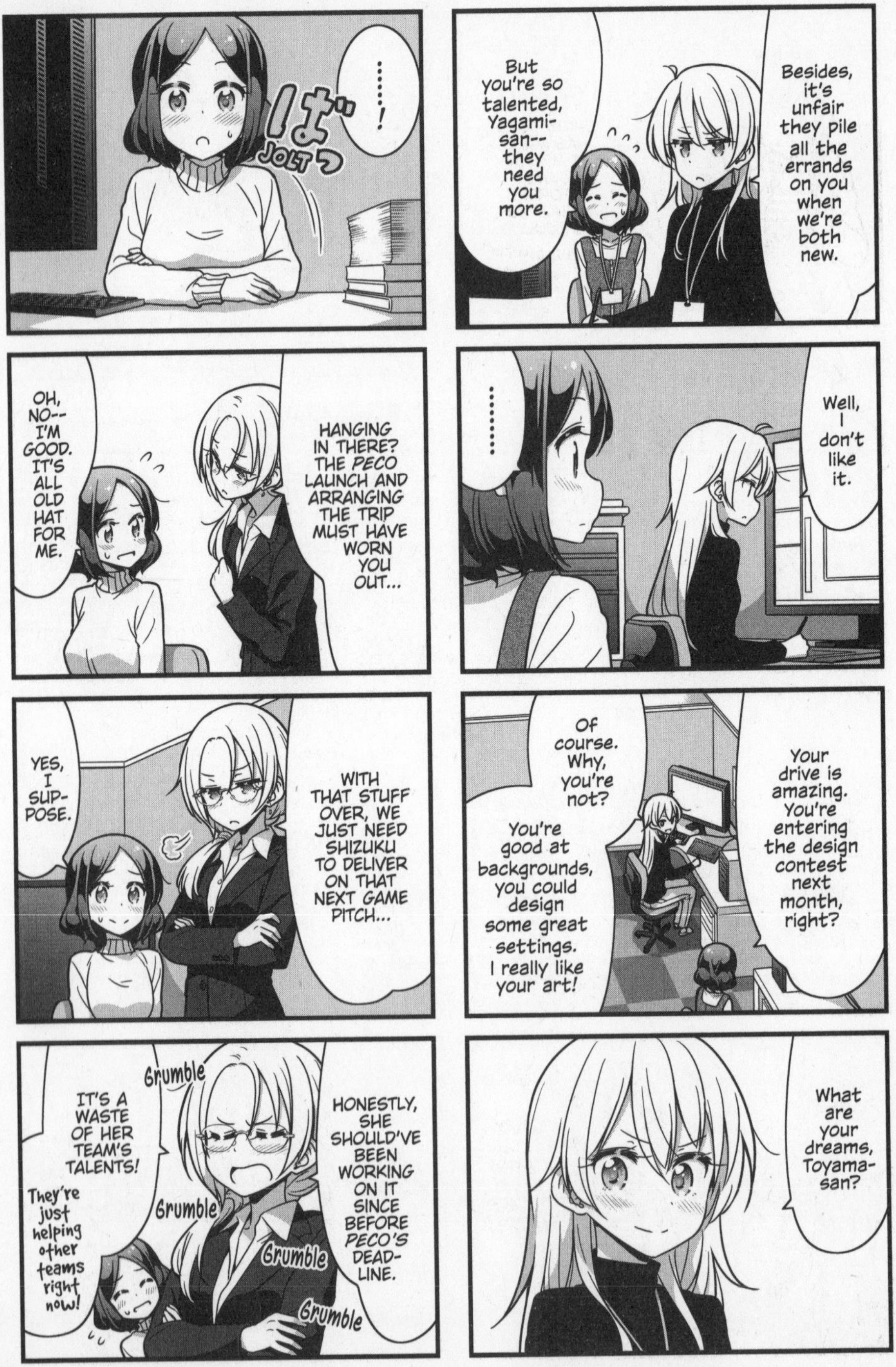
Besides, it's unfair they pile all the errands on you when we're both new.
But you're so talented, Yagami-san--they need you more.
Well, I don't like it.
......
Your drive is amazing. You're entering the design contest next month, right?
Of course. Why, you're not?
You're good at backgrounds, you could design some great settings. I really like your art!
What are your dreams, Toyama-san?
......!
ばっ
JOLT
HANGING IN THERE? THE PECO LAUNCH AND ARRANGING THE TRIP MUST HAVE WORN YOU OUT...
OH, NO--I'M GOOD. IT'S ALL OLD HAT FOR ME.
WITH THAT STUFF OVER, WE JUST NEED SHIZUKU TO DELIVER ON THAT NEXT GAME PITCH...
YES, I SUPPOSE.
HONESTLY, SHE SHOULD'VE BEEN WORKING ON IT SINCE BEFORE PECO'S DEADLINE.
Grumble
IT'S A WASTE OF HER TEAM'S TALENTS!
Grumble
Grumble
Grumble
They're just helping other teams right now!

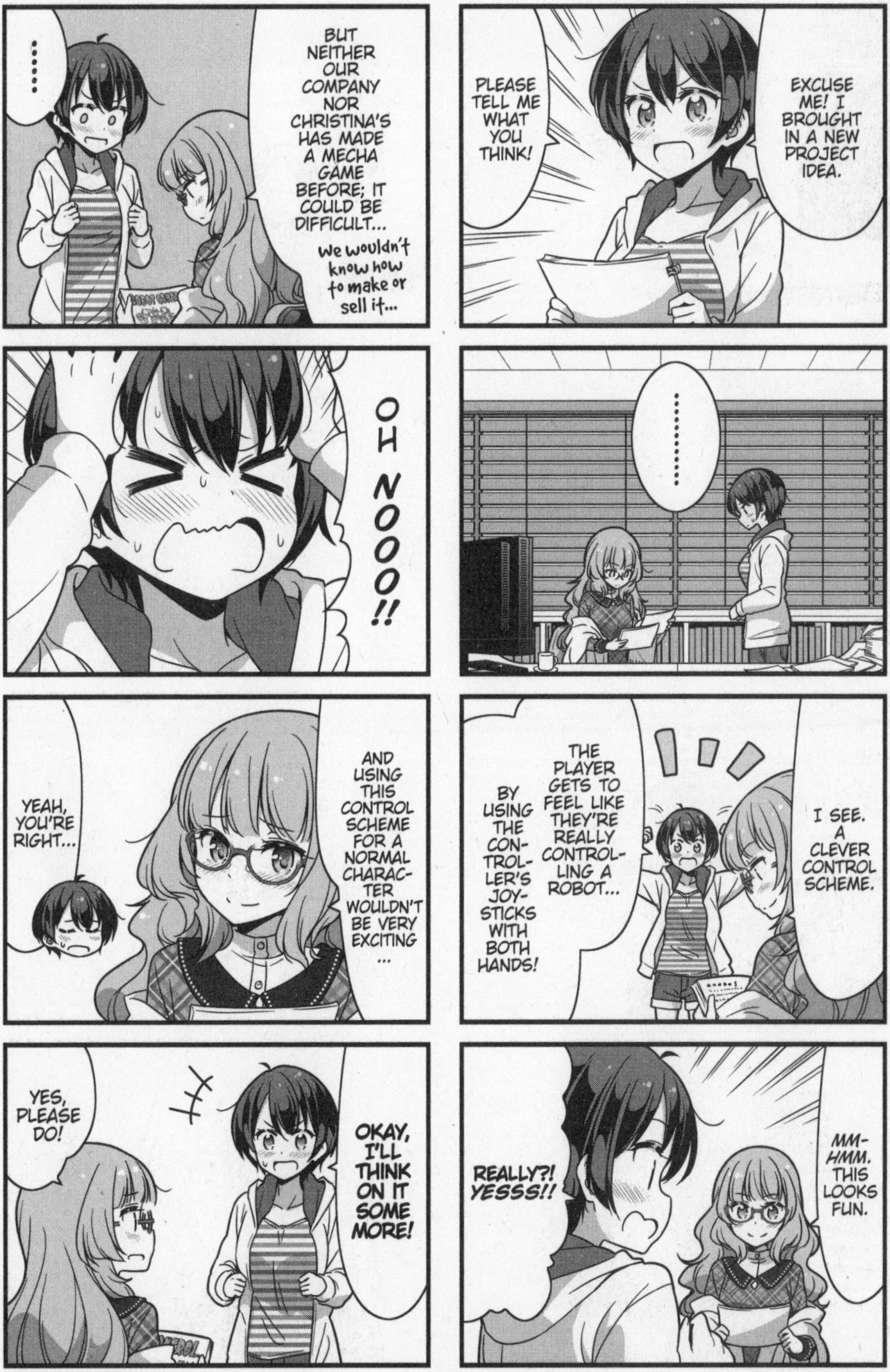
EXCUSE ME! I BROUGHT IN A NEW PROJECT IDEA.
PLEASE TELL ME WHAT YOU THINK!
BUT NEITHER OUR COMPANY NOR CHRISTINA'S HAS MADE A MECHA GAME BEFORE; IT COULD BE DIFFICULT...
we wouldn't know how to make or sell it...
......
............
OH NOOOO!!
I SEE. A CLEVER CONTROL SCHEME.
THE PLAYER GETS TO FEEL LIKE THEY'RE REALLY CONTROLLING A ROBOT...
BY USING THE CONTROLLER'S JOYSTICKS WITH BOTH HANDS!
AND USING THIS CONTROL SCHEME FOR A NORMAL CHARACTER WOULDN'T BE VERY EXCITING...
YEAH, YOU'RE RIGHT...
MM-HMM. THIS LOOKS FUN.
REALLY?! YESSS!!
OKAY, I'LL THINK ON IT SOME MORE!
YES, PLEASE DO!

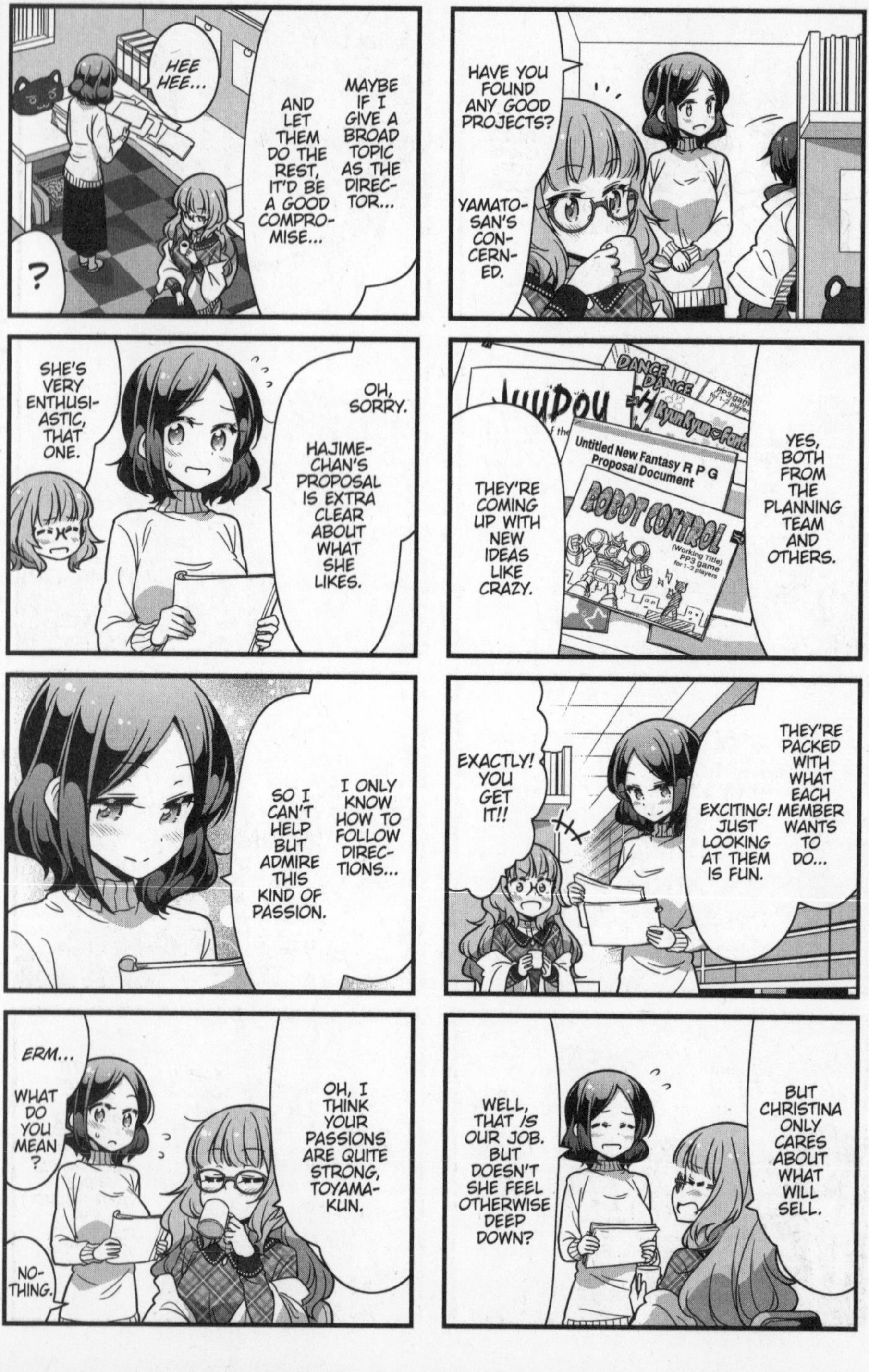
HAVE YOU FOUND ANY GOOD PROJECTS?
YAMATO-SAN'S CONCERNED.
MAYBE IF I GIVE A BROAD TOPIC AS THE DIRECTOR...
AND LET THEM DO THE REST, IT'D BE A GOOD COMPROMISE...
HEE HEE...
?
YES, BOTH FROM THE PLANNING TEAM AND OTHERS.
DANCE DANCE
PP3 game for 1-2 players
Untitled New Fantasy RPG Proposal Document
ROBOT CONTROL
(Working Title) PP3 game for 1-2 players
THEY'RE COMING UP WITH NEW IDEAS LIKE CRAZY.
OH, SORRY.
HAJIME-CHAN'S PROPOSAL IS EXTRA CLEAR ABOUT WHAT SHE LIKES.
SHE'S VERY ENTHUSIASTIC, THAT ONE.
THEY'RE PACKED WITH WHAT EACH MEMBER WANTS TO DO...
EXCITING! JUST LOOKING AT THEM IS FUN.
EXACTLY! YOU GET IT!!
I ONLY KNOW HOW TO FOLLOW DIRECTIONS...
SO I CAN'T HELP BUT ADMIRE THIS KIND OF PASSION.
BUT CHRISTINA ONLY CARES ABOUT WHAT WILL SELL.
WELL, THAT IS OUR JOB. BUT DOESN'T SHE FEEL OTHERWISE DEEP DOWN?
OH, I THINK YOUR PASSIONS ARE QUITE STRONG, TOYAMA-KUN.
ERM...
WHAT DO YOU MEAN?
NOTHING.

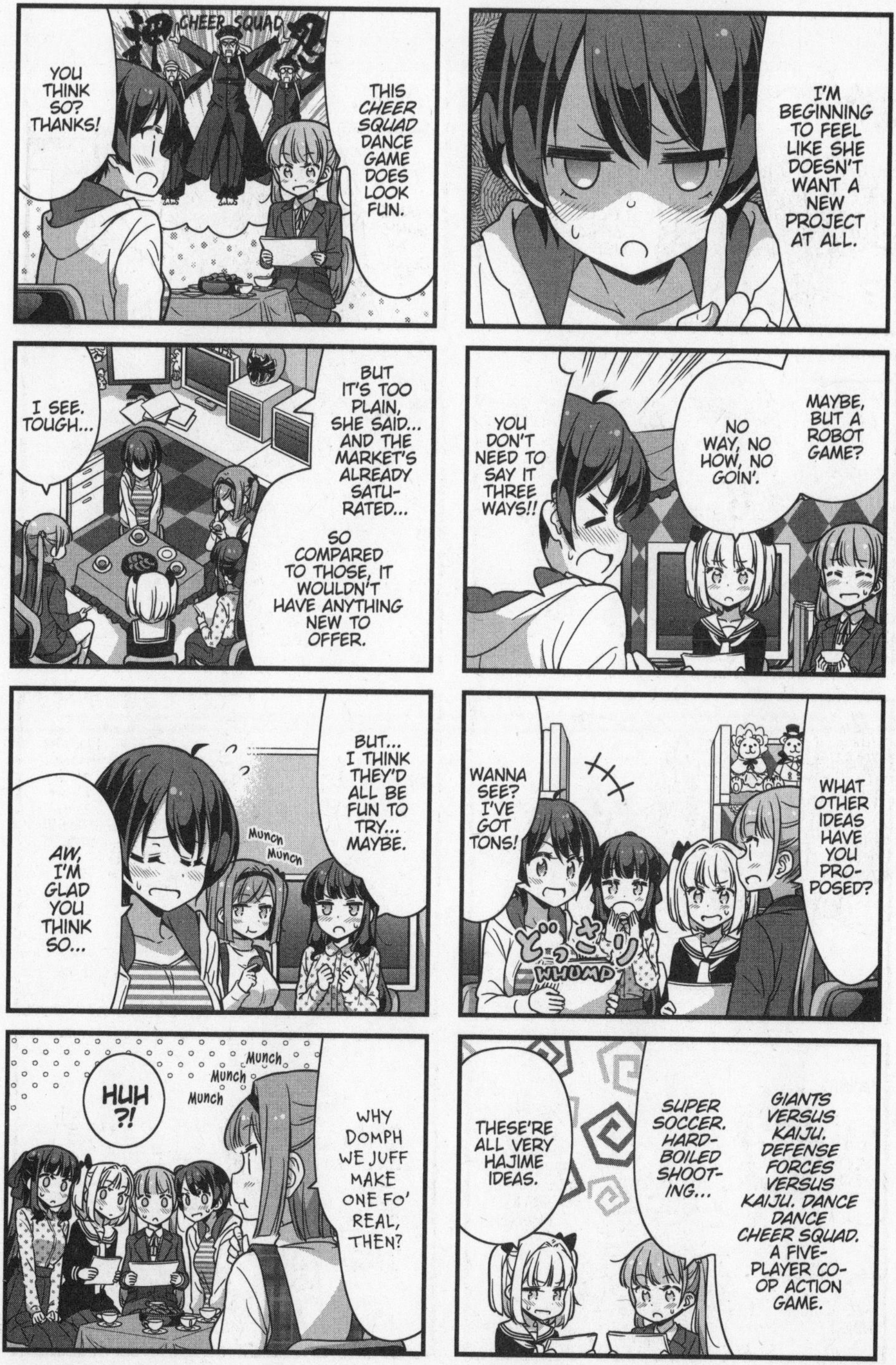
I'M BEGINNING TO FEEL LIKE SHE DOESN'T WANT A NEW PROJECT AT ALL.
MAYBE, BUT A ROBOT GAME?
NO WAY, NO HOW, NO GOIN'.
YOU DON'T NEED TO SAY IT THREE WAYS!!
WHAT OTHER IDEAS HAVE YOU PRO-POSED?
WANNA SEE? I'VE GOT TONS!
WHUMP
GIANTS VERSUS KAIJU. DEFENSE FORCES VERSUS KAIJU. DANCE DANCE CHEER SQUAD. A FIVE-PLAYER CO-OP ACTION GAME.
SUPER SOCCER. HARD-BOILED SHOOT-ING...
THESE'RE ALL VERY HAJIME IDEAS.
CHEER SQUAD
THIS CHEER SQUAD DANCE GAME DOES LOOK FUN.
YOU THINK SO? THANKS!
BUT IT'S TOO PLAIN, SHE SAID... AND THE MARKET'S ALREADY SATU-RATED...
SO COMPARED TO THOSE, IT WOULDN'T HAVE ANYTHING NEW TO OFFER.
I SEE. TOUGH...
BUT... I THINK THEY'D ALL BE FUN TO TRY... MAYBE.
Munch Munch
AW, I'M GLAD YOU THINK SO...
WHY DOMPH WE JUFF MAKE ONE FO' REAL, THEN?
Munch Munch Munch
HUH ?!

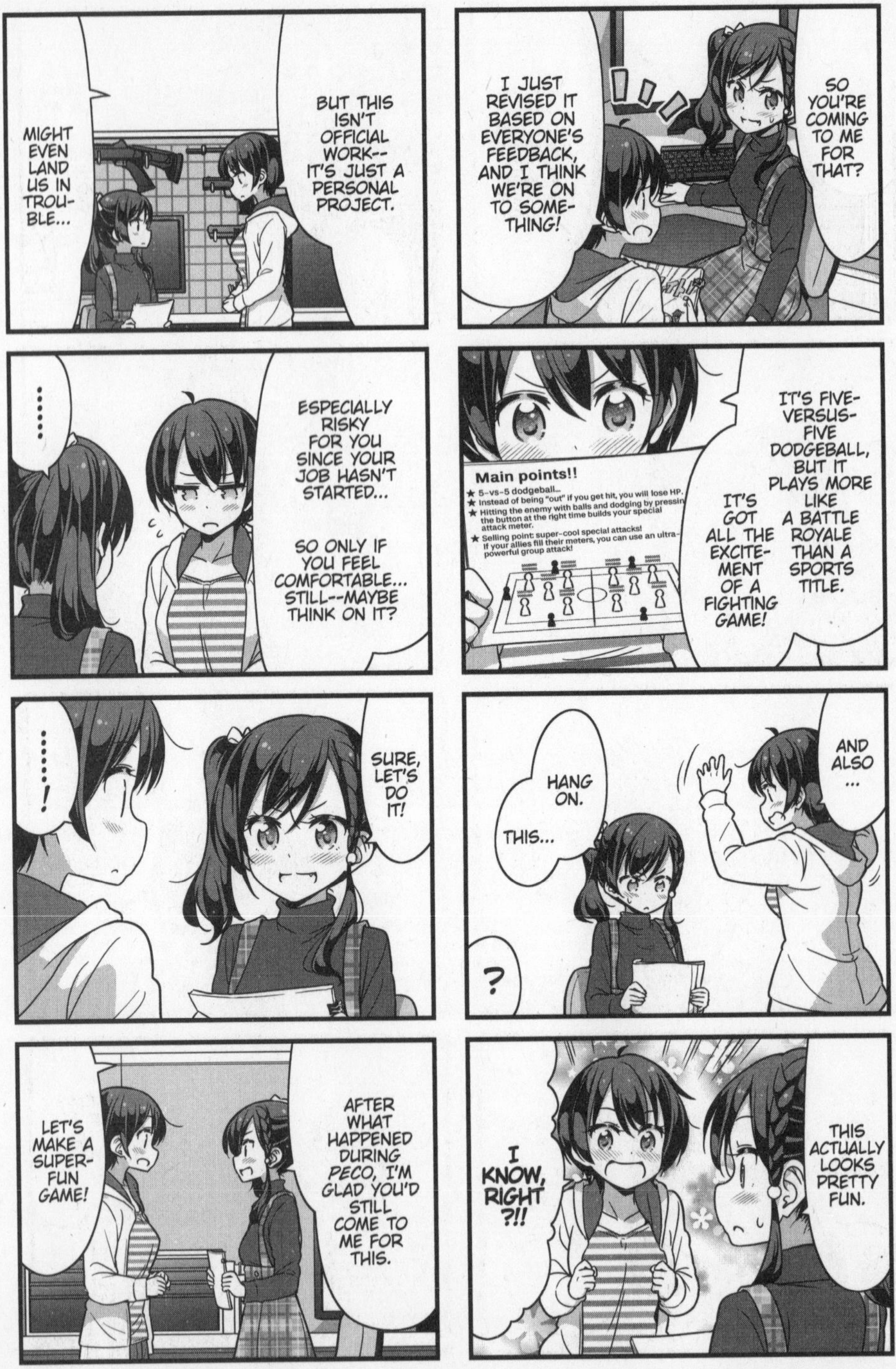
SO YOU'RE COMING TO ME FOR THAT?
I JUST REVISED IT BASED ON EVERYONE'S FEEDBACK, AND I THINK WE'RE ON TO SOMETHING!
BUT THIS ISN'T OFFICIAL WORK-- IT'S JUST A PERSONAL PROJECT.
MIGHT EVEN LAND US IN TROUBLE...
IT'S FIVE-VERSUS-FIVE DODGEBALL, BUT IT PLAYS MORE LIKE A BATTLE ROYALE THAN A SPORTS TITLE.
IT'S GOT ALL THE EXCITEMENT OF A FIGHTING GAME!
Main points!!
★ 5-vs-5 dodgeball...
★ Instead of being "out" if you get hit, you will lose HP.
★ Hitting the enemy with balls and dodging by pressin the button at the right time builds your special attack meter.
★ Selling point: super-cool special attacks! If your allies fill their meters, you can use an ultra-powerful group attack!
ESPECIALLY RISKY FOR YOU SINCE YOUR JOB HASN'T STARTED...
SO ONLY IF YOU FEEL COMFORTABLE... STILL--MAYBE THINK ON IT?
......
AND ALSO ...
HANG ON.
THIS...
?
SURE, LET'S DO IT!
......!
THIS ACTUALLY LOOKS PRETTY FUN.
I KNOW, RIGHT?!!
AFTER WHAT HAPPENED DURING PECO, I'M GLAD YOU'D STILL COME TO ME FOR THIS.
LET'S MAKE A SUPER-FUN GAME!

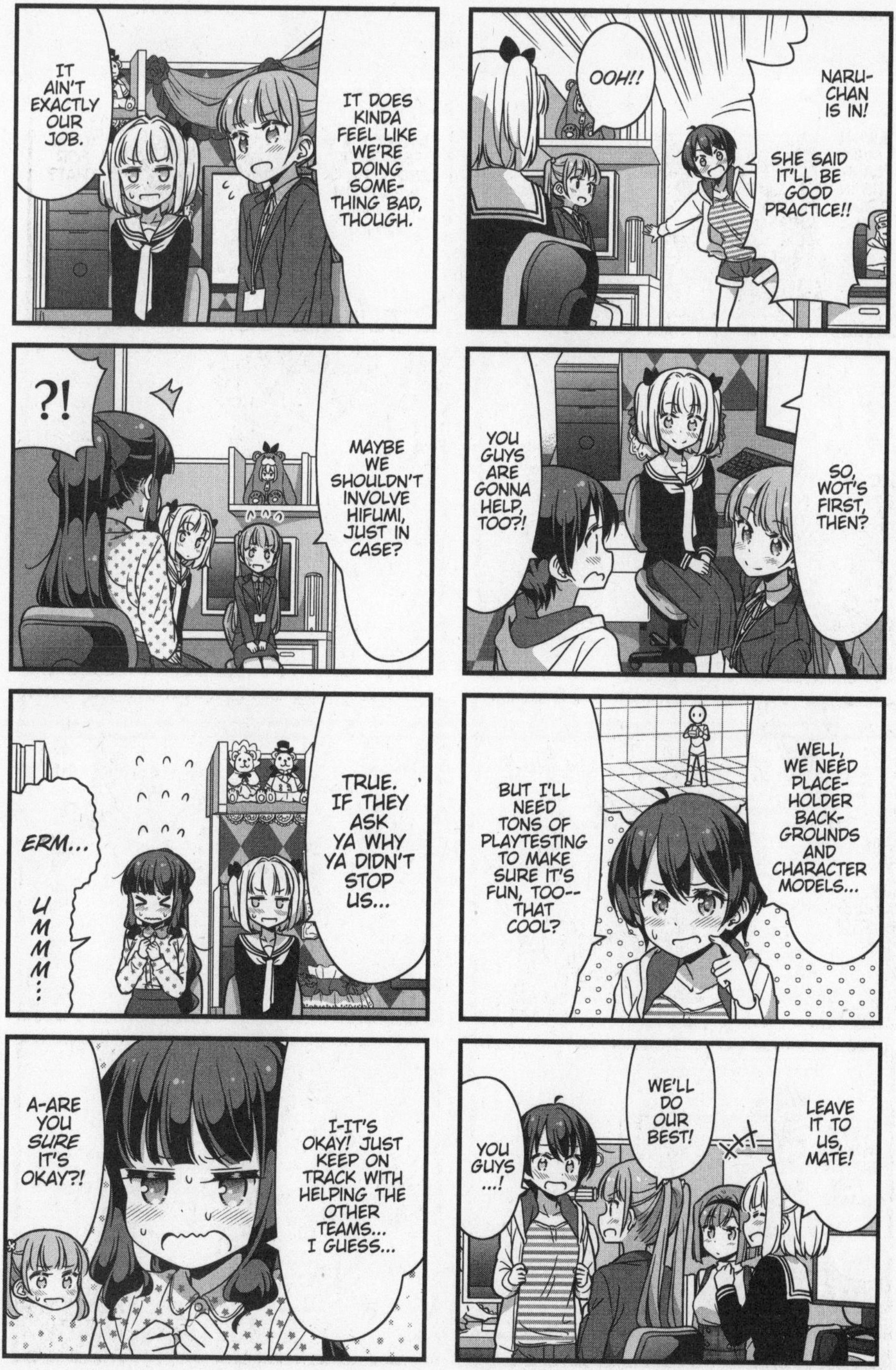
NARU-CHAN IS IN!
SHE SAID IT'LL BE GOOD PRACTICE!!
OOH!!
IT DOES KINDA FEEL LIKE WE'RE DOING SOME-THING BAD, THOUGH.
IT AIN'T EXACTLY OUR JOB.
SO, WOT'S FIRST, THEN?
YOU GUYS ARE GONNA HELP, TOO?!
MAYBE WE SHOULDN'T INVOLVE HIFUMI, JUST IN CASE?
?!
WELL, WE NEED PLACE-HOLDER BACK-GROUNDS AND CHARACTER MODELS...
BUT I'LL NEED TONS OF PLAYTESTING TO MAKE SURE IT'S FUN, TOO--THAT COOL?
TRUE. IF THEY ASK YA WHY YA DIDN'T STOP US...
ERM...
UMMMM...
LEAVE IT TO US, MATE!
WE'LL DO OUR BEST!
YOU GUYS ...!
I-IT'S OKAY! JUST KEEP ON TRACK WITH HELPING THE OTHER TEAMS... I GUESS...
A-ARE YOU SURE IT'S OKAY?!

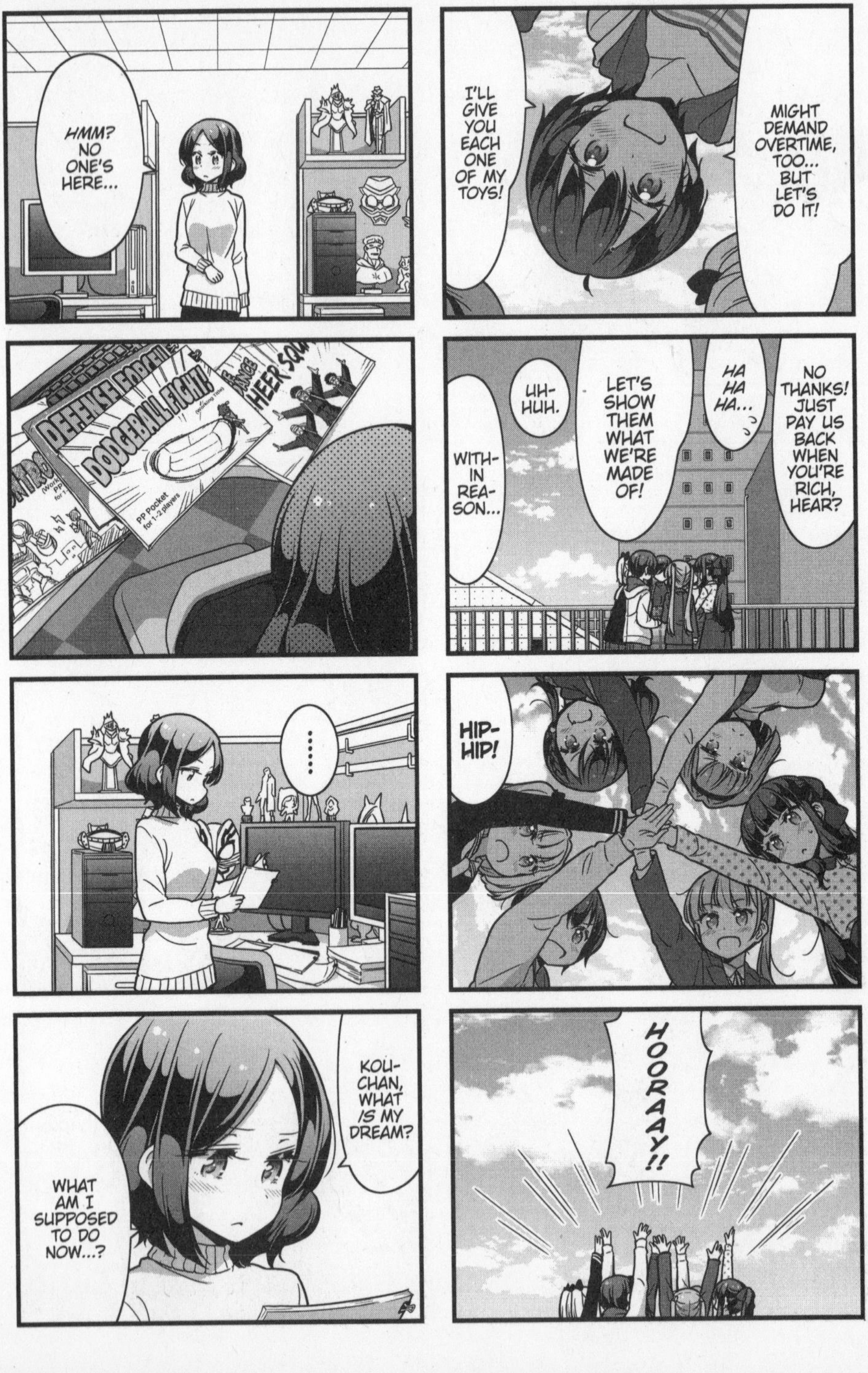

MIGHT DEMAND OVERTIME, TOO... BUT LET'S DO IT!
I'LL GIVE YOU EACH ONE OF MY TOYS!
NO THANKS! JUST PAY US BACK WHEN YOU'RE RICH, HEAR?
HA HA HA...
LET'S SHOW THEM WHAT WE'RE MADE OF!
UH-HUH.
WITH-IN REA-SON...
HIP-HIP!
HOORAAY!!
HMM? NO ONE'S HERE...
DODGEBALL FIGHT!
PP Pocket for 1-2 players
......
KOU-CHAN, WHAT IS MY DREAM?
WHAT AM I SUPPOSED TO DO NOW...?

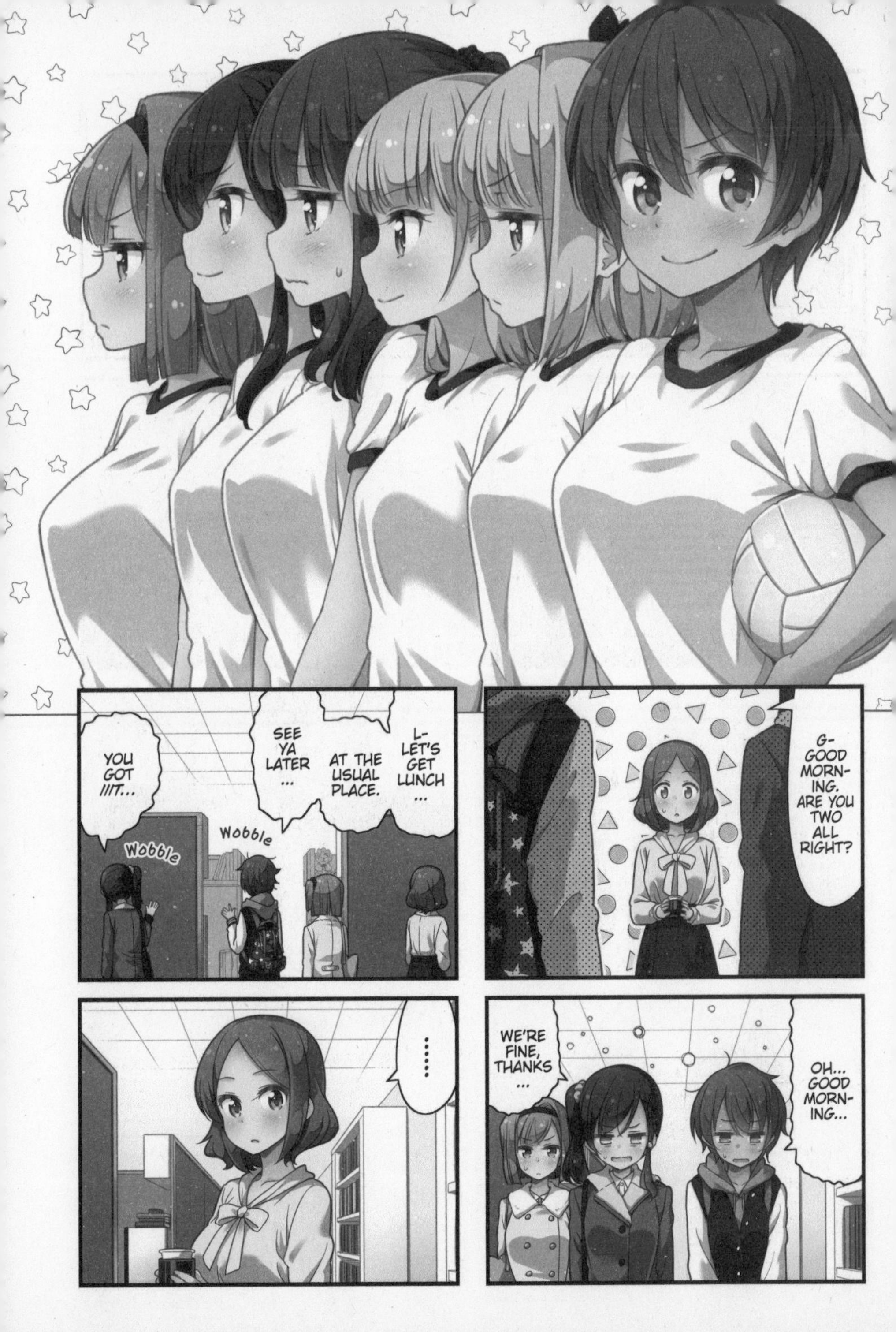
G-GOOD MORNING. ARE YOU TWO ALL RIGHT?
L-LET'S GET LUNCH ...
AT THE USUAL PLACE.
SEE YA LATER ...
YOU GOT IIIT...
Wobble
Wobble
OH... GOOD MORNING...
WE'RE FINE, THANKS ...
......

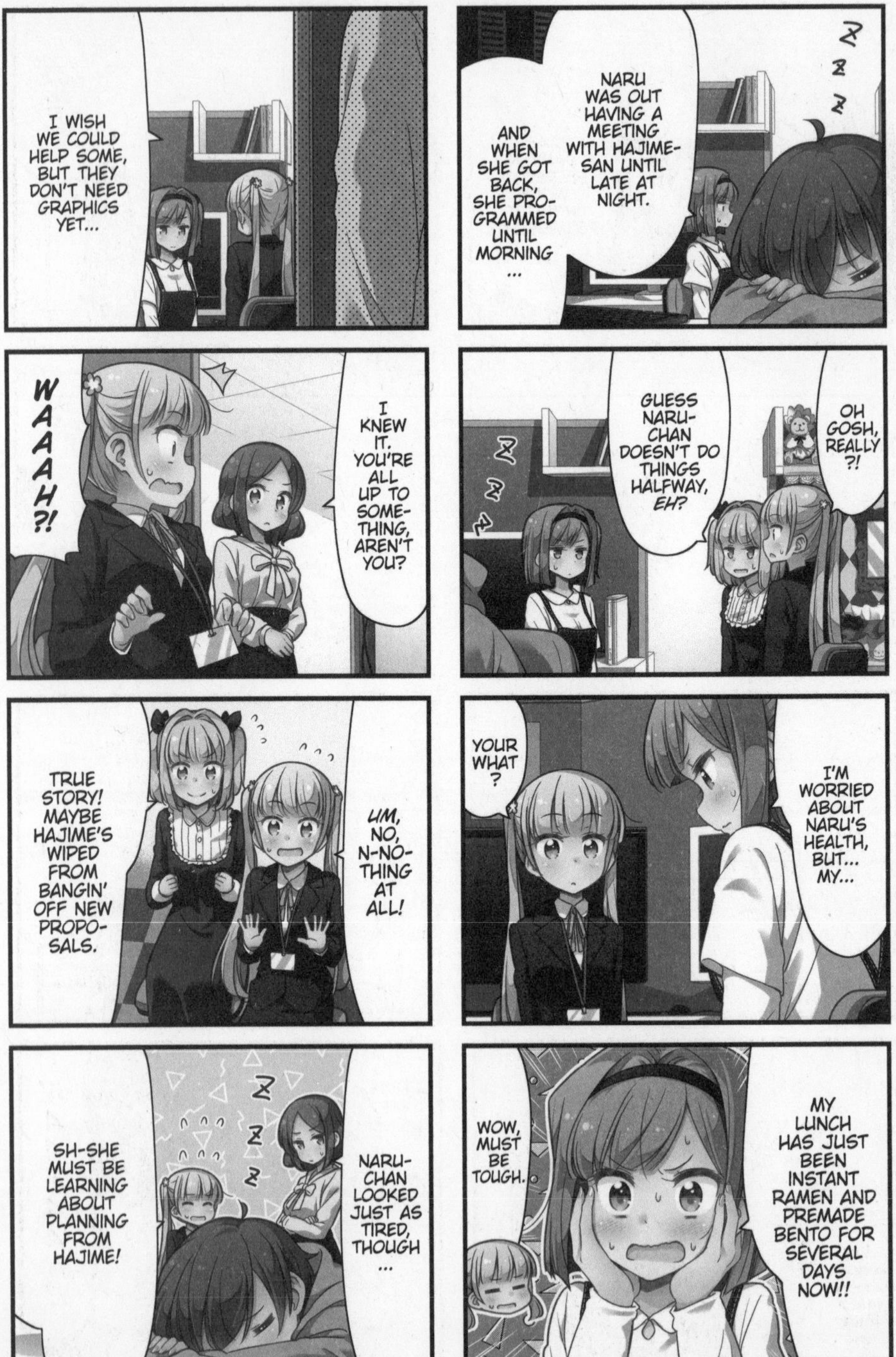
Z Z Z
NARU WAS OUT HAVING A MEETING WITH HAJIME-SAN UNTIL LATE AT NIGHT.
AND WHEN SHE GOT BACK, SHE PROGRAMMED UNTIL MORNING...
I WISH WE COULD HELP SOME, BUT THEY DON'T NEED GRAPHICS YET...
OH GOSH, REALLY?!
GUESS NARU-CHAN DOESN'T DO THINGS HALFWAY, EH?
Z Z Z
I KNEW IT. YOU'RE ALL UP TO SOMETHING, AREN'T YOU?
WAAAAH?!
I'M WORRIED ABOUT NARU'S HEALTH, BUT... MY...
YOUR WHAT?
UM, NO, N-NOTHING AT ALL!
TRUE STORY! MAYBE HAJIME'S WIPED FROM BANGIN' OFF NEW PROPOSALS.
MY LUNCH HAS JUST BEEN INSTANT RAMEN AND PREMADE BENTO FOR SEVERAL DAYS NOW!!
WOW, MUST BE TOUGH.
NARU-CHAN LOOKED JUST AS TIRED, THOUGH...
Z Z Z
SH-SHE MUST BE LEARNING ABOUT PLANNING FROM HAJIME!

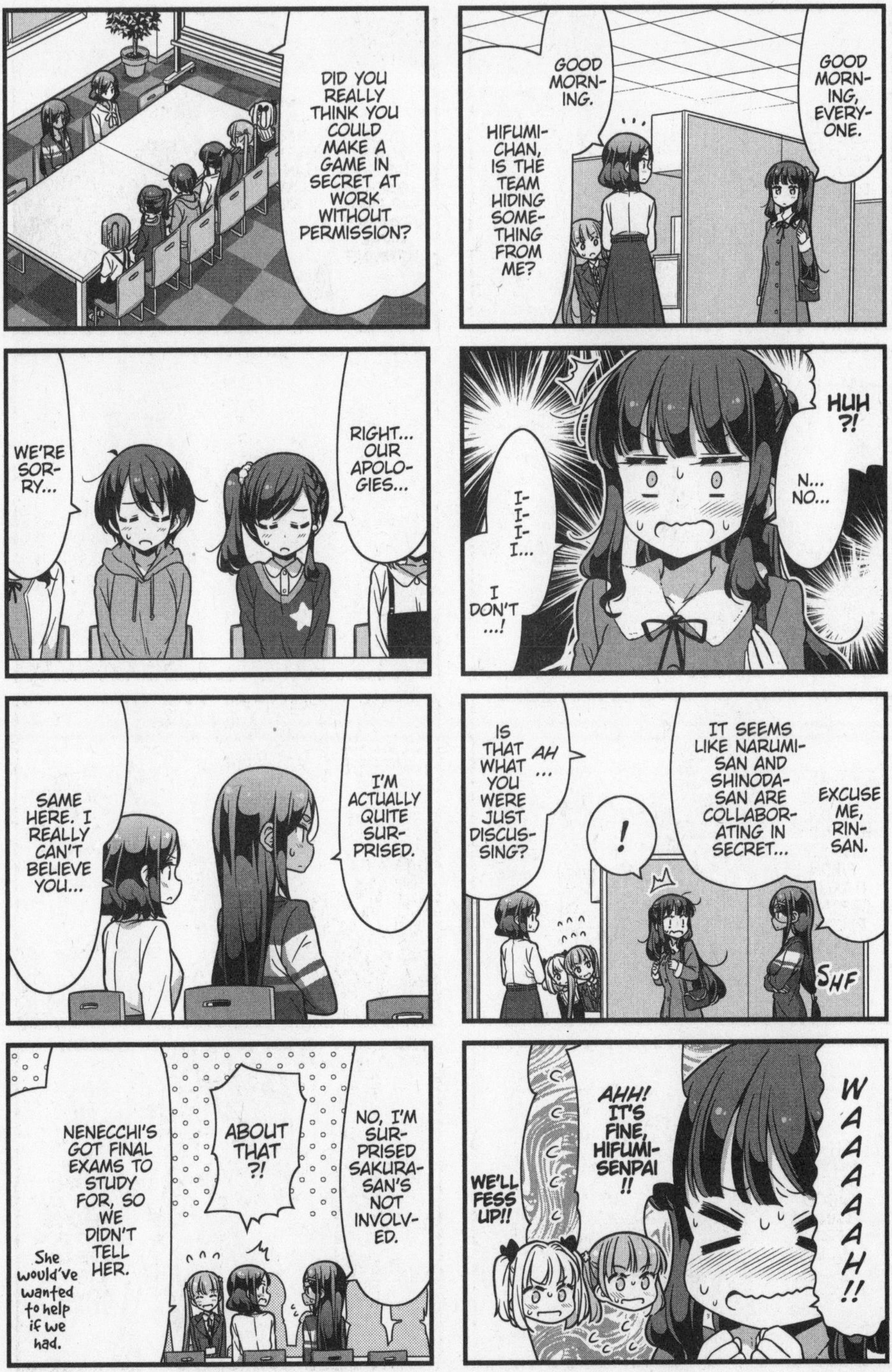
GOOD MORNING, EVERYONE.
GOOD MORNING.
HIFUMI-CHAN, IS THE TEAM HIDING SOMETHING FROM ME?
HUH ?!
N... NO...
I-I-I-I...
I DON'T ...!
EXCUSE ME, RIN-SAN.
IT SEEMS LIKE NARUMI-SAN AND SHINODA-SAN ARE COLLABORATING IN SECRET...
SHF
!
AH ...
IS THAT WHAT YOU WERE JUST DISCUSSING?
WAAAAAAH!!
AHH! IT'S FINE, HIFUMI-SENPAI!!
WE'LL FESS UP!!
DID YOU REALLY THINK YOU COULD MAKE A GAME IN SECRET AT WORK WITHOUT PERMISSION?
RIGHT... OUR APOLOGIES...
WE'RE SORRY...
I'M ACTUALLY QUITE SURPRISED.
SAME HERE. I REALLY CAN'T BELIEVE YOU...
NO, I'M SURPRISED SAKURA-SAN'S NOT INVOLVED.
ABOUT THAT?!
NENECCHI'S GOT FINAL EXAMS TO STUDY FOR, SO WE DIDN'T TELL HER.
She would've wanted to help if we had.

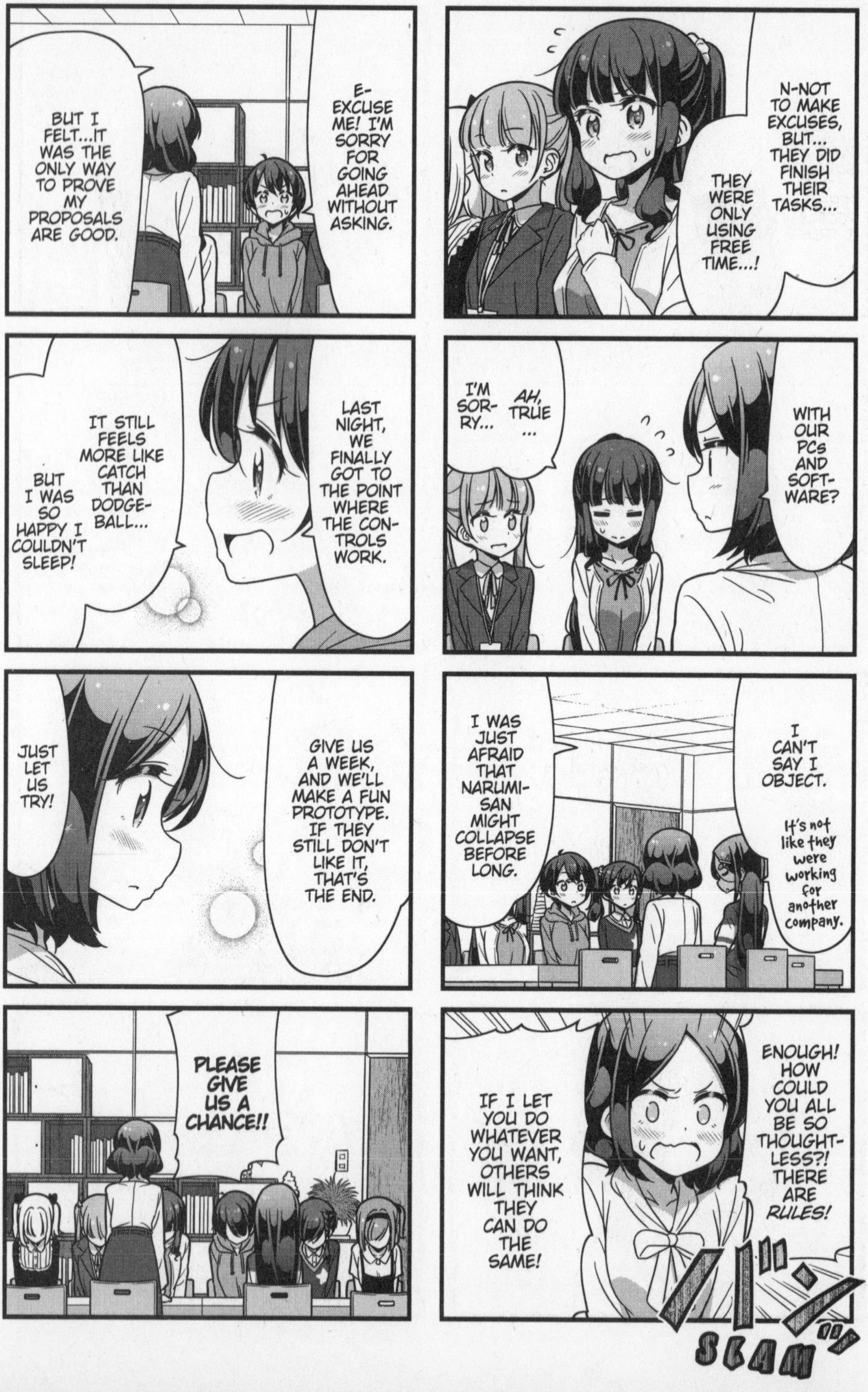
N-NOT TO MAKE EXCUSES, BUT... THEY DID FINISH THEIR TASKS...
THEY WERE ONLY USING FREE TIME...!
E-EXCUSE ME! I'M SORRY FOR GOING AHEAD WITHOUT ASKING.
BUT I FELT...IT WAS THE ONLY WAY TO PROVE MY PROPOSALS ARE GOOD.
WITH OUR PCs AND SOFT-WARE?
AH, TRUE ...
I'M SOR-RY...
LAST NIGHT, WE FINALLY GOT TO THE POINT WHERE THE CON-TROLS WORK.
IT STILL FEELS MORE LIKE CATCH THAN DODGE-BALL...
BUT I WAS SO HAPPY I COULDN'T SLEEP!
I CAN'T SAY I OBJECT.
It's not like they were working for another company.
I WAS JUST AFRAID THAT NARUMI-SAN MIGHT COLLAPSE BEFORE LONG.
GIVE US A WEEK, AND WE'LL MAKE A FUN PROTOTYPE. IF THEY STILL DON'T LIKE IT, THAT'S THE END.
JUST LET US TRY!
ENOUGH! HOW COULD YOU ALL BE SO THOUGHT-LESS?! THERE ARE RULES!
IF I LET YOU DO WHATEVER YOU WANT, OTHERS WILL THINK THEY CAN DO THE SAME!
SLAM
PLEASE GIVE US A CHANCE!!

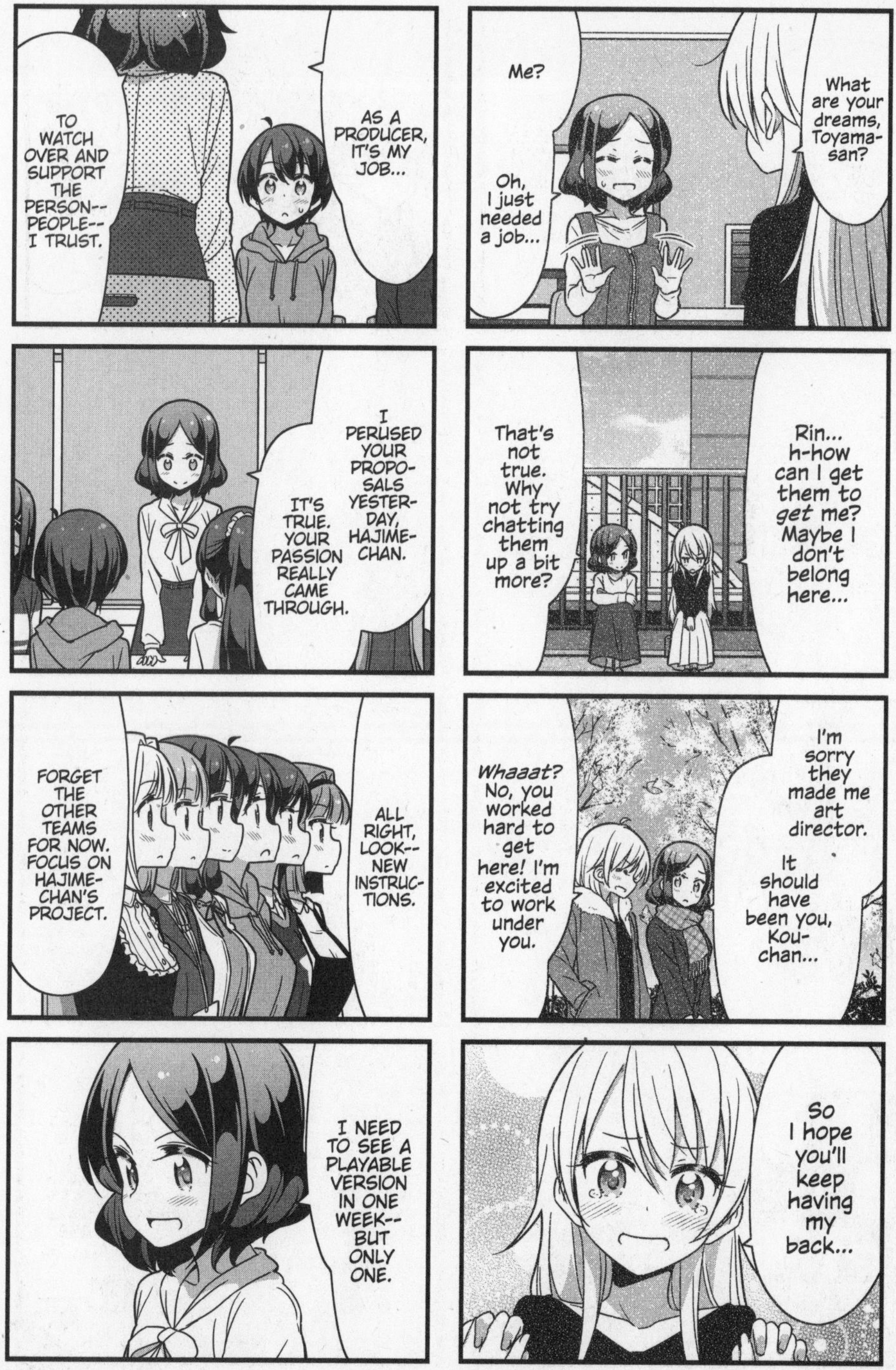
What are your dreams, Toyama-san?
Me?
Oh, I just needed a job...
Rin... h-how can I get them to *get* me? Maybe I don't belong here...
That's not true. Why not try chatting them up a bit more?
I'm sorry they made me art director.
It should have been you, Kou-chan...
*Whaaat?* No, you worked hard to get here! I'm excited to work under you.
So I hope you'll keep having my back...
AS A PRODUCER, IT'S MY JOB...
TO WATCH OVER AND SUPPORT THE PERSON-- PEOPLE-- I TRUST.
I PERUSED YOUR PROPOSALS YESTERDAY, HAJIME-CHAN.
IT'S TRUE. YOUR PASSION REALLY CAME THROUGH.
ALL RIGHT, LOOK-- NEW INSTRUCTIONS.
FORGET THE OTHER TEAMS FOR NOW. FOCUS ON HAJIME-CHAN'S PROJECT.
I NEED TO SEE A PLAYABLE VERSION IN ONE WEEK-- BUT ONLY ONE.

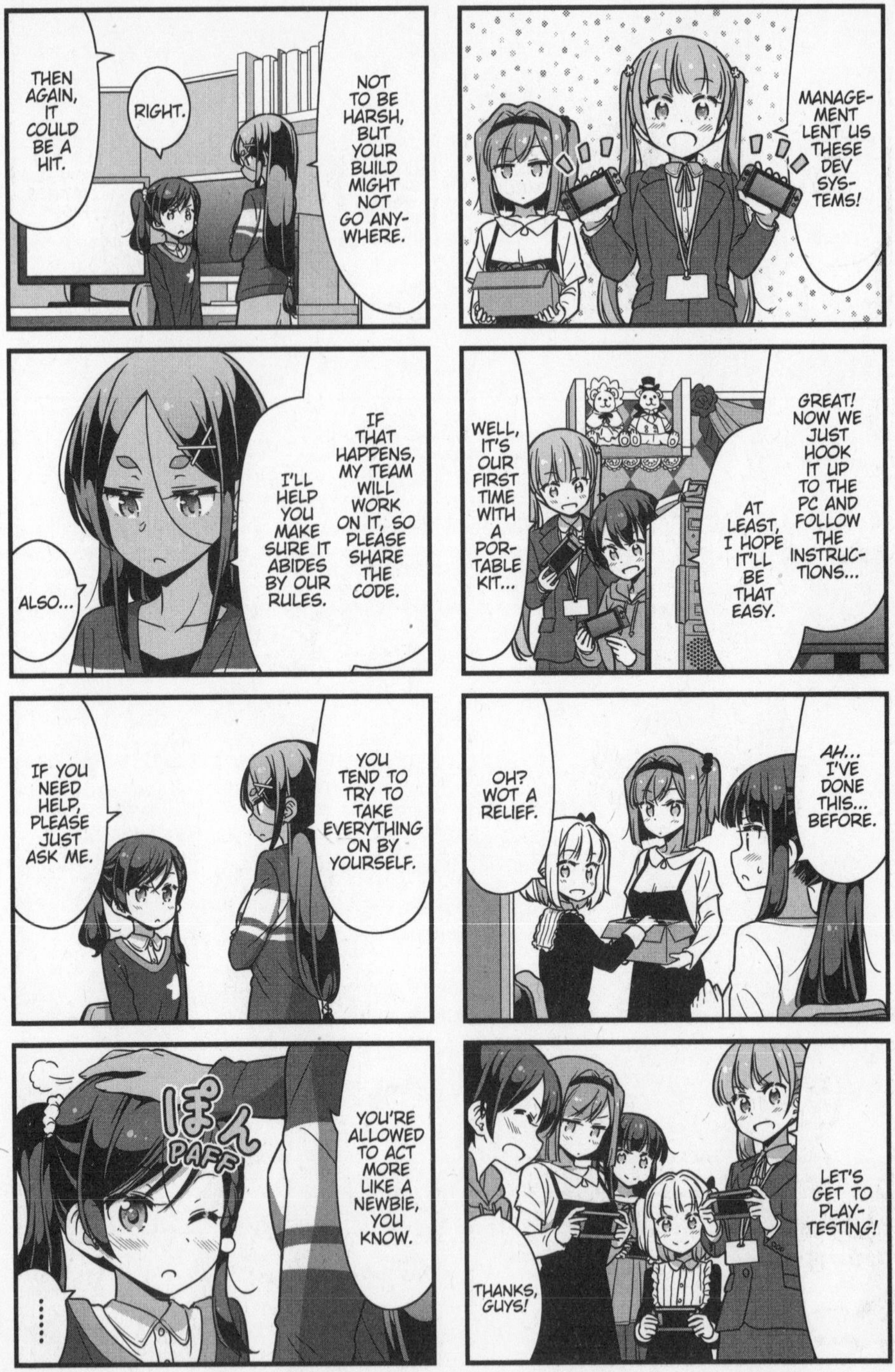
MANAGEMENT LENT US THESE DEV SYSTEMS!
GREAT! NOW WE JUST HOOK IT UP TO THE PC AND FOLLOW THE INSTRUCTIONS...
AT LEAST, I HOPE IT'LL BE THAT EASY.
WELL, IT'S OUR FIRST TIME WITH A PORTABLE KIT...
AH... I'VE DONE THIS... BEFORE.
OH? WOT A RELIEF.
LET'S GET TO PLAYTESTING!
THANKS, GUYS!
NOT TO BE HARSH, BUT YOUR BUILD MIGHT NOT GO ANYWHERE.
RIGHT.
THEN AGAIN, IT COULD BE A HIT.
IF THAT HAPPENS, MY TEAM WILL WORK ON IT, SO PLEASE SHARE THE CODE.
I'LL HELP YOU MAKE SURE IT ABIDES BY OUR RULES.
ALSO...
YOU TEND TO TRY TO TAKE EVERYTHING ON BY YOURSELF.
IF YOU NEED HELP, PLEASE JUST ASK ME.
YOU'RE ALLOWED TO ACT MORE LIKE A NEWBIE, YOU KNOW.
ぽん
PAFF
......

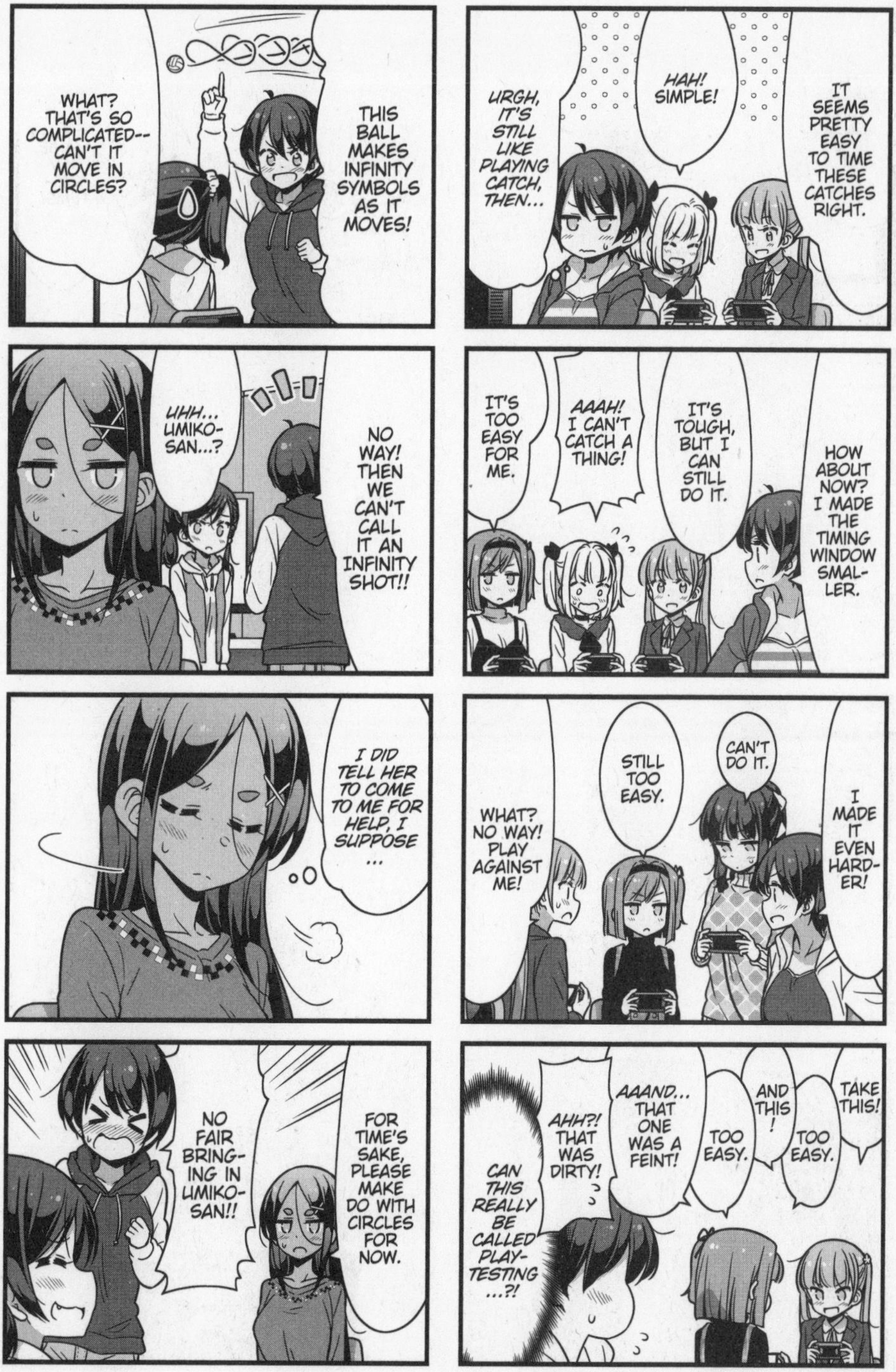
IT SEEMS PRETTY EASY TO TIME THESE CATCHES RIGHT.
HAH! SIMPLE!
URGH, IT'S STILL LIKE PLAYING CATCH, THEN...
HOW ABOUT NOW? I MADE THE TIMING WINDOW SMALLER.
IT'S TOUGH, BUT I CAN STILL DO IT.
AAAH! I CAN'T CATCH A THING!
IT'S TOO EASY FOR ME.
I MADE IT EVEN HARDER!
CAN'T DO IT.
STILL TOO EASY.
WHAT? NO WAY! PLAY AGAINST ME!
TAKE THIS!
TOO EASY.
AND THIS!
TOO EASY.
AAAND... THAT ONE WAS A FEINT!
AHH?! THAT WAS DIRTY!
CAN THIS REALLY BE CALLED PLAY-TESTING...?!
THIS BALL MAKES INFINITY SYMBOLS AS IT MOVES!
WHAT? THAT'S SO COMPLICATED--CAN'T IT MOVE IN CIRCLES?
NO WAY! THEN WE CAN'T CALL IT AN INFINITY SHOT!!
UHH... UMIKO-SAN...?
I DID TELL HER TO COME TO ME FOR HELP, I SUPPOSE...
FOR TIME'S SAKE, PLEASE MAKE DO WITH CIRCLES FOR NOW.
NO FAIR BRINGING IN UMIKO-SAN!!

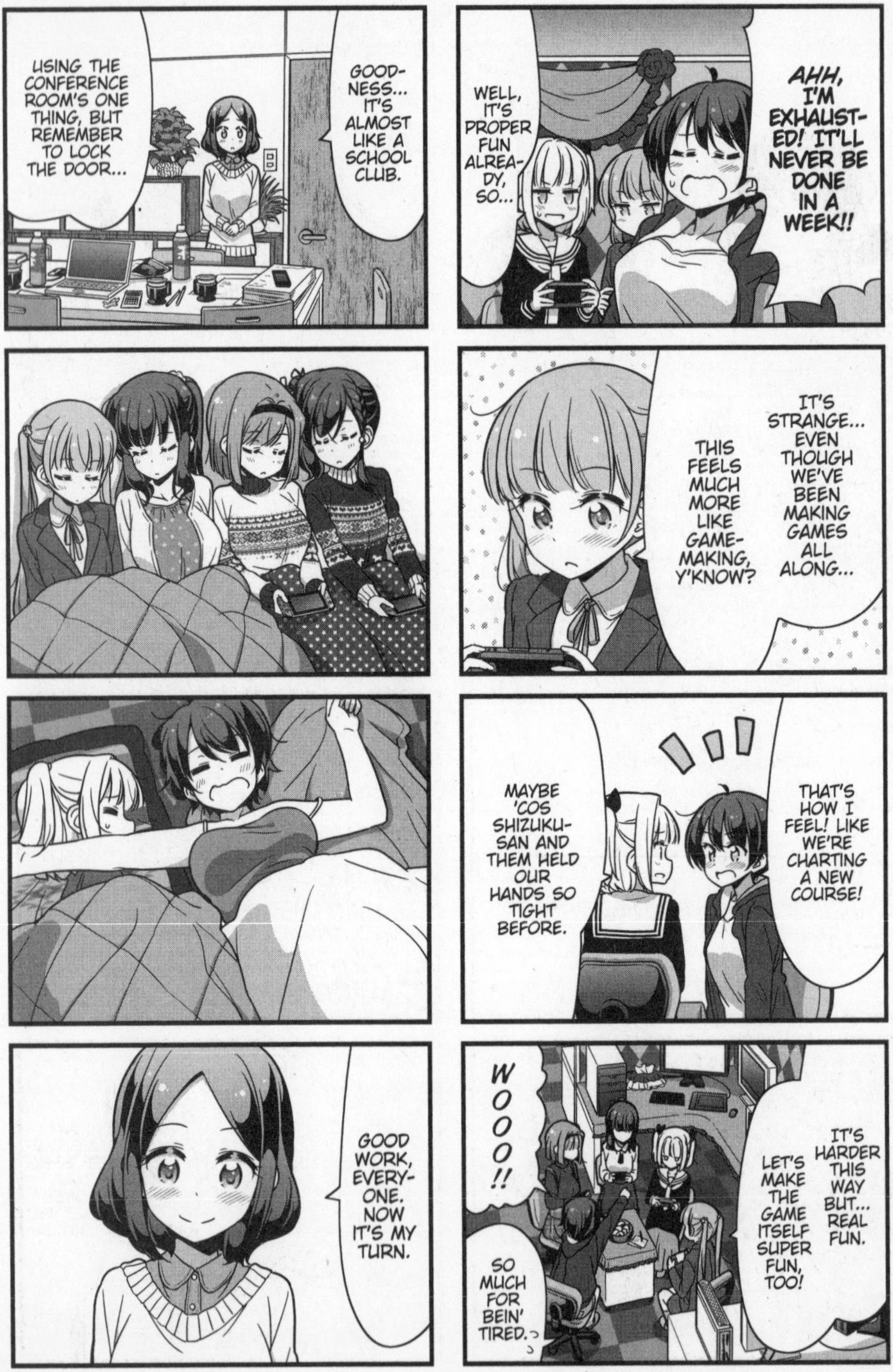
AHH, I'M EXHAUSTED! IT'LL NEVER BE DONE IN A WEEK!!
WELL, IT'S PROPER FUN ALREADY, SO...
GOODNESS... IT'S ALMOST LIKE A SCHOOL CLUB.
USING THE CONFERENCE ROOM'S ONE THING, BUT REMEMBER TO LOCK THE DOOR...
IT'S STRANGE... EVEN THOUGH WE'VE BEEN MAKING GAMES ALL ALONG...
THIS FEELS MUCH MORE LIKE GAME-MAKING, Y'KNOW?
THAT'S HOW I FEEL! LIKE WE'RE CHARTING A NEW COURSE!
MAYBE 'COS SHIZUKU-SAN AND THEM HELD OUR HANDS SO TIGHT BEFORE.
IT'S HARDER THIS WAY BUT... REAL FUN.
LET'S MAKE THE GAME ITSELF SUPER FUN, TOO!
WOOOO!!
SO MUCH FOR BEIN' TIRED.
GOOD WORK, EVERYONE. NOW IT'S MY TURN.

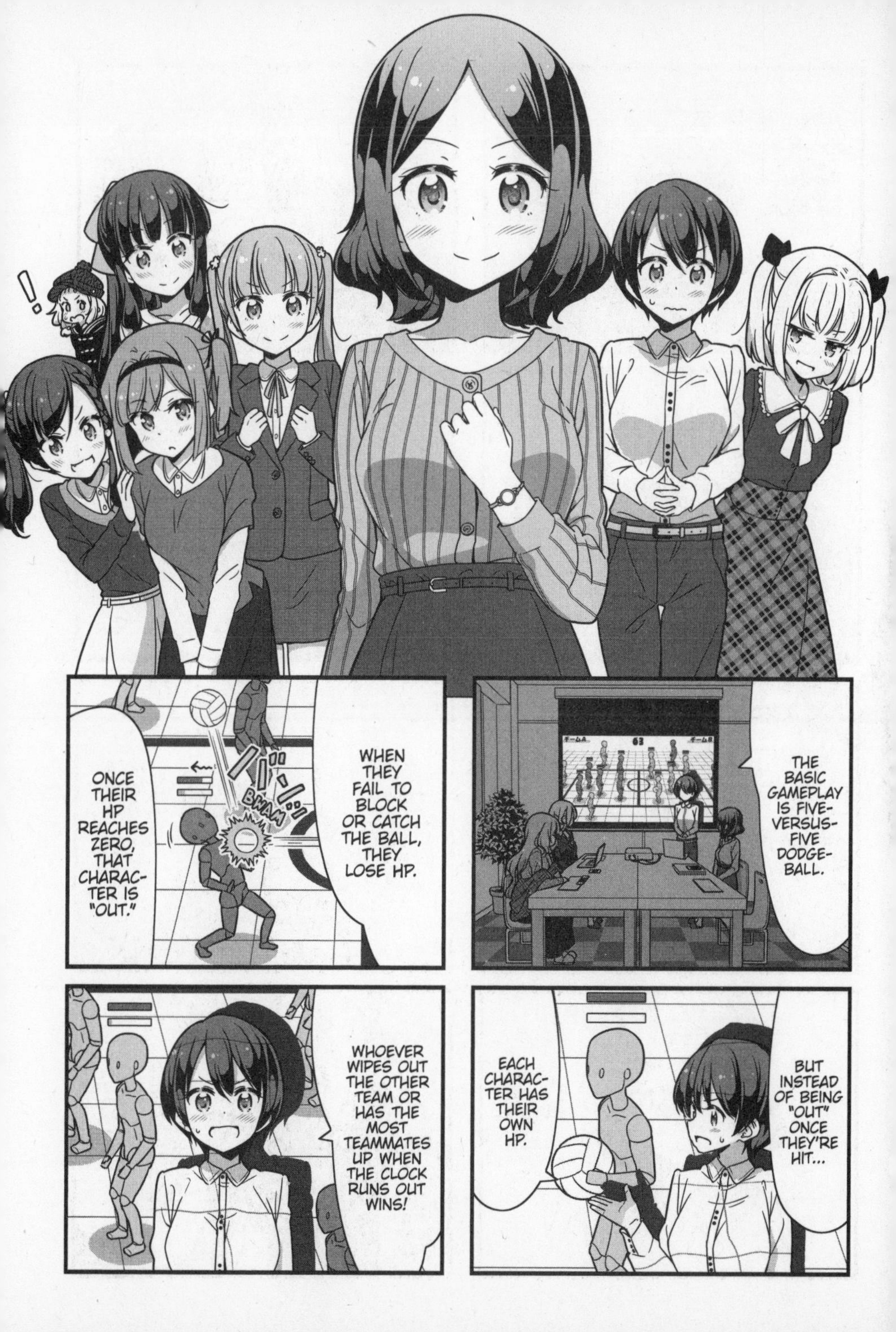
!
THE BASIC GAMEPLAY IS FIVE-VERSUS-FIVE DODGEBALL.
WHEN THEY FAIL TO BLOCK OR CATCH THE BALL, THEY LOSE HP.
BWAM
ONCE THEIR HP REACHES ZERO, THAT CHARACTER IS "OUT."
BUT INSTEAD OF BEING "OUT" ONCE THEY'RE HIT...
EACH CHARACTER HAS THEIR OWN HP.
WHOEVER WIPES OUT THE OTHER TEAM OR HAS THE MOST TEAMMATES UP WHEN THE CLOCK RUNS OUT WINS!

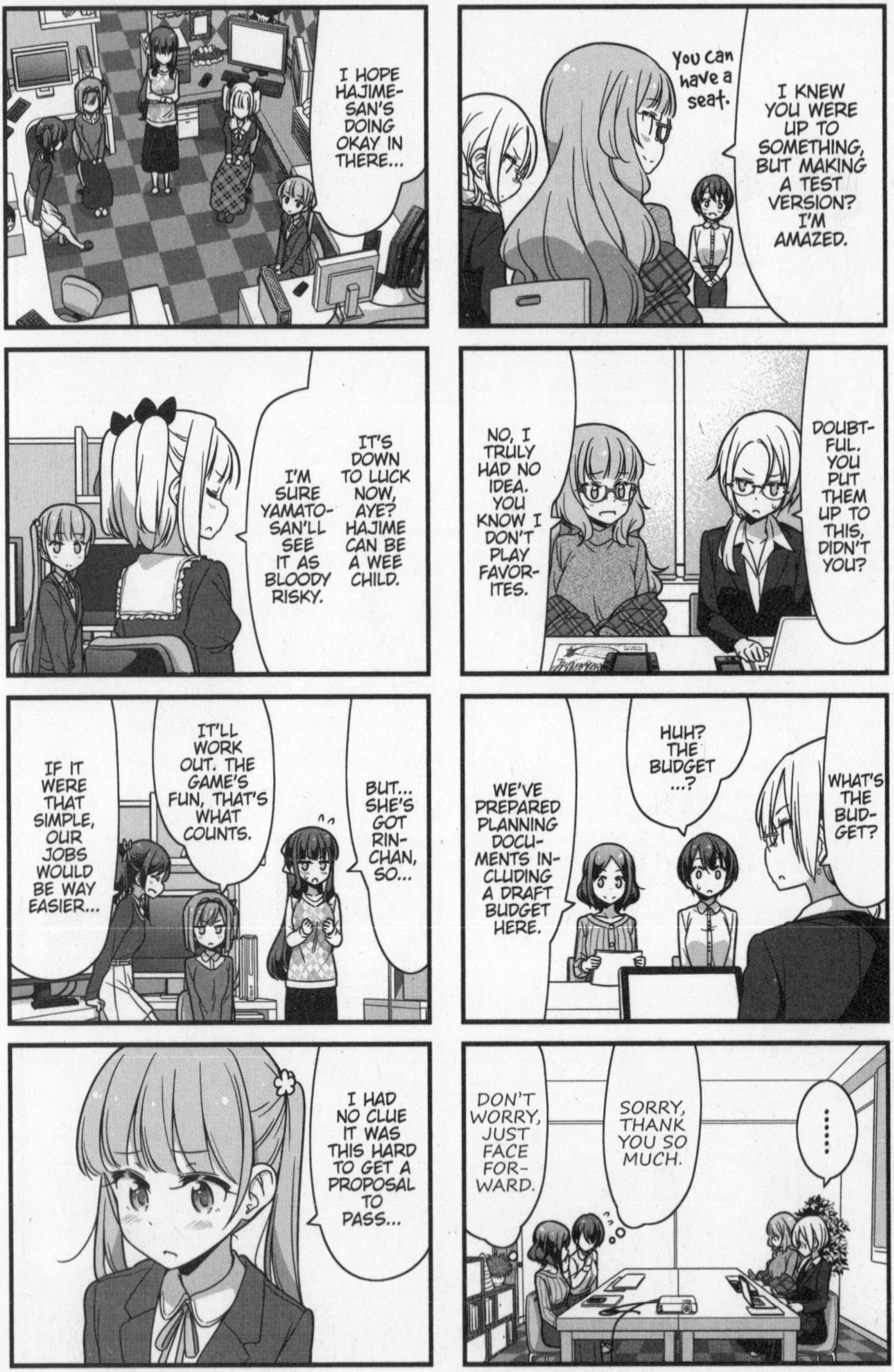
I KNEW YOU WERE UP TO SOMETHING, BUT MAKING A TEST VERSION? I'M AMAZED.
You can have a seat.
I HOPE HAJIME-SAN'S DOING OKAY IN THERE...
DOUBTFUL. YOU PUT THEM UP TO THIS, DIDN'T YOU?
NO, I TRULY HAD NO IDEA. YOU KNOW I DON'T PLAY FAVORITES.
IT'S DOWN TO LUCK NOW, AYE? HAJIME CAN BE A WEE CHILD.
I'M SURE YAMATO-SAN'LL SEE IT AS BLOODY RISKY.
WHAT'S THE BUDGET?
HUH? THE BUDGET...?
WE'VE PREPARED PLANNING DOCUMENTS INCLUDING A DRAFT BUDGET HERE.
BUT... SHE'S GOT RIN-CHAN, SO...
IT'LL WORK OUT. THE GAME'S FUN, THAT'S WHAT COUNTS.
IF IT WERE THAT SIMPLE, OUR JOBS WOULD BE WAY EASIER...
......
SORRY, THANK YOU SO MUCH.
DON'T WORRY, JUST FACE FORWARD.
I HAD NO CLUE IT WAS THIS HARD TO GET A PROPOSAL TO PASS...

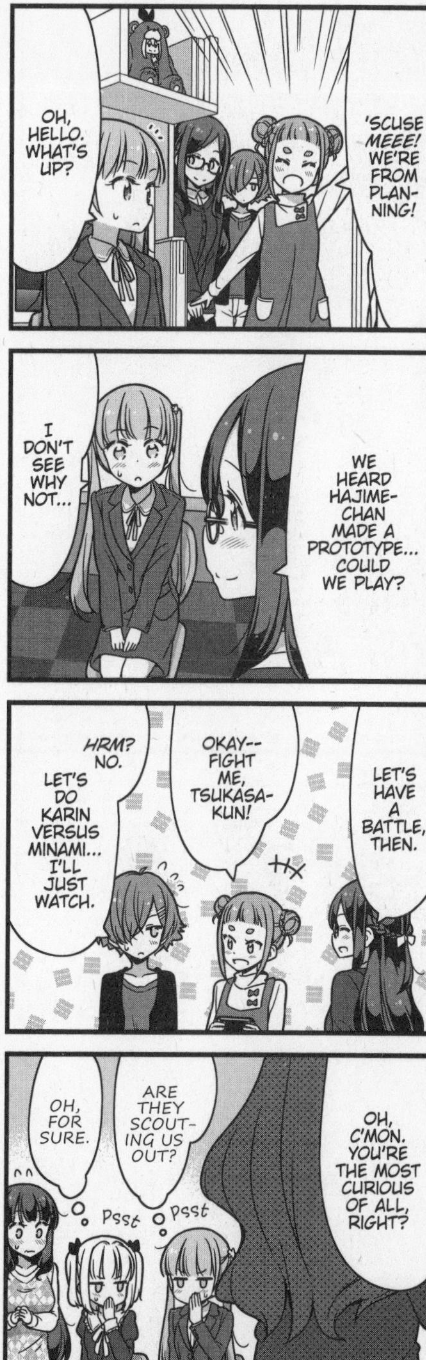
'SCUSE MEEE! WE'RE FROM PLANNING!
OH, HELLO. WHAT'S UP?
WE HEARD HAJIME-CHAN MADE A PROTOTYPE... COULD WE PLAY?
I DON'T SEE WHY NOT...
LET'S HAVE A BATTLE, THEN.
OKAY--FIGHT ME, TSUKASA-KUN!
HRM? NO. LET'S DO KARIN VERSUS MINAMI... I'LL JUST WATCH.
OH, C'MON. YOU'RE THE MOST CURIOUS OF ALL, RIGHT?
ARE THEY SCOUTING US OUT?
Psst
Psst
OH, FOR SURE.
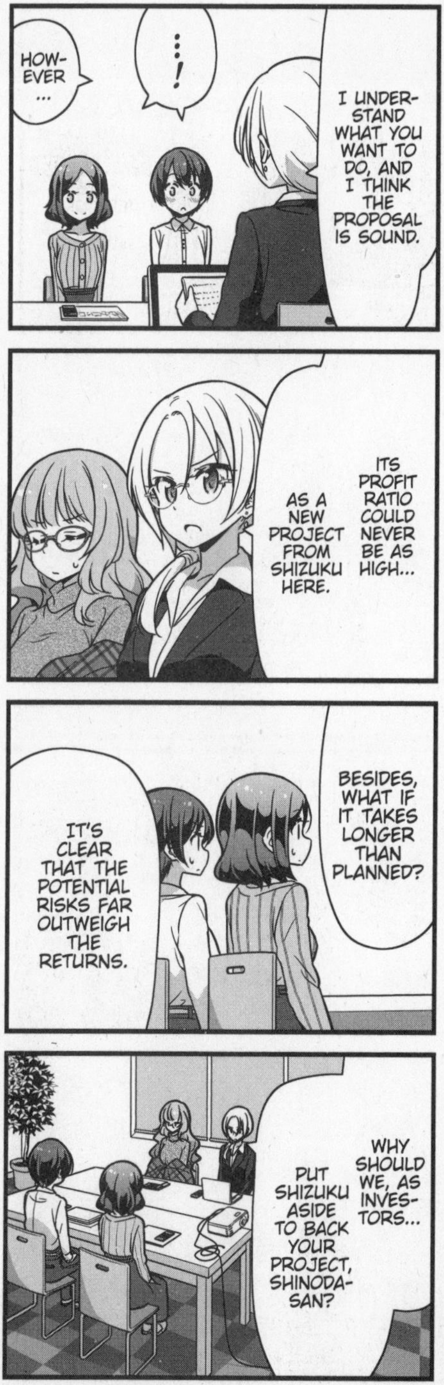
I UNDERSTAND WHAT YOU WANT TO DO, AND I THINK THE PROPOSAL IS SOUND.
...!
HOWEVER...
ITS PROFIT RATIO COULD NEVER BE AS HIGH...
AS A NEW PROJECT FROM SHIZUKU HERE.
BESIDES, WHAT IF IT TAKES LONGER THAN PLANNED?
IT'S CLEAR THAT THE POTENTIAL RISKS FAR OUTWEIGH THE RETURNS.
WHY SHOULD WE, AS INVESTORS...
PUT SHIZUKU ASIDE TO BACK YOUR PROJECT, SHINODA-SAN?

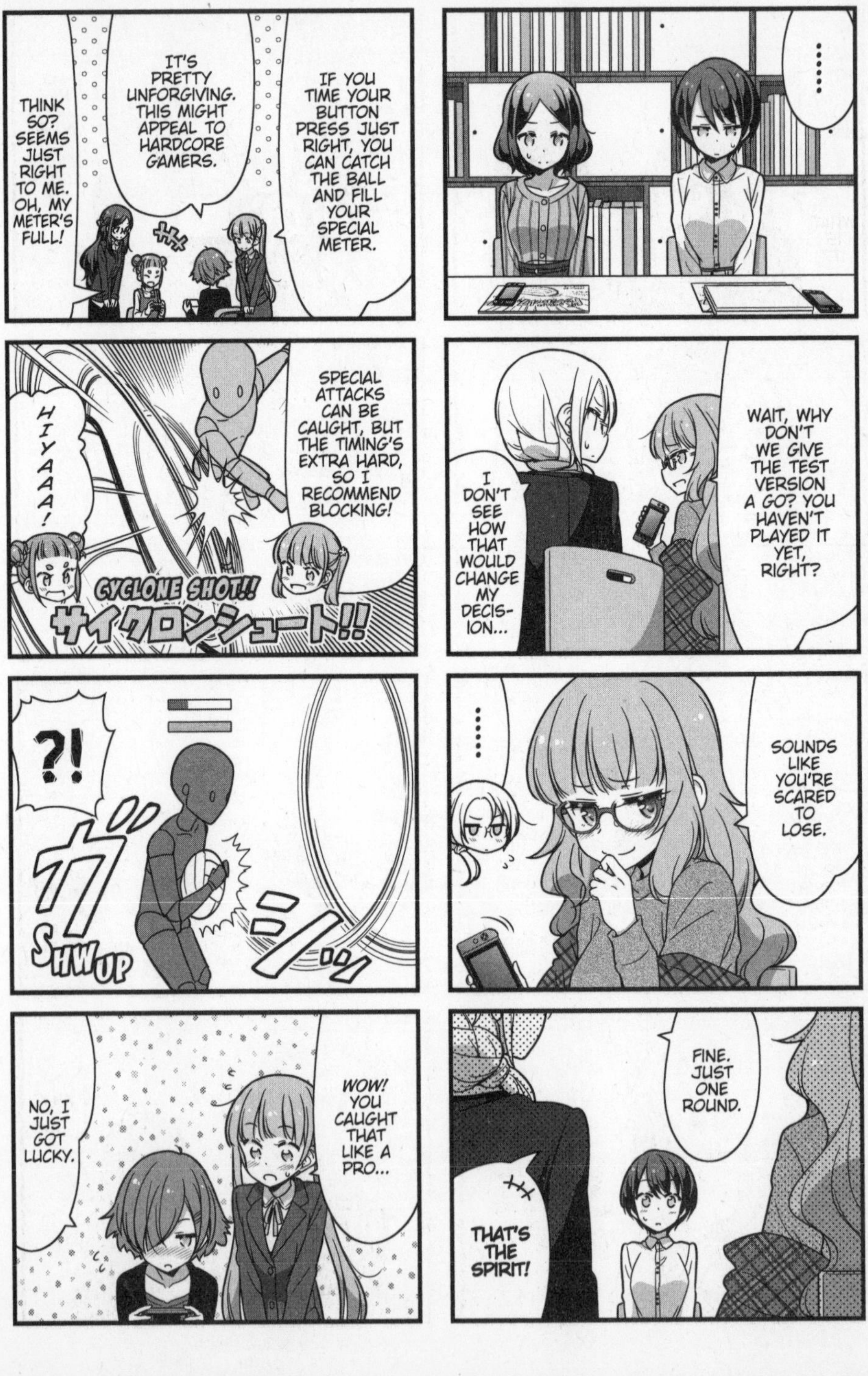
......
WAIT, WHY DON'T WE GIVE THE TEST VERSION A GO? YOU HAVEN'T PLAYED IT YET, RIGHT?
I DON'T SEE HOW THAT WOULD CHANGE MY DECISION...
SOUNDS LIKE YOU'RE SCARED TO LOSE.
......
FINE. JUST ONE ROUND.
THAT'S THE SPIRIT!
IF YOU TIME YOUR BUTTON PRESS JUST RIGHT, YOU CAN CATCH THE BALL AND FILL YOUR SPECIAL METER.
IT'S PRETTY UNFORGIVING. THIS MIGHT APPEAL TO HARDCORE GAMERS.
THINK SO? SEEMS JUST RIGHT TO ME. OH, MY METER'S FULL!
SPECIAL ATTACKS CAN BE CAUGHT, BUT THE TIMING'S EXTRA HARD, SO I RECOMMEND BLOCKING!
HIYAAAA!
CYCLONE SHOT!!
サイクロンシュート!!
?!
SHWUP
WOW! YOU CAUGHT THAT LIKE A PRO...
NO, I JUST GOT LUCKY.

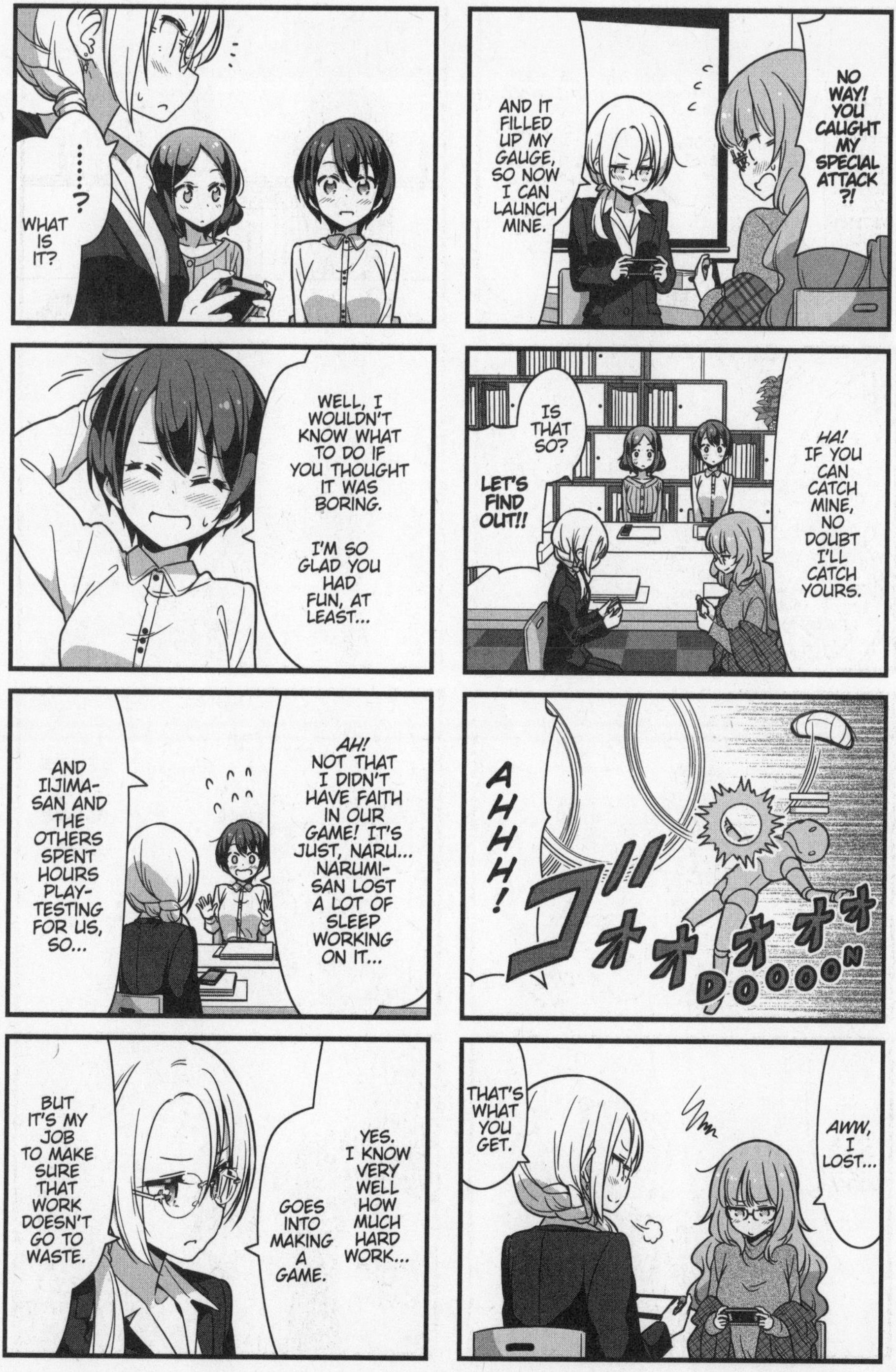
NO WAY! YOU CAUGHT MY SPECIAL ATTACK?!
AND IT FILLED UP MY GAUGE, SO NOW I CAN LAUNCH MINE.
HA! IF YOU CAN CATCH MINE, NO DOUBT I'LL CATCH YOURS.
IS THAT SO?
LET'S FIND OUT!!
AHHHH!
ゴォオオオオオ
DOOOOON
AWW, I LOST...
THAT'S WHAT YOU GET.
......?
WHAT IS IT?
WELL, I WOULDN'T KNOW WHAT TO DO IF YOU THOUGHT IT WAS BORING.
I'M SO GLAD YOU HAD FUN, AT LEAST...
AH! NOT THAT I DIDN'T HAVE FAITH IN OUR GAME! IT'S JUST, NARU... NARUMI-SAN LOST A LOT OF SLEEP WORKING ON IT...
AND IIJIMA-SAN AND THE OTHERS SPENT HOURS PLAY-TESTING FOR US, SO...
YES. I KNOW VERY WELL HOW MUCH HARD WORK...
GOES INTO MAKING A GAME.
BUT IT'S MY JOB TO MAKE SURE THAT WORK DOESN'T GO TO WASTE.

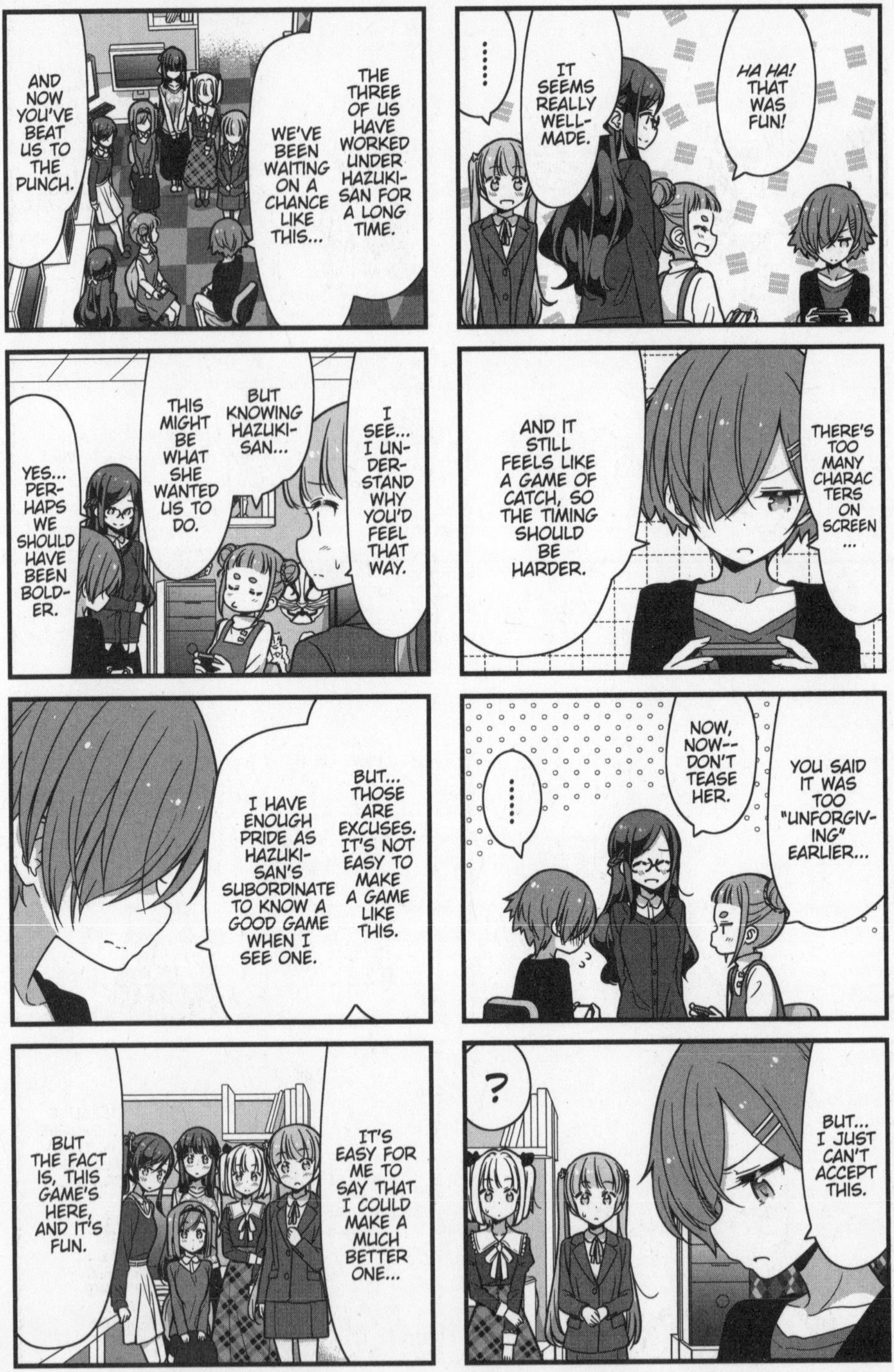
HA HA! THAT WAS FUN!
IT SEEMS REALLY WELL-MADE.
......
THE THREE OF US HAVE WORKED UNDER HAZUKI-SAN FOR A LONG TIME.
WE'VE BEEN WAITING ON A CHANCE LIKE THIS...
AND NOW YOU'VE BEAT US TO THE PUNCH.
THERE'S TOO MANY CHARACTERS ON SCREEN...
AND IT STILL FEELS LIKE A GAME OF CATCH, SO THE TIMING SHOULD BE HARDER.
I SEE... I UNDERSTAND WHY YOU'D FEEL THAT WAY.
BUT KNOWING HAZUKI-SAN...
THIS MIGHT BE WHAT SHE WANTED US TO DO.
YES... PERHAPS WE SHOULD HAVE BEEN BOLDER.
YOU SAID IT WAS TOO "UNFORGIVING" EARLIER...
NOW, NOW-- DON'T TEASE HER.
......
BUT... THOSE ARE EXCUSES. IT'S NOT EASY TO MAKE A GAME LIKE THIS.
I HAVE ENOUGH PRIDE AS HAZUKI-SAN'S SUBORDINATE TO KNOW A GOOD GAME WHEN I SEE ONE.
?
BUT... I JUST CAN'T ACCEPT THIS.
IT'S EASY FOR ME TO SAY THAT I COULD MAKE A MUCH BETTER ONE...
BUT THE FACT IS, THIS GAME'S HERE, AND IT'S FUN.

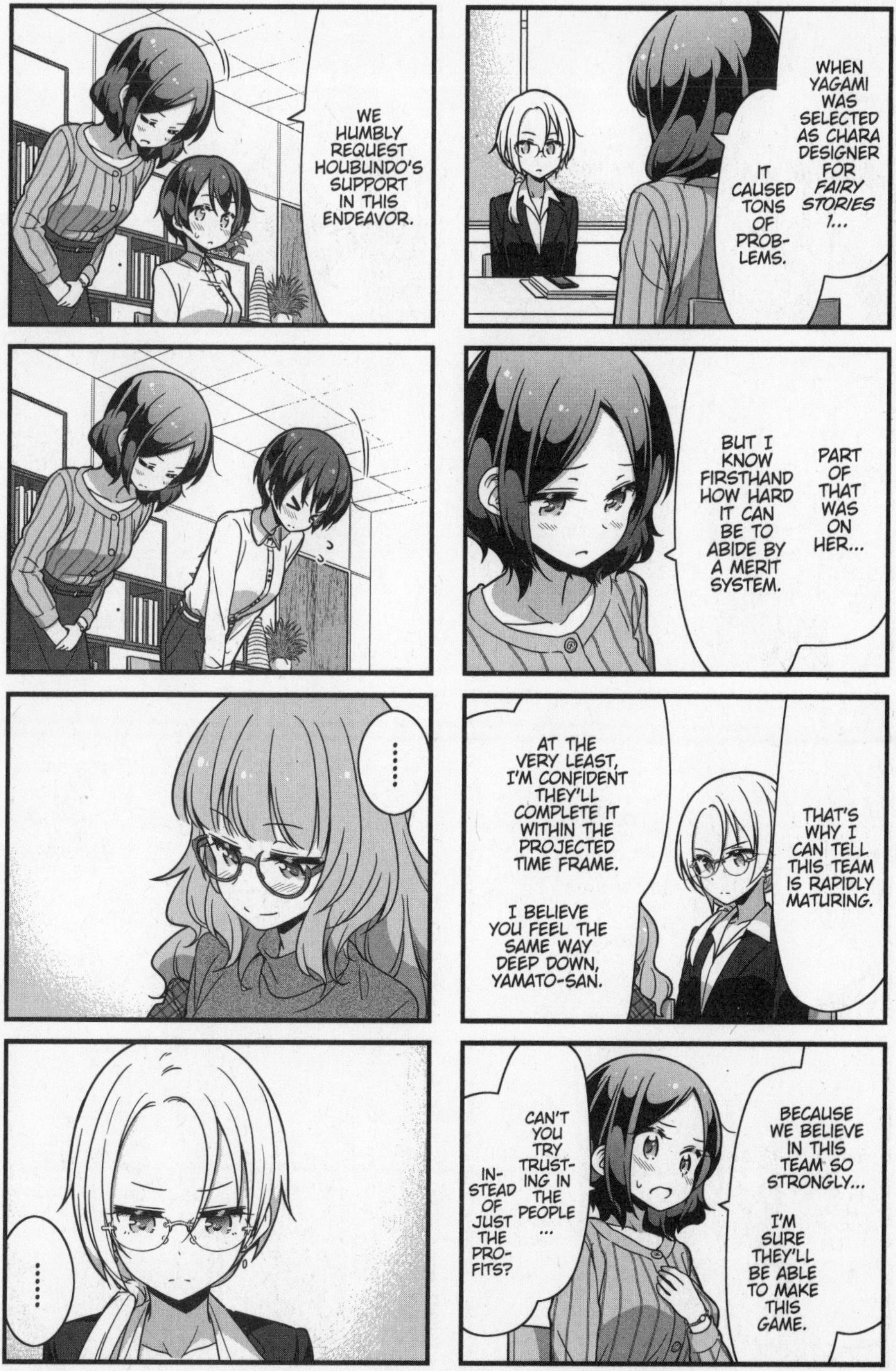
WHEN YAGAMI WAS SELECTED AS CHARA DESIGNER FOR *FAIRY STORIES 1*...
IT CAUSED TONS OF PROB-LEMS.
WE HUMBLY REQUEST HOUBUNDO'S SUPPORT IN THIS ENDEAVOR.
PART OF THAT WAS ON HER...
BUT I KNOW FIRSTHAND HOW HARD IT CAN BE TO ABIDE BY A MERIT SYSTEM.
THAT'S WHY I CAN TELL THIS TEAM IS RAPIDLY MATURING.
AT THE VERY LEAST, I'M CONFIDENT THEY'LL COMPLETE IT WITHIN THE PROJECTED TIME FRAME.
I BELIEVE YOU FEEL THE SAME WAY DEEP DOWN, YAMATO-SAN.
......
BECAUSE WE BELIEVE IN THIS TEAM SO STRONGLY...
I'M SURE THEY'LL BE ABLE TO MAKE THIS GAME.
CAN'T YOU TRY TRUSTING IN THE PEOPLE...
IN-STEAD OF JUST THE PRO-FITS?
......

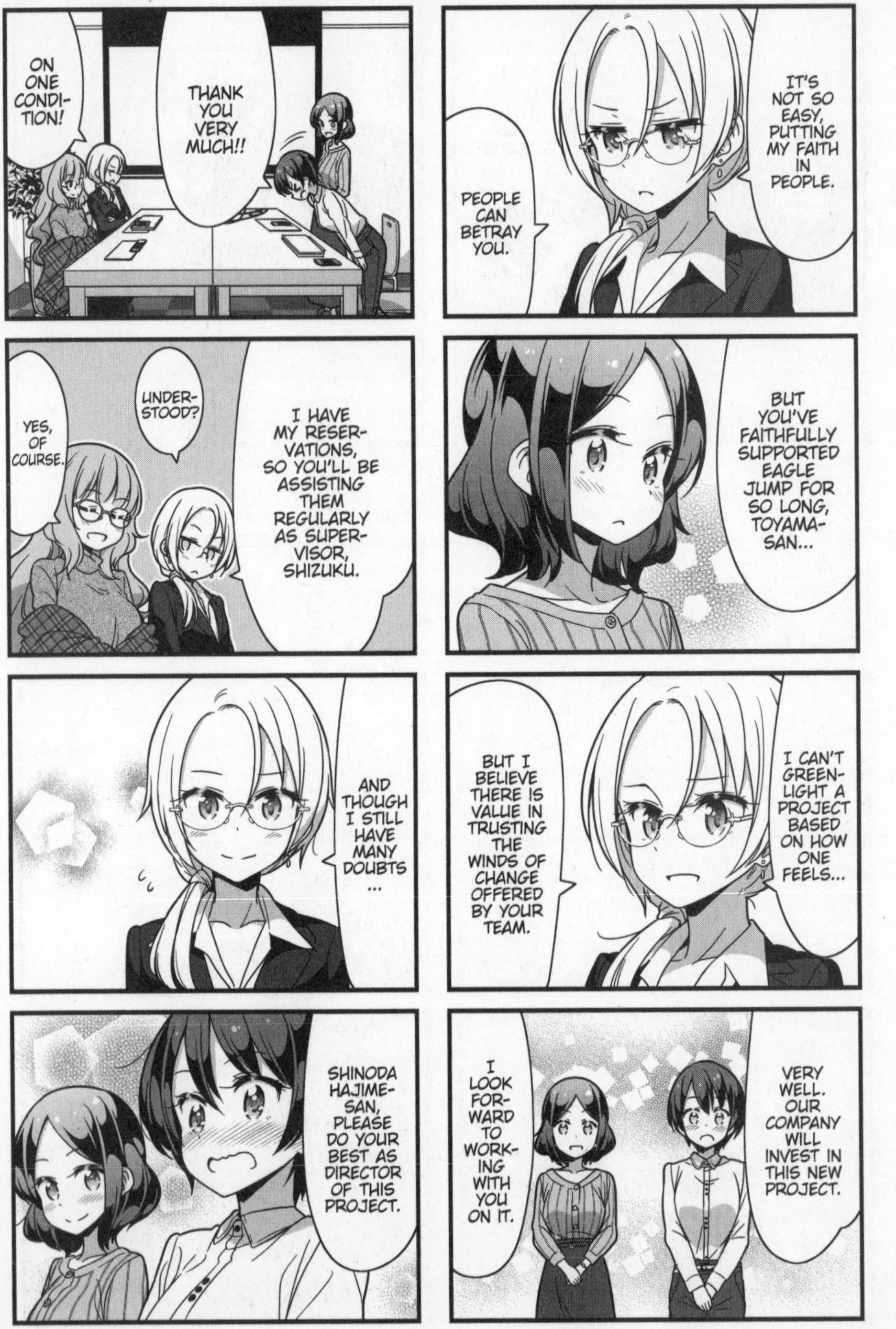
IT'S NOT SO EASY, PUTTING MY FAITH IN PEOPLE.
PEOPLE CAN BETRAY YOU.
THANK YOU VERY MUCH!!
ON ONE CONDITION!
BUT YOU'VE FAITHFULLY SUPPORTED EAGLE JUMP FOR SO LONG, TOYAMA-SAN...
I HAVE MY RESERVATIONS, SO YOU'LL BE ASSISTING THEM REGULARLY AS SUPERVISOR, SHIZUKU.
UNDERSTOOD?
YES, OF COURSE.
I CAN'T GREENLIGHT A PROJECT BASED ON HOW ONE FEELS...
BUT I BELIEVE THERE IS VALUE IN TRUSTING THE WINDS OF CHANGE OFFERED BY YOUR TEAM.
AND THOUGH I STILL HAVE MANY DOUBTS...
VERY WELL. OUR COMPANY WILL INVEST IN THIS NEW PROJECT.
I LOOK FORWARD TO WORKING WITH YOU ON IT.
SHINODA HAJIME-SAN, PLEASE DO YOUR BEST AS DIRECTOR OF THIS PROJECT.

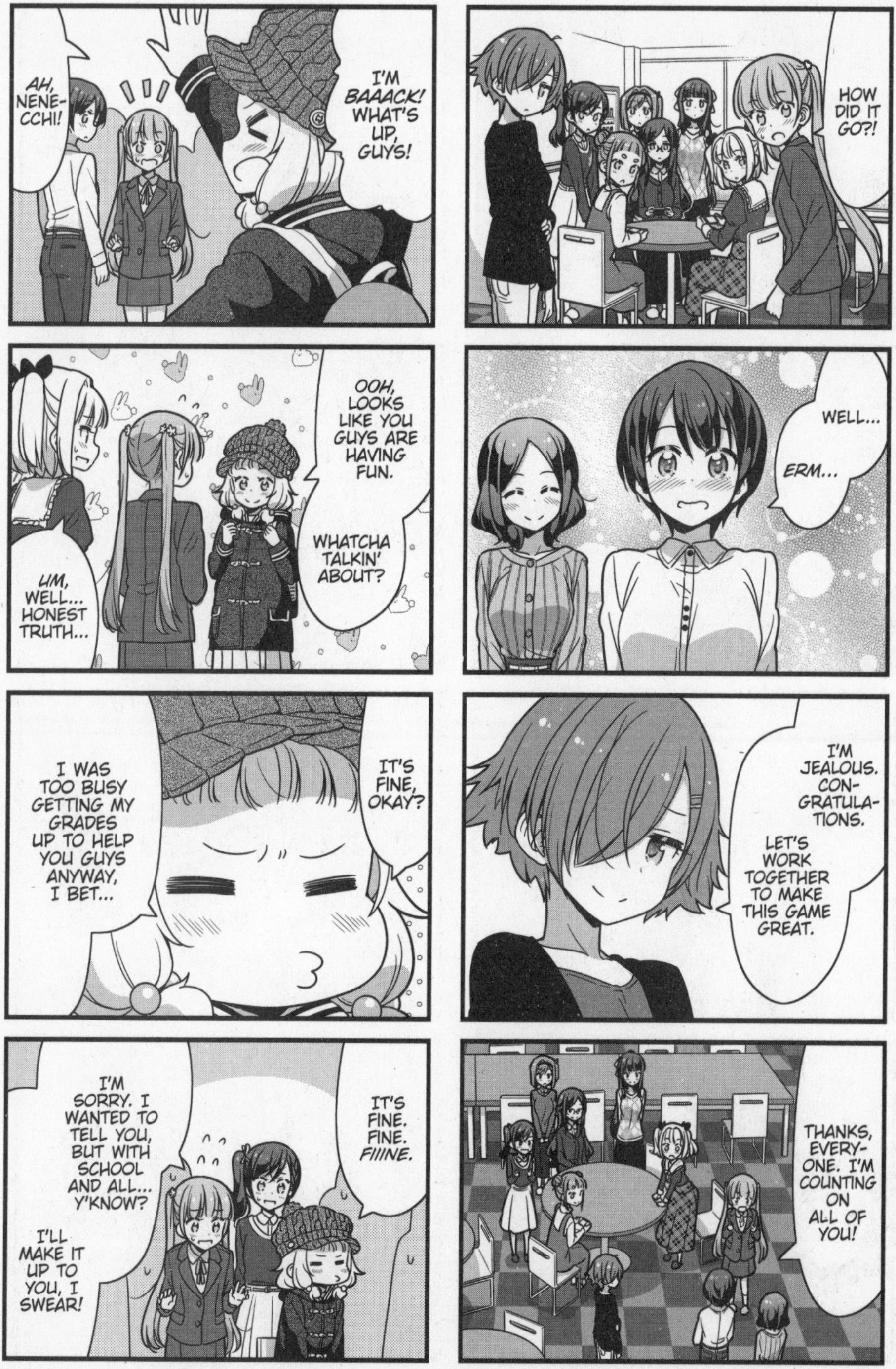
HOW DID IT GO?!
I'M BAAACK! WHAT'S UP, GUYS!
AH, NENE-CCHI!
WELL... ERM...
OOH, LOOKS LIKE YOU GUYS ARE HAVING FUN.
WHATCHA TALKIN' ABOUT?
UM, WELL... HONEST TRUTH...
I'M JEALOUS. CON-GRATULA-TIONS.
LET'S WORK TOGETHER TO MAKE THIS GAME GREAT.
IT'S FINE, OKAY?
I WAS TOO BUSY GETTING MY GRADES UP TO HELP YOU GUYS ANYWAY, I BET...
THANKS, EVERY-ONE. I'M COUNTING ON ALL OF YOU!
IT'S FINE. FINE. FIIINE.
I'M SORRY. I WANTED TO TELL YOU, BUT WITH SCHOOL AND ALL... Y'KNOW?
I'LL MAKE IT UP TO YOU, I SWEAR!

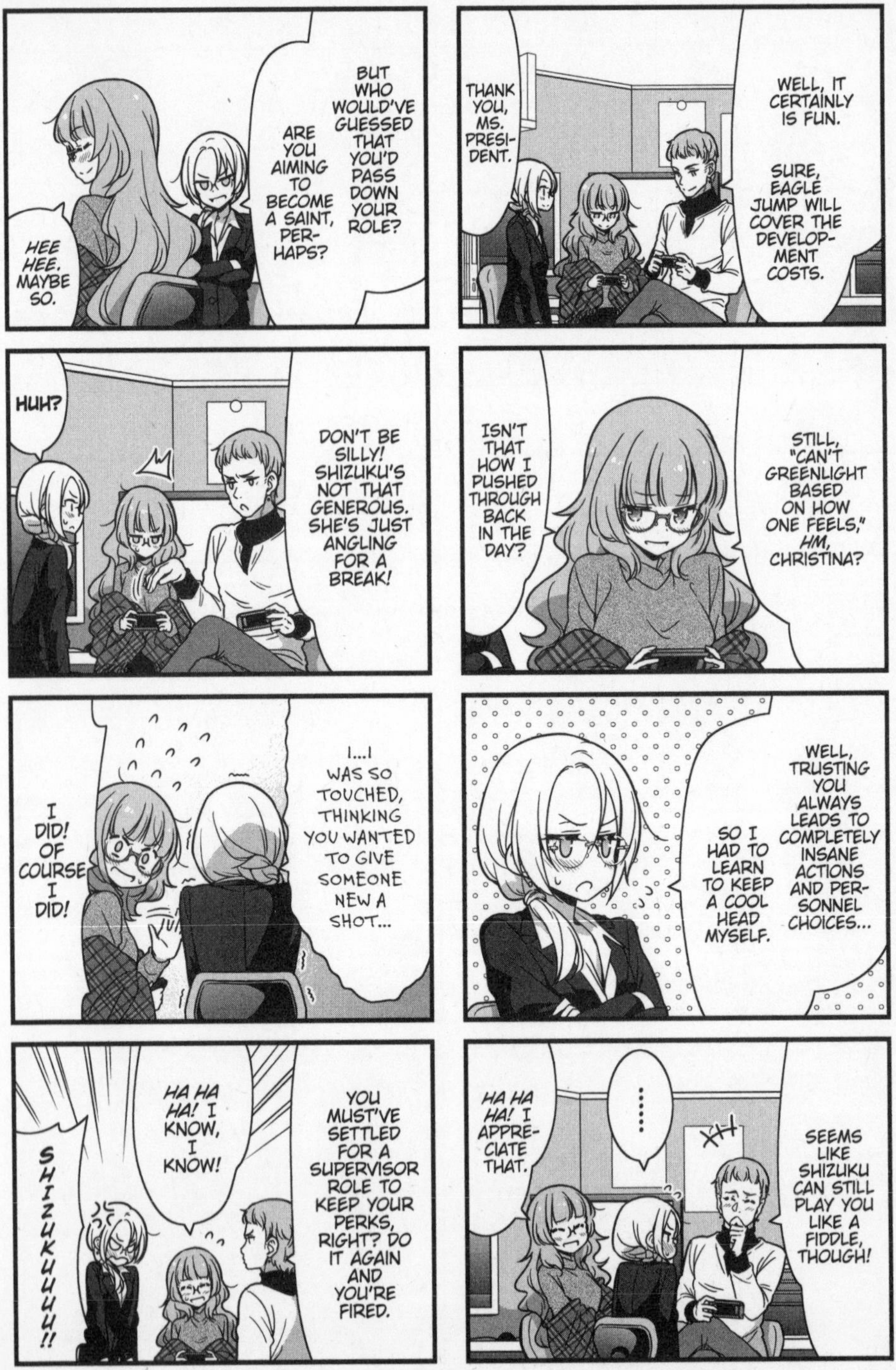
WELL, IT CERTAINLY IS FUN.
SURE, EAGLE JUMP WILL COVER THE DEVELOPMENT COSTS.
THANK YOU, MS. PRESIDENT.
STILL, "CAN'T GREENLIGHT BASED ON HOW ONE FEELS," *HM*, CHRISTINA?
ISN'T THAT HOW I PUSHED THROUGH BACK IN THE DAY?
WELL, TRUSTING YOU ALWAYS LEADS TO COMPLETELY INSANE ACTIONS AND PERSONNEL CHOICES...
SO I HAD TO LEARN TO KEEP A COOL HEAD MYSELF.
SEEMS LIKE SHIZUKU CAN STILL PLAY YOU LIKE A FIDDLE, THOUGH!
*HA HA HA!* I APPRECIATE THAT.
......
BUT WHO WOULD'VE GUESSED THAT YOU'D PASS DOWN YOUR ROLE?
ARE YOU AIMING TO BECOME A SAINT, PERHAPS?
*HEE HEE.* MAYBE SO.
DON'T BE SILLY! SHIZUKU'S NOT THAT GENEROUS. SHE'S JUST ANGLING FOR A BREAK!
HUH?
I...I WAS SO TOUCHED, THINKING YOU WANTED TO GIVE SOMEONE NEW A SHOT...
I DID! OF COURSE I DID!
YOU MUST'VE SETTLED FOR A SUPERVISOR ROLE TO KEEP YOUR PERKS, RIGHT? DO IT AGAIN AND YOU'RE FIRED.
*HA HA HA!* I KNOW, I KNOW!
SHIZUKUUUUU!!

NEW GAME!

NEW GAME!

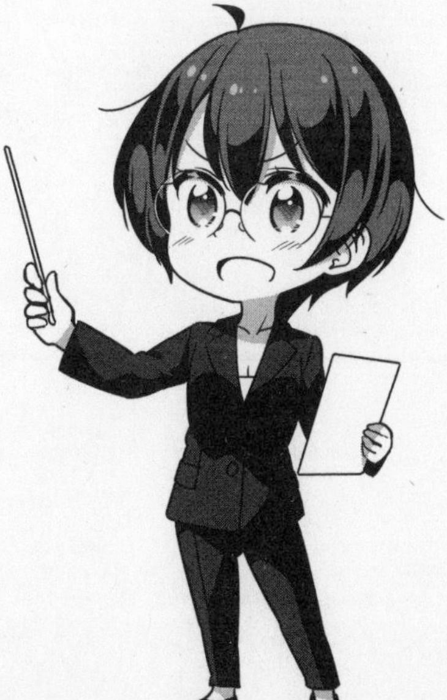

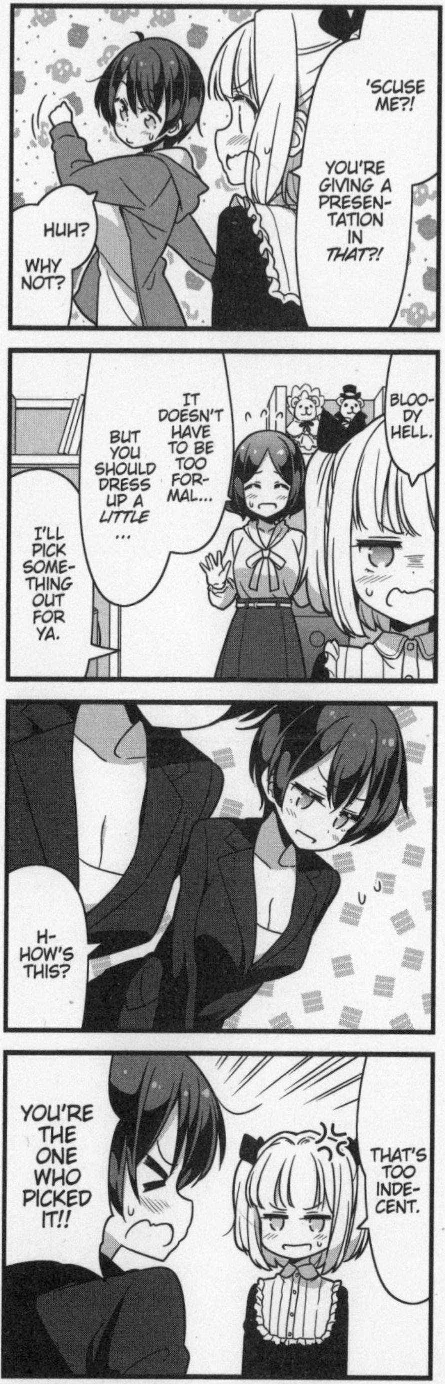
'SCUSE ME?!
YOU'RE GIVING A PRESENTATION IN *THAT*?!
HUH?
WHY NOT?
BLOODY HELL.
IT DOESN'T HAVE TO BE TOO FORMAL...
BUT YOU SHOULD DRESS UP A *LITTLE* ...
I'LL PICK SOMETHING OUT FOR YA.
H-HOW'S THIS?
THAT'S TOO INDECENT.
YOU'RE THE ONE WHO PICKED IT!!

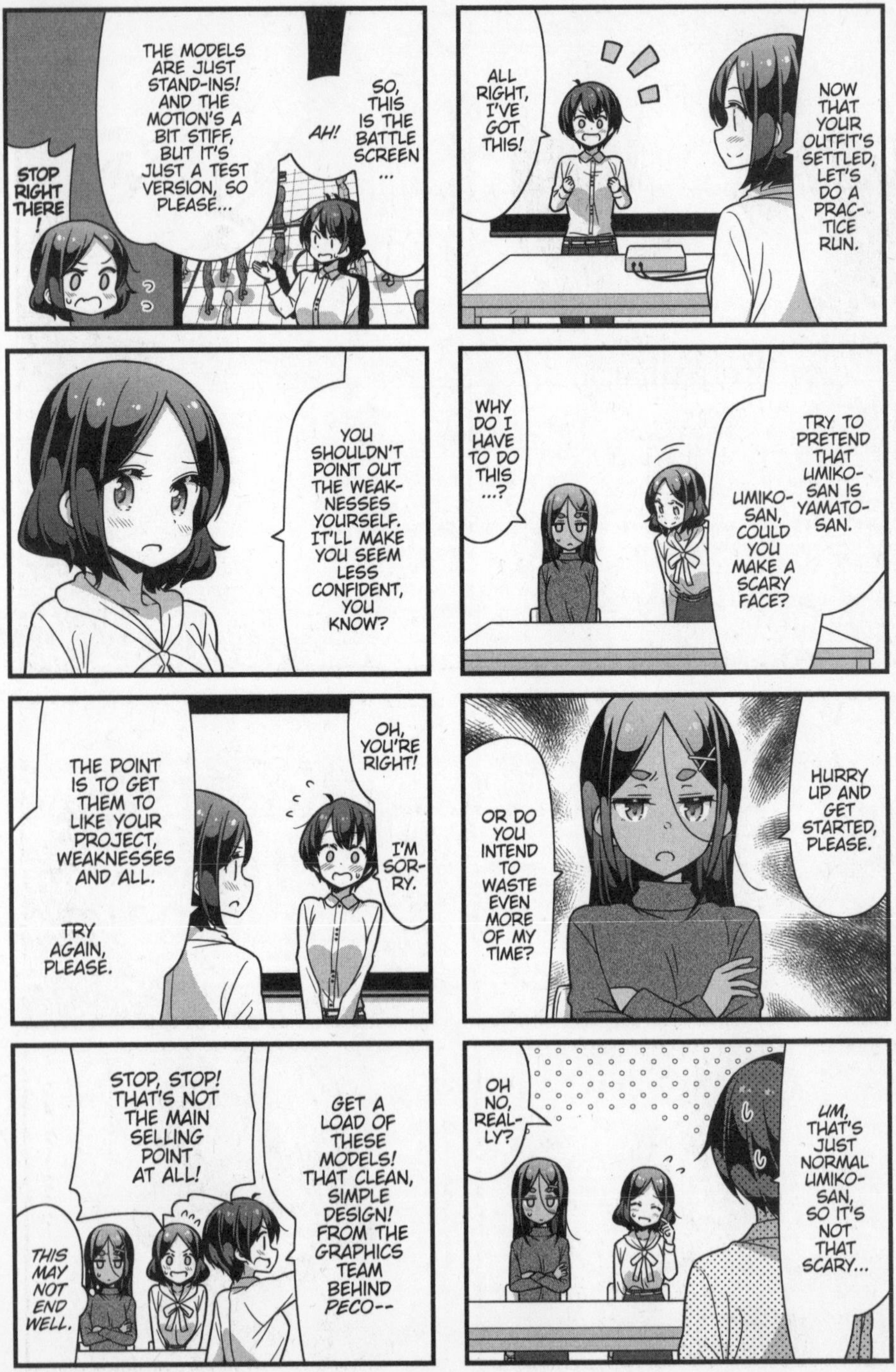
NOW THAT YOUR OUTFIT'S SETTLED, LET'S DO A PRACTICE RUN.
ALL RIGHT, I'VE GOT THIS!
SO, THIS IS THE BATTLE SCREEN...
AH!
THE MODELS ARE JUST STAND-INS! AND THE MOTION'S A BIT STIFF, BUT IT'S JUST A TEST VERSION, SO PLEASE...
STOP RIGHT THERE!
TRY TO PRETEND THAT UMIKO-SAN IS YAMATO-SAN.
UMIKO-SAN, COULD YOU MAKE A SCARY FACE?
WHY DO I HAVE TO DO THIS...?
YOU SHOULDN'T POINT OUT THE WEAKNESSES YOURSELF. IT'LL MAKE YOU SEEM LESS CONFIDENT, YOU KNOW?
HURRY UP AND GET STARTED, PLEASE.
OR DO YOU INTEND TO WASTE EVEN MORE OF MY TIME?
OH, YOU'RE RIGHT!
I'M SORRY.
THE POINT IS TO GET THEM TO LIKE YOUR PROJECT, WEAKNESSES AND ALL.
TRY AGAIN, PLEASE.
UM, THAT'S JUST NORMAL UMIKO-SAN, SO IT'S NOT THAT SCARY...
OH NO, REALLY?
GET A LOAD OF THESE MODELS! THAT CLEAN, SIMPLE DESIGN! FROM THE GRAPHICS TEAM BEHIND PECO--
STOP, STOP! THAT'S NOT THE MAIN SELLING POINT AT ALL!
THIS MAY NOT END WELL.

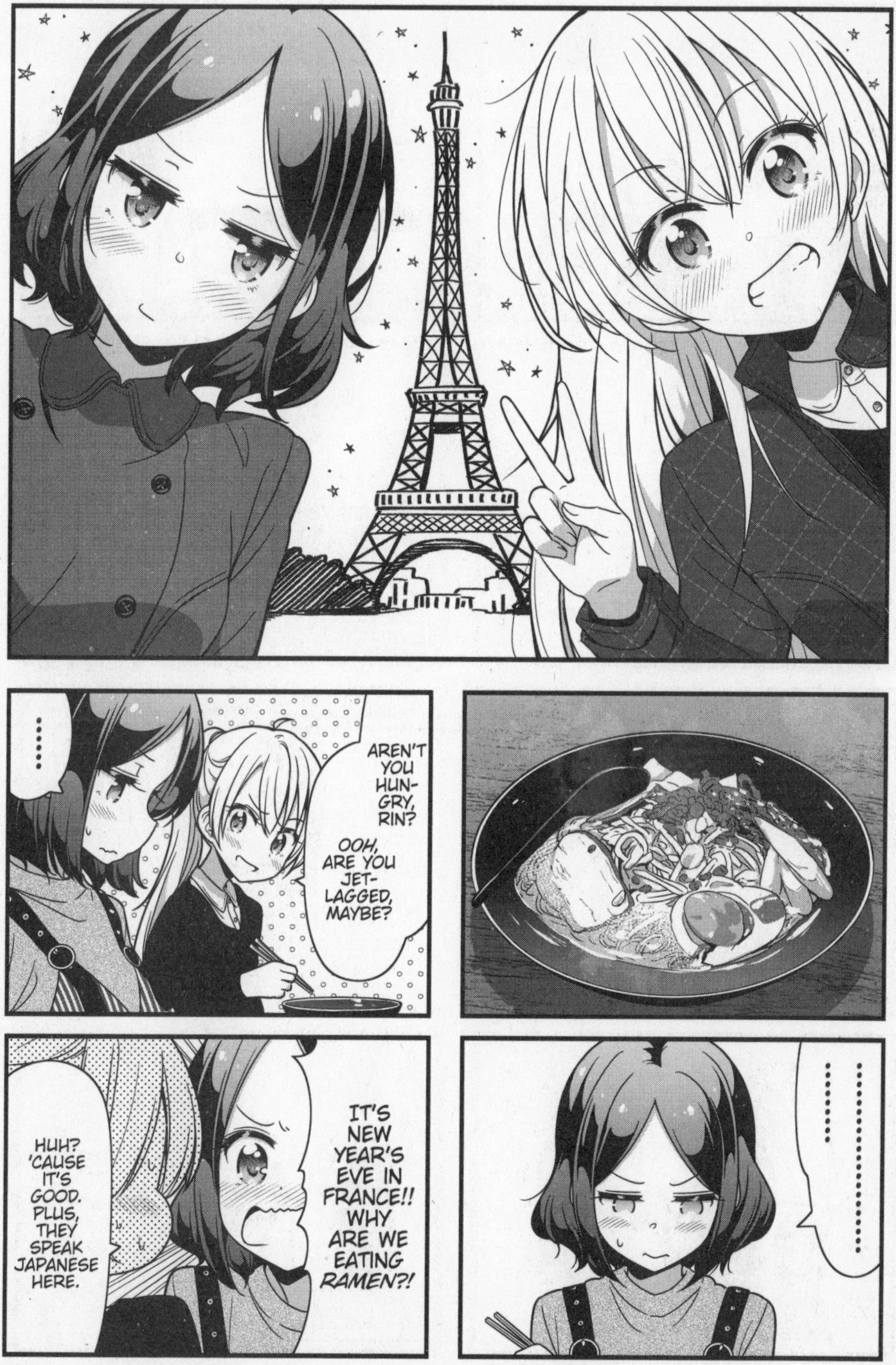
AREN'T YOU HUN-GRY, RIN?
OOH, ARE YOU JET-LAGGED, MAYBE?
......
..........
IT'S NEW YEAR'S EVE IN FRANCE!! WHY ARE WE EATING *RAMEN*?!
HUH? 'CAUSE IT'S GOOD. PLUS, THEY SPEAK JAPANESE HERE.

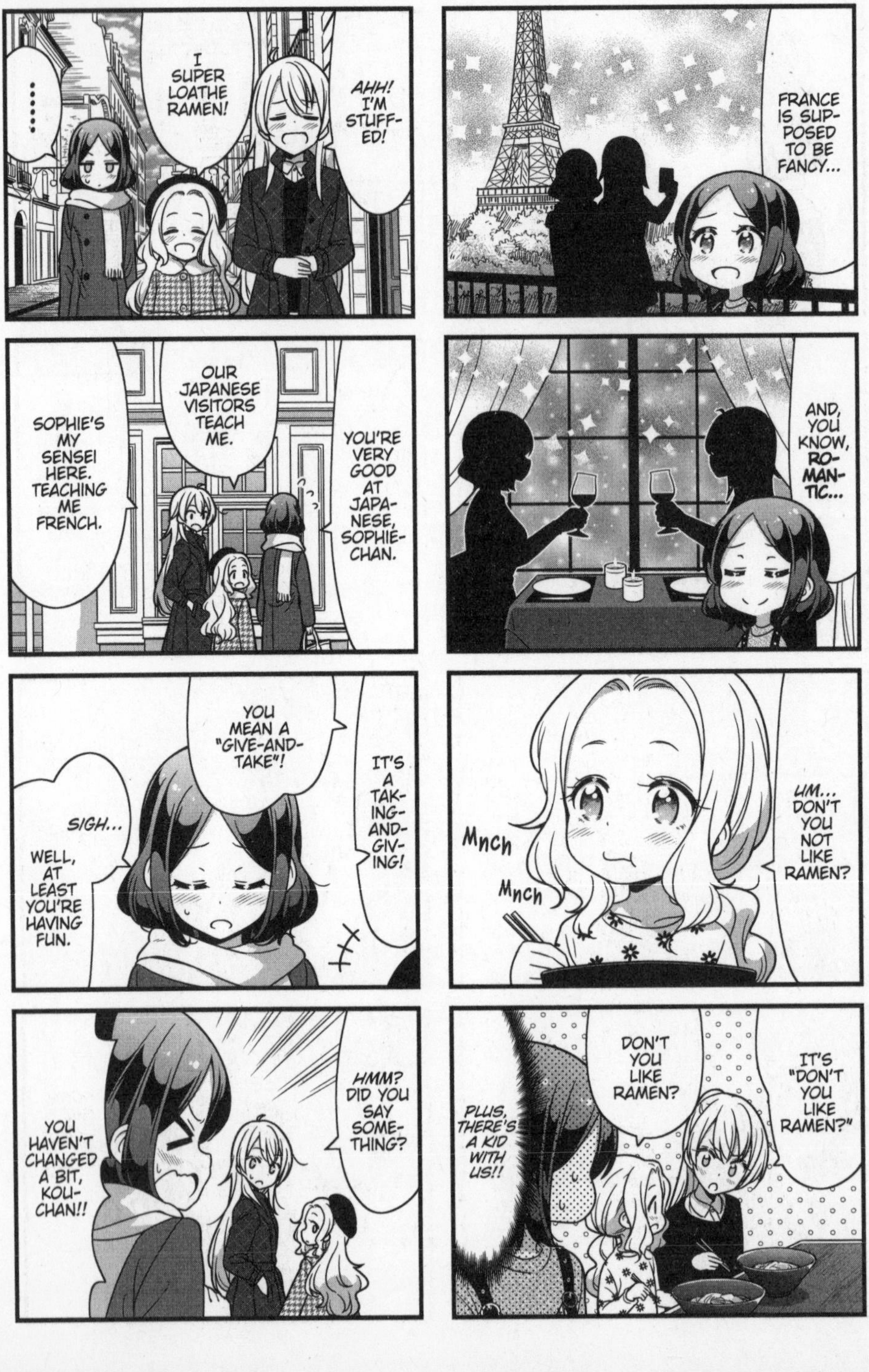
FRANCE IS SUP-POSED TO BE FANCY...
AHH! I'M STUFF-ED!
I SUPER LOATHE RAMEN!
......
AND, YOU KNOW, RO-MAN-TIC...
YOU'RE VERY GOOD AT JAPA-NESE, SOPHIE-CHAN.
OUR JAPANESE VISITORS TEACH ME.
SOPHIE'S MY SENSEI HERE. TEACHING ME FRENCH.
UM... DON'T YOU NOT LIKE RAMEN?
Mnch
Mnch
IT'S A TAKING-AND-GIV-ING!
YOU MEAN A "GIVE-AND-TAKE"!
SIGH...
WELL, AT LEAST YOU'RE HAVING FUN.
IT'S "DON'T YOU LIKE RAMEN?"
DON'T YOU LIKE RAMEN?
PLUS, THERE'S A KID WITH US!!
HMM? DID YOU SAY SOME-THING?
YOU HAVEN'T CHANGED A BIT, KOU-CHAN!!

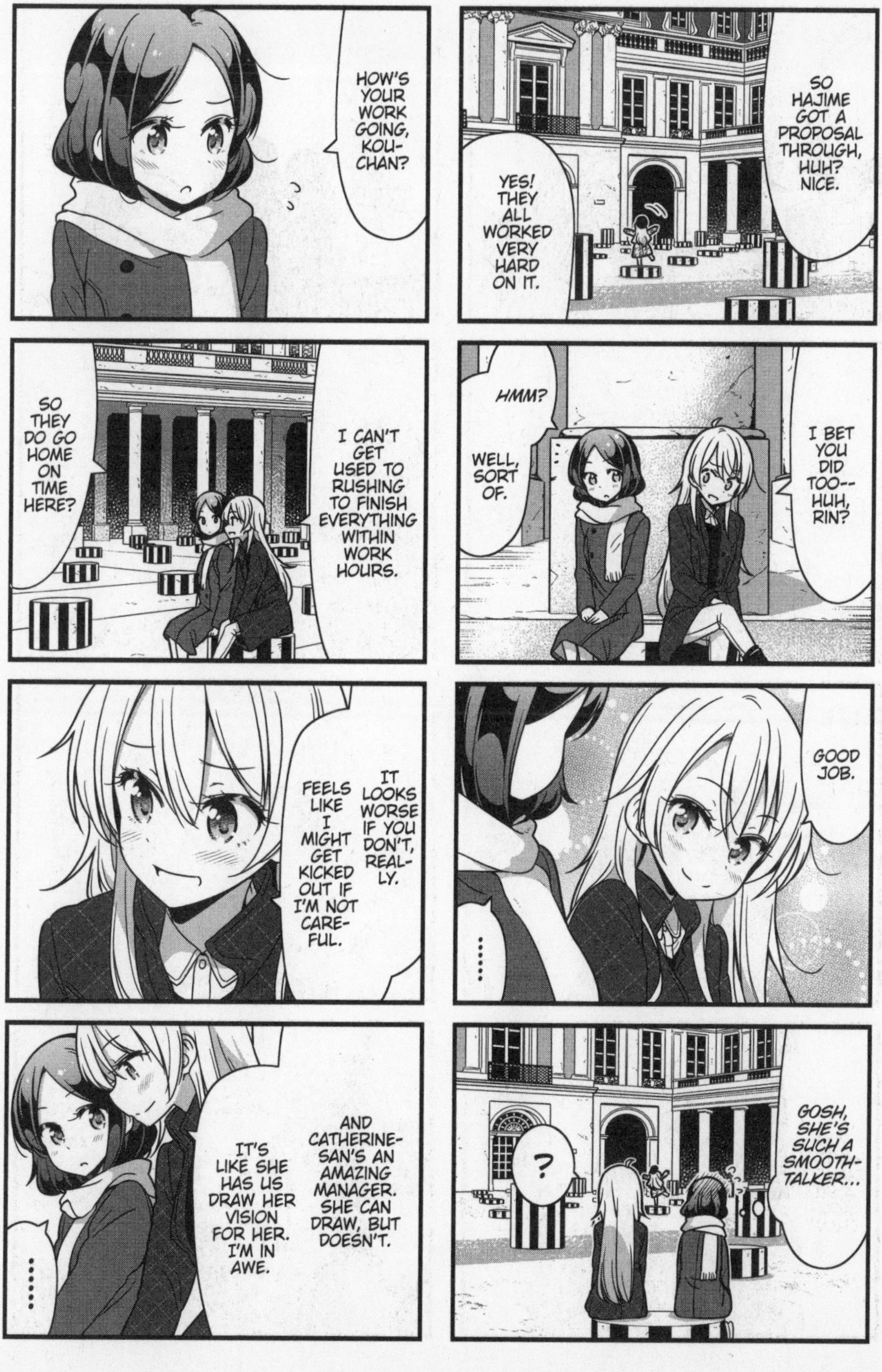
SO HAJIME GOT A PROPOSAL THROUGH, HUH? NICE.
YES! THEY ALL WORKED VERY HARD ON IT.
HOW'S YOUR WORK GOING, KOU-CHAN?
I BET YOU DID TOO--HUH, RIN?
HMM?
WELL, SORT OF.
I CAN'T GET USED TO RUSHING TO FINISH EVERYTHING WITHIN WORK HOURS.
SO THEY DO GO HOME ON TIME HERE?
GOOD JOB.
......
IT LOOKS WORSE IF YOU DON'T, REALLY.
FEELS LIKE I MIGHT GET KICKED OUT IF I'M NOT CAREFUL.
GOSH, SHE'S SUCH A SMOOTH-TALKER...
?
AND CATHERINE-SAN'S AN AMAZING MANAGER. SHE CAN DRAW, BUT DOESN'T.
IT'S LIKE SHE HAS US DRAW HER VISION FOR HER. I'M IN AWE.
......

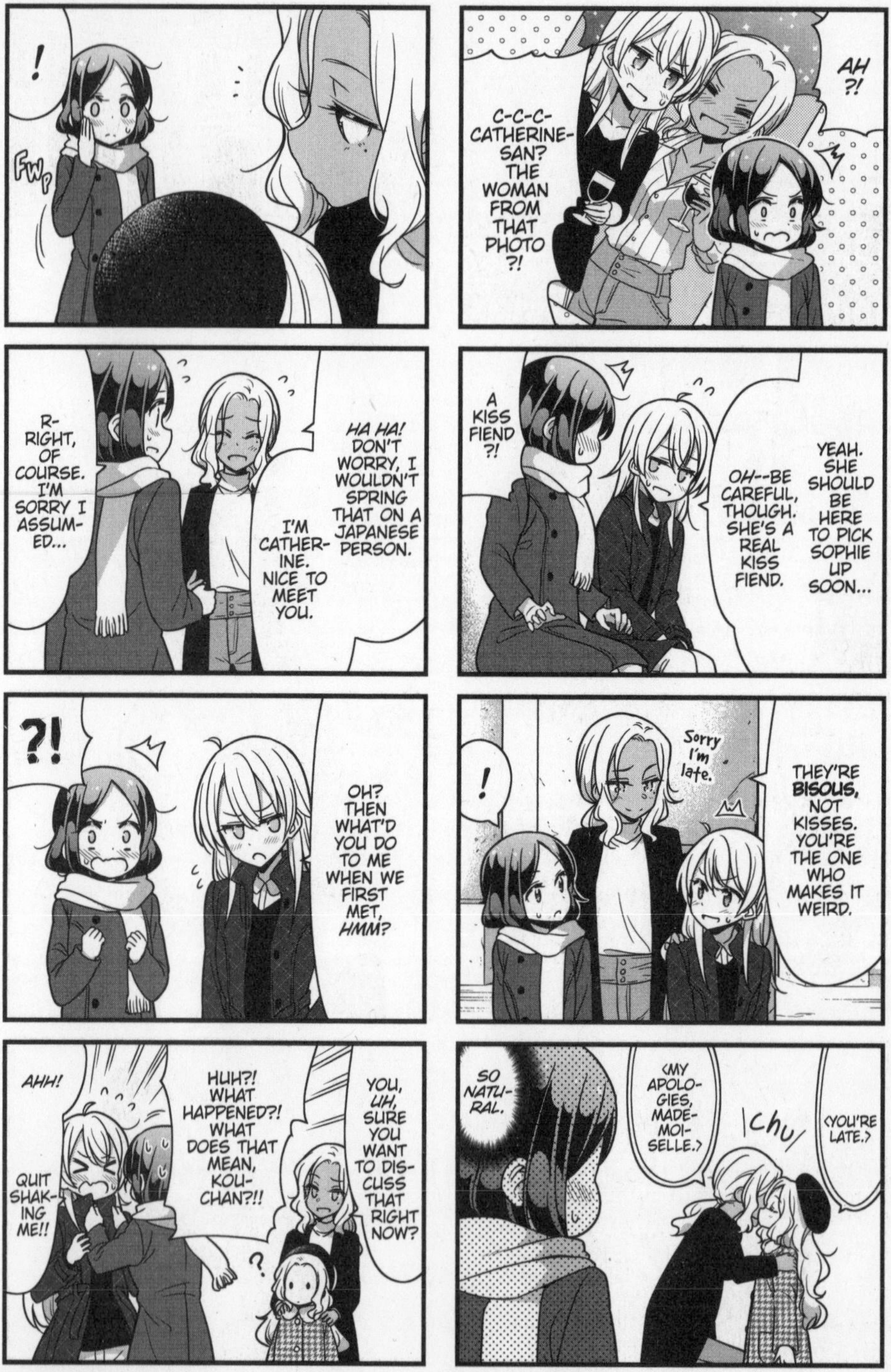
AH?!
C-C-C-CATHERINE-SAN? THE WOMAN FROM THAT PHOTO?!
YEAH. SHE SHOULD BE HERE TO PICK SOPHIE UP SOON...
OH--BE CAREFUL, THOUGH. SHE'S A REAL KISS FIEND.
A KISS FIEND?!
THEY'RE BISOUS, NOT KISSES. YOU'RE THE ONE WHO MAKES IT WEIRD.
Sorry I'm late.
!
<YOU'RE LATE.>
CHU
<MY APOLOGIES, MADEMOISELLE.>
SO NATURAL.
!
FWP
HA HA! DON'T WORRY, I WOULDN'T SPRING THAT ON A JAPANESE PERSON.
I'M CATHERINE. NICE TO MEET YOU.
R-RIGHT, OF COURSE. I'M SORRY I ASSUMED...
OH? THEN WHAT'D YOU DO TO ME WHEN WE FIRST MET, HMM?
?!
YOU, UH, SURE YOU WANT TO DISCUSS THAT RIGHT NOW?
HUH?! WHAT HAPPENED?! WHAT DOES THAT MEAN, KOU-CHAN?!!
AHH!
QUIT SHAKING ME!!
?

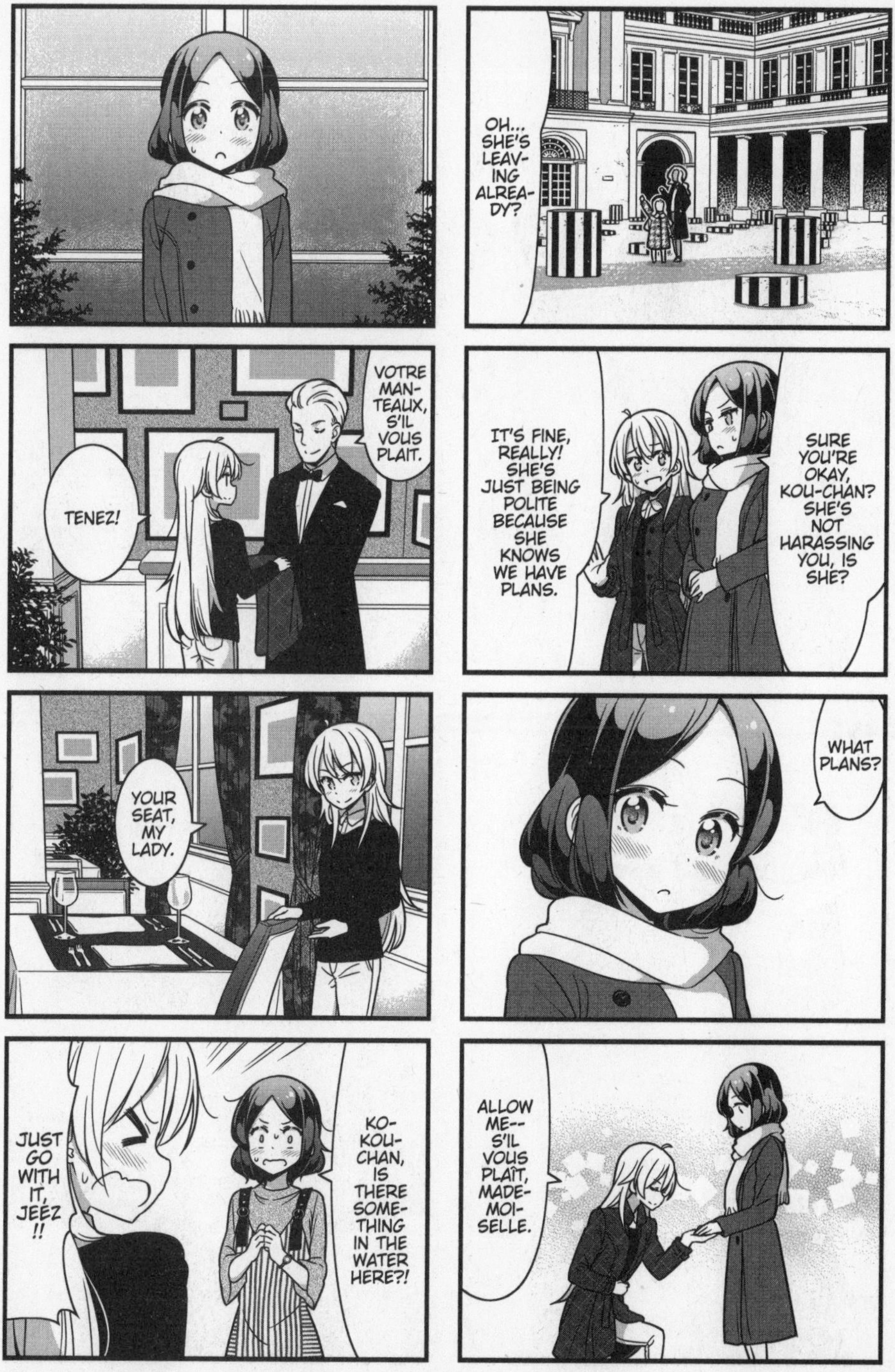
OH... SHE'S LEAVING ALREADY?
SURE YOU'RE OKAY, KOU-CHAN? SHE'S NOT HARASSING YOU, IS SHE?
IT'S FINE, REALLY! SHE'S JUST BEING POLITE BECAUSE SHE KNOWS WE HAVE PLANS.
VOTRE MANTEAUX, S'IL VOUS PLAIT.
TENEZ!
WHAT PLANS?
YOUR SEAT, MY LADY.
ALLOW ME-- S'IL VOUS PLAÎT, MADEMOISELLE.
KO-KOU-CHAN, IS THERE SOMETHING IN THE WATER HERE?!
JUST GO WITH IT, JEEZ!!

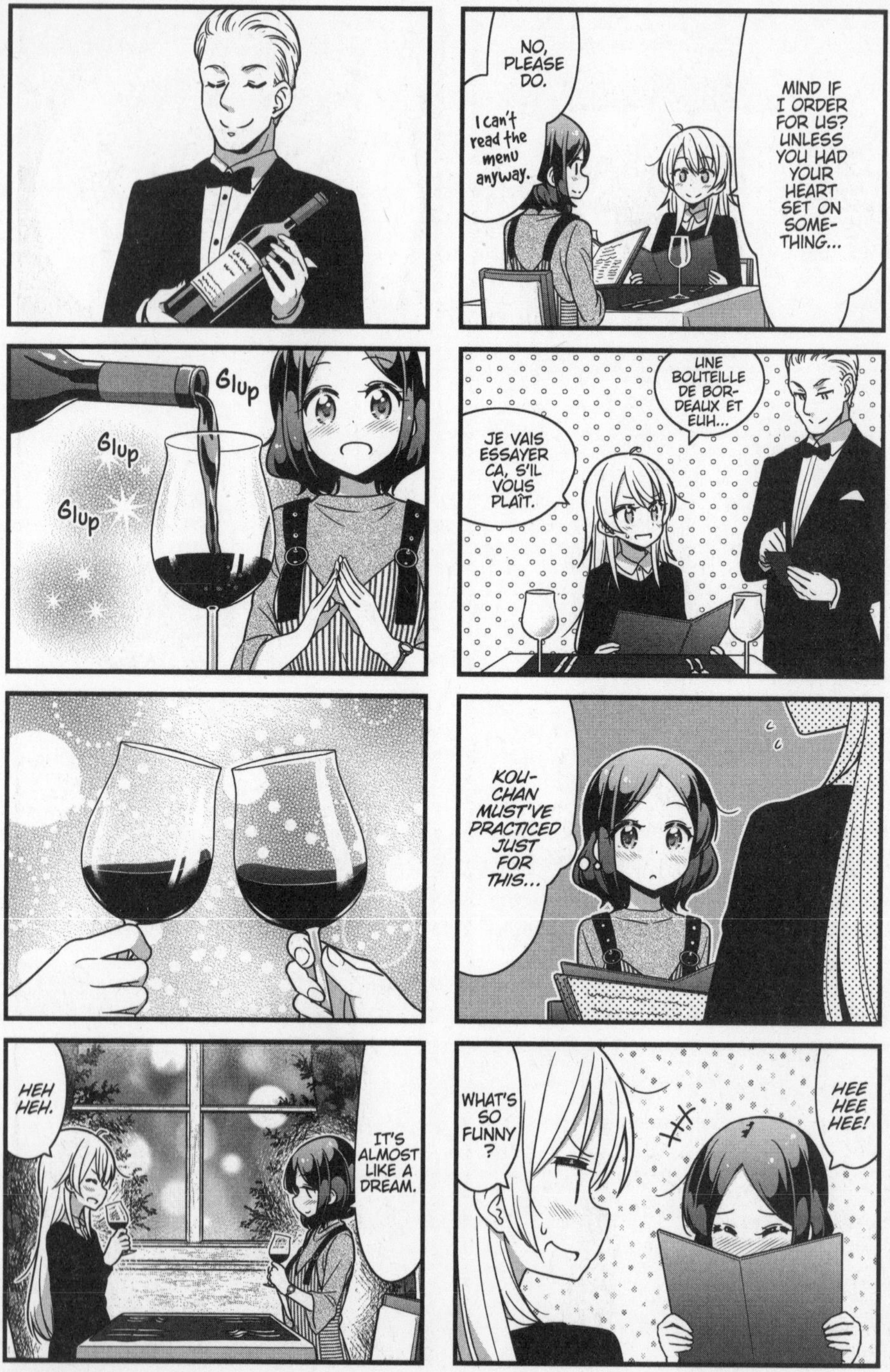
MIND IF I ORDER FOR US? UNLESS YOU HAD YOUR HEART SET ON SOMETHING...
NO, PLEASE DO.
I can't read the menu anyway.
UNE BOUTEILLE DE BORDEAUX ET EUH...
JE VAIS ESSAYER CA, S'IL VOUS PLAÎT.
Glup
Glup
Glup
KOU-CHAN MUST'VE PRACTICED JUST FOR THIS...
HEE HEE HEE!
WHAT'S SO FUNNY?
IT'S ALMOST LIKE A DREAM.
HEH HEH.

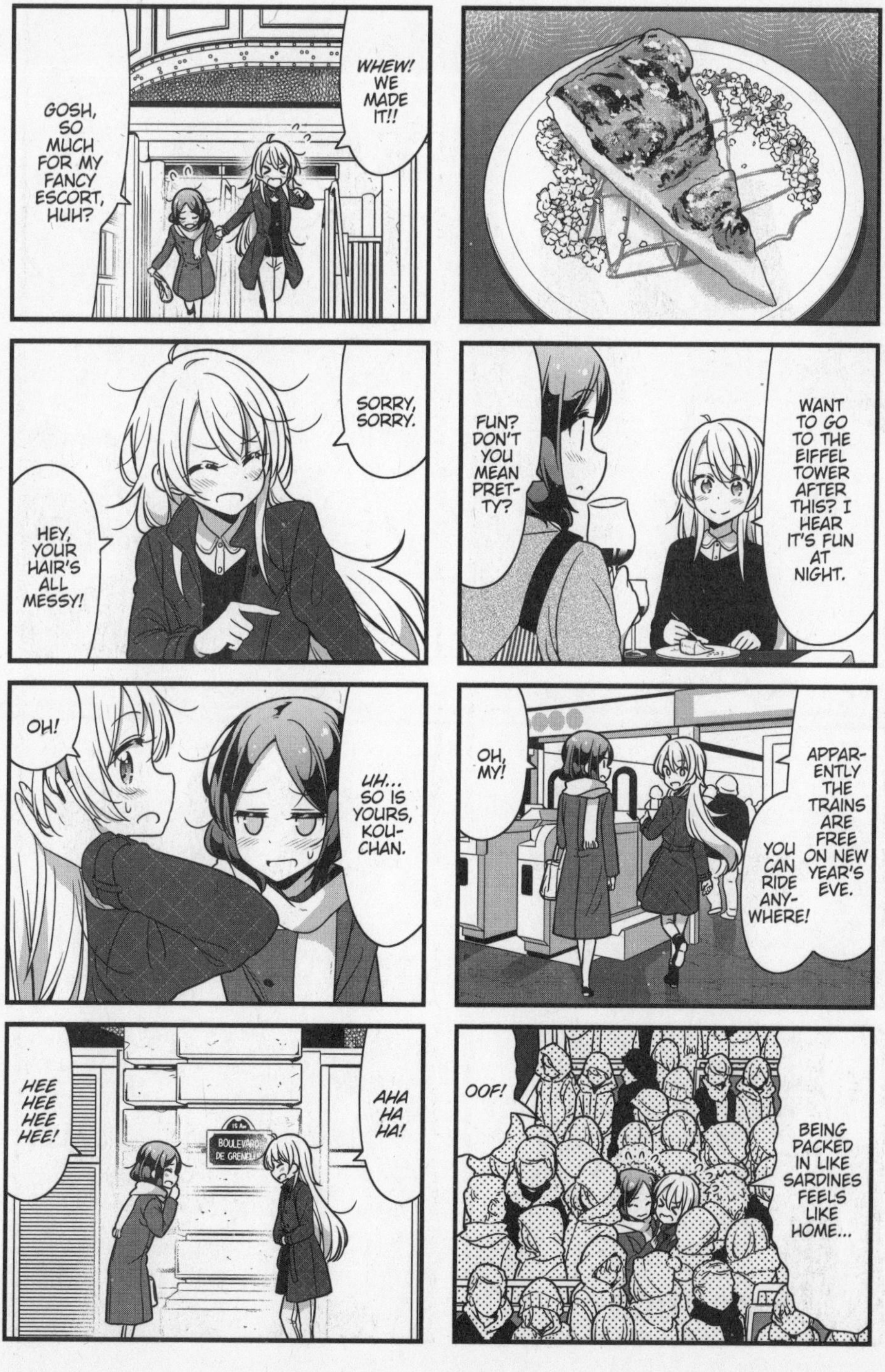
WHEW! WE MADE IT!!
GOSH, SO MUCH FOR MY FANCY ESCORT, HUH?
WANT TO GO TO THE EIFFEL TOWER AFTER THIS? I HEAR IT'S FUN AT NIGHT.
FUN? DON'T YOU MEAN PRETTY?
SORRY, SORRY.
HEY, YOUR HAIR'S ALL MESSY!
APPARENTLY THE TRAINS ARE FREE ON NEW YEAR'S EVE.
YOU CAN RIDE ANYWHERE!
OH, MY!
UH... SO IS YOURS, KOU-CHAN.
OH!
BEING PACKED IN LIKE SARDINES FEELS LIKE HOME...
OOF!
AHA HA HA!
HEE HEE HEE HEE!
BOULEVARD DE GRENEL

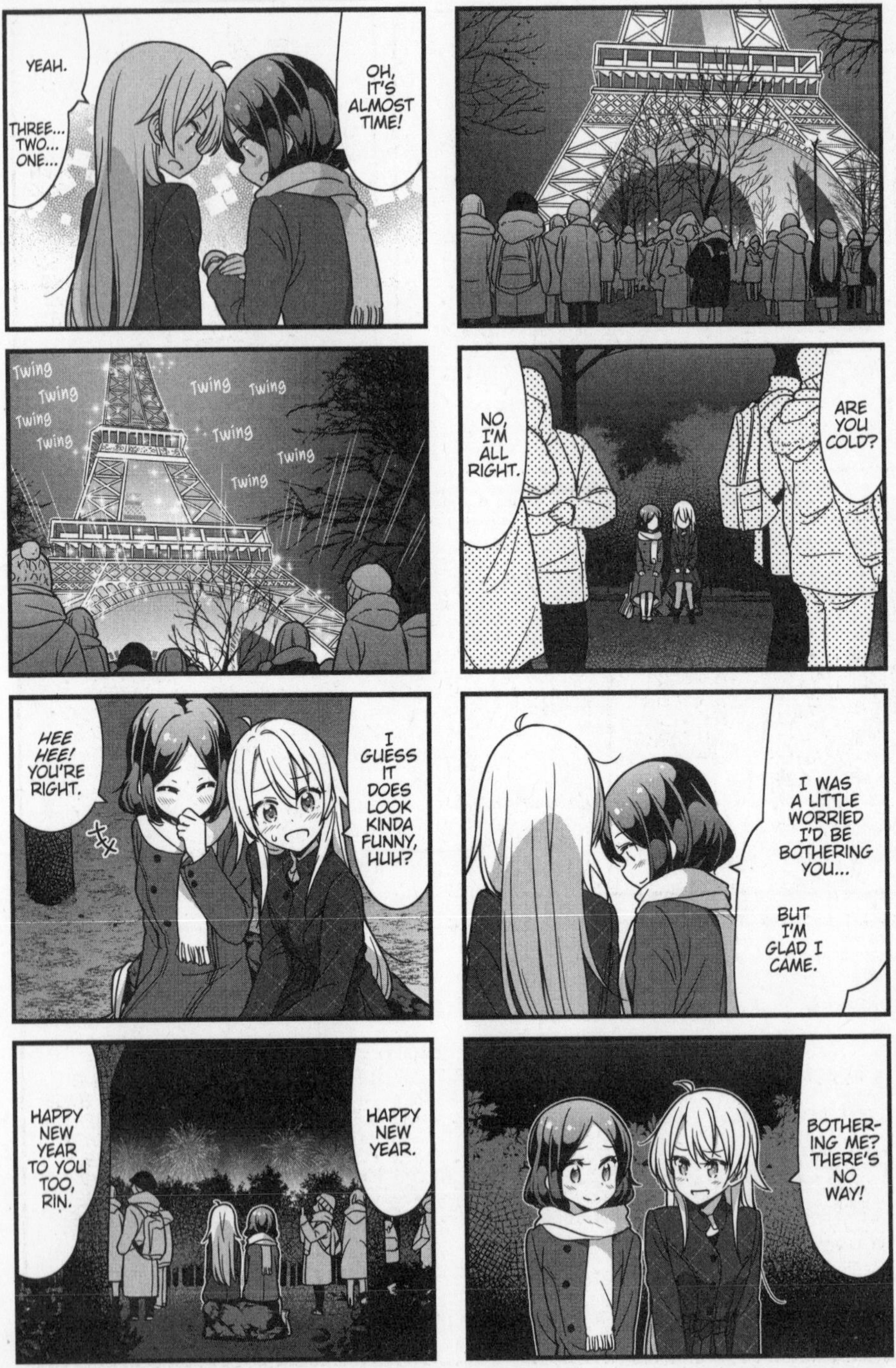
OH, IT'S ALMOST TIME!
YEAH.
THREE... TWO... ONE...
ARE YOU COLD?
NO, I'M ALL RIGHT.
Twing Twing Twing Twing Twing Twing Twing Twing
I WAS A LITTLE WORRIED I'D BE BOTHERING YOU...
BUT I'M GLAD I CAME.
I GUESS IT DOES LOOK KINDA FUNNY, HUH?
HEE HEE! YOU'RE RIGHT.
BOTHERING ME? THERE'S NO WAY!
HAPPY NEW YEAR.
HAPPY NEW YEAR TO YOU TOO, RIN.

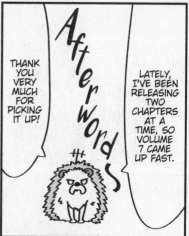

Afterword~
LATELY, I'VE BEEN RELEASING TWO CHAPTERS AT A TIME, SO VOLUME 7 CAME UP FAST.
THANK YOU VERY MUCH FOR PICKING IT UP!
A FEW OF THESE CHAPTERS TAKE PLACE IN FRANCE, SO I WENT THERE FOR REAL FROM AFTER CHRISTMAS 2016 THROUGH TO NEW YEAR'S.
IT WASN'T A DATE, THOUGH--IT WAS A SOLO TRIP. I LIKE TRAVELING ALONE, THAT'S WHY. (KOFF...)
I SKIPPED CHRISTMAS BECAUSE, WHEN I WENT TO EXPERIENCE IT IN GERMANY A FEW YEARS AGO, EVERYONE WENT HOME AT NIGHT, SO IT WAS A PRETTY LONELY HOLIDAY.
All the stores close up on Christmas night...
I GOT THE IMPRESSION THAT IN EUROPE, PEOPLE SPEND CHRISTMAS WITH THEIR FAMILIES AND THAT NEW YEAR'S IS MORE LIKE A FESTIVAL--THE OPPOSITE OF JAPAN, BASICALLY.
Christmas was really festive until night-time, though.
THE RAMEN SHOP, THE CROWDED FREE TRAINS, AND THE SPARKLING EIFFEL TOWER WERE ALL BASED ON MY REAL-LIFE EXPERIENCES, SO I THOUGHT I'D TALK ABOUT MY TRIP A BIT HERE.
Twing
Twing
Twing
It's pretty... kinda?!
BY THE WAY, IF YOU LOOK TOWARD THE ARC DE TRIOMPHE FROM THE BASE OF THE EIFFEL TOWER, YOU CAN BARELY SEE AND HEAR THE FIREWORKS, SO THAT PART'S FICTIONALIZED.
THE EIFFEL TOWER SPARKLES PERIODICALLY LEADING UP TO MIDNIGHT, SO IT MIGHT BE MORE FUN TO GO TO THE ARC DE TRIOMPHE FOR THE COUNTDOWN ITSELF.
WELL, THAT TURNED INTO A TRAVEL REVIEW. ANYWAY--SEASON 2 OF THE ANIME WAS WELL-RECEIVED, SO I'M VERY GRATEFUL!
I HOPE YOU'LL CONTINUE TO SUPPORT *NEW GAME*. SEE YOU IN VOLUME 8!
\BOW/

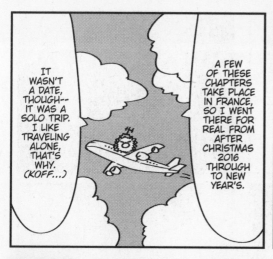

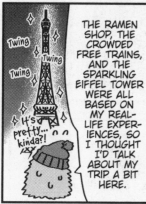

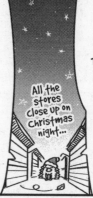

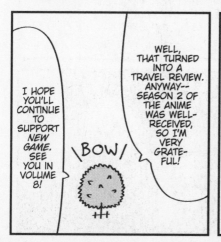

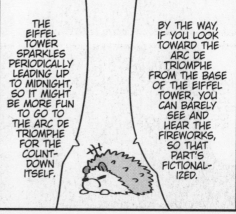

## Buggy Rangers Insect Five (1)

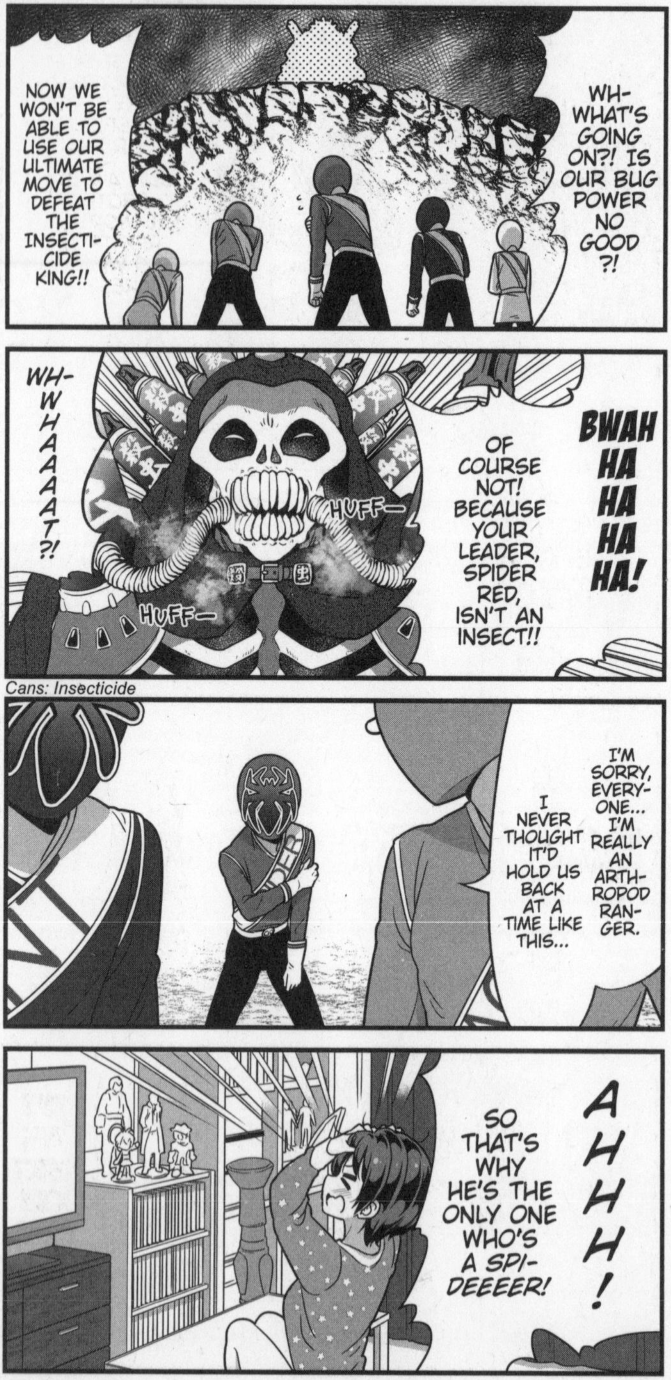
WH-WHAT'S GOING ON?! IS OUR BUG POWER NO GOOD?!
NOW WE WON'T BE ABLE TO USE OUR ULTIMATE MOVE TO DEFEAT THE INSECTICIDE KING!!
BWAH HA HA HA HA HA!
OF COURSE NOT! BECAUSE YOUR LEADER, SPIDER RED, ISN'T AN INSECT!!
HUFF—
HUFF—
WH-WHAAAAAT?!
Cans: Insecticide
I'M SORRY, EVERYONE... I'M REALLY AN ARTHROPOD RANGER.
I NEVER THOUGHT IT'D HOLD US BACK AT A TIME LIKE THIS...
AHHH!
SO THAT'S WHY HE'S THE ONLY ONE WHO'S A SPIDEEEER!

Buggy Rangers Insect Five (2)

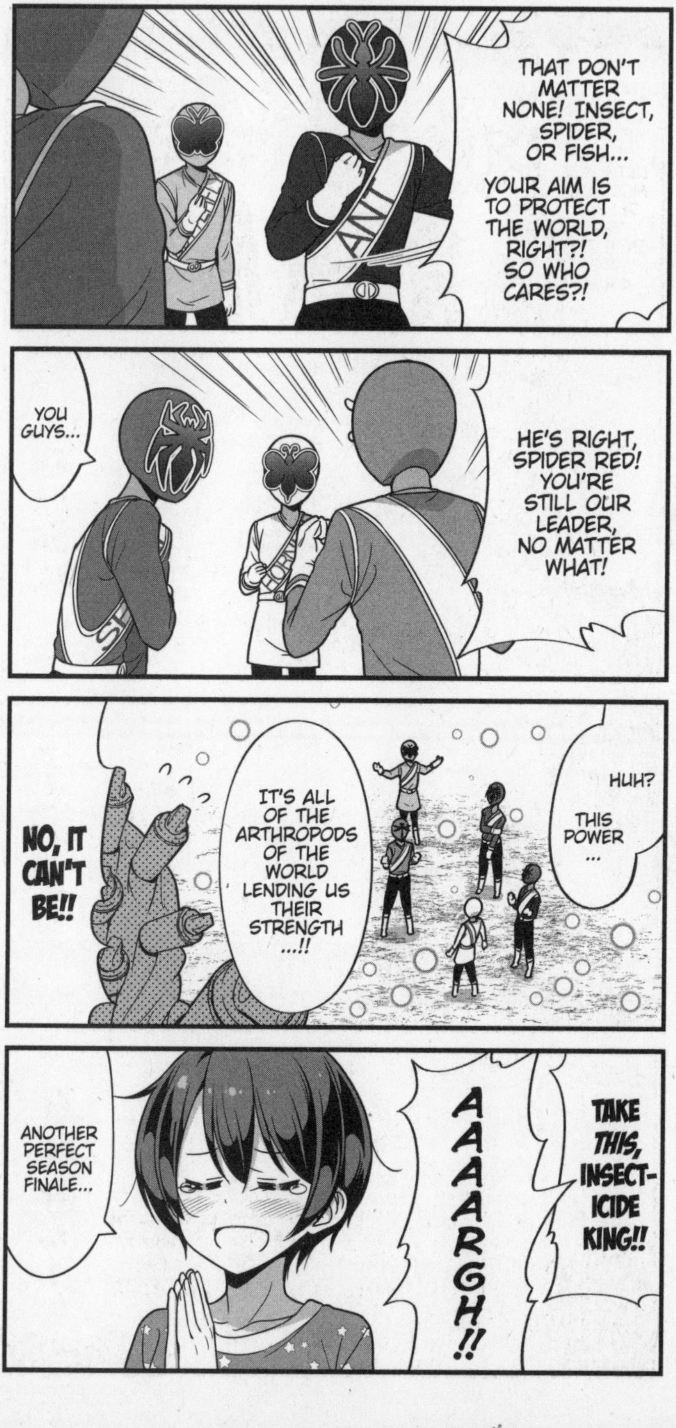
THAT DON'T MATTER NONE! INSECT, SPIDER, OR FISH...
YOUR AIM IS TO PROTECT THE WORLD, RIGHT?! SO WHO CARES?!
HE'S RIGHT, SPIDER RED! YOU'RE STILL OUR LEADER, NO MATTER WHAT!
YOU GUYS...
HUH?
THIS POWER ...
IT'S ALL OF THE ARTHROPODS OF THE WORLD LENDING US THEIR STRENGTH ...!!
NO, IT CAN'T BE!!
TAKE THIS, INSECT-ICIDE KING!!
AAAARGH!!
ANOTHER PERFECT SEASON FINALE...

# SEVEN SEAS ENTERTAINMENT PRESENTS

# NEW GAME!

story & art by **SHOTARO TOKUNO**

**VOLUME 7**

TRANSLATION
**Jenny McKeon**

ADAPTATION
**Jamal Joseph Jr.**

LETTERING AND RETOUCH
**Courtney Williams**

COVER DESIGN
**Nicky Lím**

PROOFREADER
**Danielle King**
**Dayna Abel**

EDITOR
**Jenn Grunigen**

PRODUCTION MANAGER
**Lissa Pattillo**

MANAGING EDITOR
**Julie Davis**

EDITOR-IN-CHIEF
**Adam Arnold**

PUBLISHER
**Jason DeAngelis**

NEW GAME! VOLUME 7
© Shotaro Tokuno 2018
First published in 2018 by Houbunsha Co., LTD. Tokyo, Japan.
English translation rights arranged with Houbunsha Co., LTD.

Seven Seas press and purchase enquiries can be sent to Marketing Manager Lianne Sentar at press@gomanga.com. Information regarding the distribution and purchase of digital editions is available from Digital Manager CK Russell at digital@gomanga.com.

Seven Seas and the Seven Seas logo are trademarks of Seven Seas Entertainment. All rights reserved.

ISBN: 978-1-64275-711-8

Printed in Canada

First Printing: October 2019

10 9 8 7 6 5 4 3 2 1

**FOLLOW US ONLINE: www.sevenseasentertainment.com**

# READING DIRECTIONS

This book reads from *right to left*, Japanese style. If this is your first time reading manga, you start reading from the top right panel on each page and take it from there. If you get lost, just follow the numbered diagram here. It may seem backwards at first, but you'll get the hang of it! Have fun!!

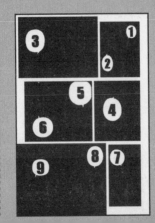